"Lesbian nuns I know are going to dance! In convents this book will go around like hotcakes, just the way THE HITE REPORT did. Everybody read it. Lesbian nuns will be more self-conscious about this book. They're also going to be listening for the response from other members of the community and praying to God it's okay.

The book will also be an occasion for confronting a lot of pain. Lesbian sisters who are not out in their communities (and I don't know anybody who is out) will have to listen to homophobic reactions. But it will be a catalyst. All hell's going to break loose. Religious communities are going to have to discuss the book. They're going to have to respond to the reality, and they've never had to do that."

Sister Sara, 1958–Present

LESBIAN NUNS: BREAKING SILENCE

LESBIAN NUNS: BREAKING SILENCE

edited by
Rosemary Curb &
Nancy Manahan

The Naiad Press Inc.
1985

Printed in the United States of America
First Edition

First Printing, February, 1985
Second Printing, March, 1985
Third Printing, April, 1985

Cover and title page design by Tee A. Corinne
Typesetting by Sandi Stancil

Library of Congress Cataloging in Publication Data

Main entry under title:

Lesbian nuns: breaking silence.

    Bibliography: p.
    Includes index.
    1. Lesbian nuns—United States—Biography—
Addresses, essays, lectures. I. Curb, Rosemary,
1940–   . II. Manahan, Nancy, 1946–
BX4225.L47 1985   255'.9'0088006643   84-29594
ISBN 0-930044-63-0
ISBN 0-930044-62-2 (pbk.)

NANCY MANAHAN and ROSEMARY CURB, June 1982
(Photograph taken in Peg Cruikshank's San Francisco apartment by photographer Barbara Hammer.)

CONTENTS

PRELIMINARIES

Acknowledgements .... *xv*

What Is a Lesbian Nun?
  Rosemary Keefe Curb (1958–1965) .... *xix*

What Silence Does This Book Break?
  Nancy Manahan (1966–1967) .... *xxxv*

SECTION I: VOICES FROM GHOSTS 1

My Immaculate Heart
  Jeanne Cordova (1966–1967) 3

Journal of a Novice
  Barbara MacKenna (1964–1967) 17

Not Even an Altar Girl
  Diana T. Di Prima (1960–1962) 29

(Dates indicate years in religious life.)

Examen of Consciousness
    Judy Smith (1959–1968) 35
Voices from Ghosts, Including the Holy
    Wendy Sequoia (1958–1967) 41

SECTION II: RACE, CLASS, AND CULTURE 49
Get Rid of That Nun
    Marie Dennis (1960–1968) 51
From Convent to Coven: A Working Life
    Kevyn Lutton (1960–1967) 55
What Was a Nice Jewish Girl Like Me Doing
in a Convent?
    Ayyelet Hashachar* (1962–1968) 65
So Good, So Right
    Jessie (1959–1967) 73

SECTION III: THEY SHALL NOT TOUCH 79
They Shall Not Touch, Even in Jest
    Margaret* (1963–1965) 81
Certified Straight
    Kate Quigley* (1961–1966) 87
Fresh Starts
    Betsy Snider (1964–1967) 99
Finding Myself in Harlem
    Marie* (1952–1970) 103
My Art and My Spirit
    Sonja Meidell (1965–1970) 113
Dissolving My Masculine Alter Ego
    Jane E. McLarson* (1964–1970) 117

*Indicates pseudonym.

SECTION IV: DON'T BE TOO RIGID IN YOUR UNDERSTANDING OF CHASTITY 125

Don't Be Too Rigid in Your Understanding
of Chastity
    Sister Agatha* (1957-present) 127
Gay and Celibate at Sixty-Five
    Sister Marla* (1935-present) 133
The Gift of Sexuality in the Spirit of Celibacy
    Sister Hana Zarinah* (1963-present) 139
The Awakening
    Sister Maria Nuscera* (1976-present) 145
Love That Lesbian Music
    Sister Sara* (1958-present) 149

SECTION V: SURPRISES AND CONTRADICTIONS 157

Second Generation
    Mary Alice Scully (1961-1979) 159
Union Activists, Lovers, and Parents
    Christine (1971-1972) and Sheila (1960-1981) . . 163
Cozier That Way
    Terry (1969-1971) 169
Two Closet Doors
    Charlotte Doclar (1952-1981) 175
Revolving Doors
    Coriander (1962-1968) 181

SECTION VI: CLOISTERED SENSUALITY 195

Finding My Way
    Mary Brady* (1956-1970) 197

Recognizing Myself as Lesbian
    Susan Weaver (1948–1954) 205
South American Lawyer in the Cloister
    Maria Cristina (1963–1975) 209
Convent Reminiscences
    H. M. Fairfield-Hickey (1947–1953) 219
Cloistered Sensuality
    Monique DuBois* (1964–1976) 223
God Was an Innocent Bystander
    Jean O'Leary (1966–1971) as told to Jan
    Holden 231

SECTION VII: HEALING IN THE DARK 241
God's Love Is Priceless
    Ann Campbell* (1955–1971) 243
Agoraphobia
    Teresa O'Herlihy (1972–1978) 253
I Always Knew You Would
    Helen Horigan (1963–1968) 261
Myth for Winter's Eve
    Elizabeth Malloy (1952–1967) 271
From German Lutheran to Ex-Nun Psychic
    Helga Dietzel (1959–1966) 277
Healing in the Dark
    Mab Maher (1956–1974) 285

SECTION VIII: ON THE BOUNDARY 293
To Shed the Veil of Anonymity
    Sister Esperanza Fuerte* (1967–present) 295
Dream Journey to Myself
    Sister Pat O'Donnell (1955–present) 301
Alternative Community
    Sister Anne* (1963–present) 307

Lesbian Nun on the Boundary
    Sister Eileen Brady (1969–present) 315

**SECTION IX: CONVENT VALUES AND LESBIAN
ETHICS** 319
The Grace to Empower
    Virginia Apuzzo (1966–1969) 321
Life-Long Lovers
    Mary Mendola (1967–1970) 327
Nun Dreams: Allegory of Spiritual Transformation
    Joanne Marrow (1964–1966) 331
Mysticism: Love or Suffering?
    Hannah Blue Heron (1951–1967) 341
No Circle of Woman Arms under Moonlight
    Joyce (1967–1972) 345
Convent Values and Lesbian Ethics
    Janice Raymond (1960–1972) and
    Patricia Hynes (1965–1970) 349

Glossary 363

Additional Reading and Resources 373

ACKNOWLEDGEMENTS

Creating this book has been a transcontinental quilting party. More friends, relatives, and colleagues than we can name helped with a scrap of fabric or a stitch in time. Thanks first to Peg Cruikshank for proposing the book and introducing us to each other and to Barbara Grier for offering to publish before we knew if there were any contributors. Thanks to the hundreds of Lesbian former and present nuns who called and wrote, told others about the project, started local networks, opened hearts and homes to us, and contributed the sacred hidden fragments of lives.

Friends and family critiqued and proofread the book at various stages. Nancy thanks Ruth Baetz, Ellen Brannick, Carol Brockfield, Lauren Coodley, Peg Cruikshank, Robin Ruth Linden, Susan Rothbaum, Karen Vertin, the Manahan family, and especially partner Barbara Evans, whose editing skills polished nearly every piece. Rosemary thanks her convent particular friend J. A. for her silent presence and continuing practical advice; colleagues at Rollins College, especially English Department Chair Cary Ser; friends Tina Beer, Lynn Butler, Joanne Glasgow, Rochelle Baluch, and Fairolyn Livingston for reading stories and offering advice; editorial assistant Kathleen O'Shea for entering stories on the computer and creating an initial draft of the glossary; and especially daughter Lisa Curb, who acted as go-for, message-taker, and soother of a slightly bezerk mom.

Thanks also to Rollins College, Napa Valley College, and Colgate University, where computer services made it possible to revise portions of the book eight or ten times in our effort to condense each piece and include as many diverse accounts as possible.

Although during most of our two and one-half years of editing, we worked separately or by phone between Florida and California, we met for six editing sessions: 1) in June 1982 at Nancy and Barbara's home in Napa, California; 2) at Winter Solstice 1982 as guests of Sky, Blue, Barbara Deming and Jane Gapen in Sugarloaf Key, Florida; 3) in May 1983 at Peg Cruikshank's home in San Francisco; 4) in August 1983 in the offices and home of Sharon Postma and Jim Manahan, Nancy's brother, who gave us access to typewriters, word processor, copier, and floor space for sleeping at their offices in Mankato, Minnesota; 5) in April/May 1984 at Matile Poor's home in San Francisco; and 6) in July 1984 at Rosemary's home in Winter Park, Florida.

Finally, we salute the forty-nine former and present nuns whose stories appear in this book. Thank you, sisters, for breaking silence.

Rosemary Keefe Curb, 1963

Jerry Keefe (father)

WHAT IS A LESBIAN NUN?

Rosemary Keefe Curb
(Sister Mary Geralda, O.P., 1958–1965)

My mother warned me not to do this book: "Why bother? Everyone thinks convents are full of Lesbians. Don't you know you're committing professional suicide? And why hurt those nice people in the Catholic Church? They just might decide to fight back." Let me introduce these silence-shattering stories by responding to my mother and to anyone with similar questions about why we bothered, who we are, how we worked, and just what effect I imagine this book will have.

Is this a dangerous book? I think so, but not in the way my mother suspects. My mother worries that I will be hurt — professionally and perhaps physically. She doesn't want her daughter to be one breaking centuries of silence. I think fears like hers perpetuate the silence that keeps the closet locked, whereas telling the truth about our lives can set us free.

If our culture defines normality in terms of male experience and values only women who relate to men, both nuns and Lesbians tend to be ridiculed or dismissed as irrelevant to the strides of history. Perceiving the whole female sex as servile and dependent bolsters the faith of our fathers. The very existence of autonomous communities of women threatens patriarchal arrogance. And a collection of autobiographical stories from Lesbian nuns not only violates patriarchal taboo, it is unimaginable in our polarized society.

Ironically groups of nuns or Lesbians are often mistaken for one another today, since we often travel in female packs oblivious to male attention or needs. Eschewing the cosmetics and costumes of the commercially promoted feminine mystique, both nuns and Lesbians are emotionally inaccessible to male coercion. Time and energy which heterosexual women devote to catering to men can be focused on private or communal projects. Despite similarities, a male-defined culture which moralizes about "sins of the flesh" and the pollution and evil of women's carnal desires sees both nuns and Lesbians as "unnatural" but at opposite poles on a scale of female virtue.

We use the term *Lesbian nun* both for Lesbians still in religious communities as well as for those who left several decades ago. We use the word *nun* in its popular sense, meaning all women who take vows of poverty, chastity, and obedience in religious communities, even though the Roman Catholic Church considers only those who take solemn vows and live completely cloistered lives as *nuns* and other women in religious life as *sisters*. The word *Lesbian* reveals our primary spiritual and political commitment to loving women as well as our sexual orientation, but not necessarily our sexual activity.

How does one become a Lesbian nun? Let me introduce

myself. From age eight in Chicago, when I first heard God's call to the religious life, I trudged off daily to the seven o'clock Mass. I was the most devoutly religious member of my family. On the snowiest mornings, my mother's hot Cream of Wheat lures only strengthened my will to resist the temptations of the flesh.

Three months after high school graduation, I entered the Dominican Sisters. I was tossing aside the vanities of the world in the form of a promising acting career. Neither my hard-won Actors Equity card nor my flirtation with fantasy stardom diverted me from my religious vocation. Through every opening night and curtain call, I knew where I was really going. I planned to stay hidden from the world through a long life of prayer and service and to be buried in the cemetery at the Motherhouse.

I loved religious life and my sisters. Receiving the Dominican habit and my religious name was the purest happiness I have ever known. Although devoted to religious life, I had an emotionally consuming clandestine relationship with an older sister during my sixth and seventh years in the convent. I will not narrate my convent story here because I found fragments of it in almost every story in this collection.

I left the convent just before taking final vows because I found religious life emotionally stifling. Removing the many layers of the white wool habit and stiff medieval black veil for the flesh-baring clothes fashionable in the mid-sixties, I felt I was defaulting on a promise made to God. I was conditioned in conformity and ignorant of my sexuality — even my simplest emotional needs. I have not returned to the Motherhouse at Sinsinawa, Wisconsin, since I left in August 1965, but I can still smell the wax shining along those silent corridors, see the serpentine line of black veils in funeral processions to the cemetery, hear the faint click of our long rosaries as we made a middle inclination to chant the doxology "Gloria patri et filio-o-o" at the end of each psalm in the Little Office of the Blessed Virgin. (Religious terms are defined in the Glossary.)

I was lucky to find a job teaching high school biology in rural northern Nebraska. I married an English professor teaching at a nearby college and had a daughter the following year. Four years later in Arkansas, I left my husband. Three years after that, in 1973, I declared myself a Lesbian.

During this past decade, while completing a doctorate in literature, beginning my career as a college English professor, speaking and publishing as an "out" Lesbian/feminist activist, and living as a single Lesbian mother with my daughter (who is graduating from high school in 1985), I have been wondering if choosing to live in a religious community of women twenty-five years ago stemmed from my then unknown Lesbianism. How many women of my generation became nuns because we were already Lesbians? I wanted to find my Lesbian sisters who had entered the convent, not only as a response to a call from God, but as a refuge from heterosexuality, Catholic marriage, and exhausting motherhood.

In June 1981, at the National Women's Studies Association conference in Connecticut, Peg Cruikshank introduced me to Nancy Manahan. We both had autobiographical stories in *The Lesbian Path*, edited by Peg, who urged us to collaborate on editing a collection of stories from Lesbians who were nuns. In an effort to reconcile her religious past with her present radical feminism, Nancy had already begun to search for Lesbian ex-nuns. (Recent and historical studies are listed under Additional Readings.)

In October 1981, when Barbara Grier of Naiad Press invited Nancy and me to edit this collection, none of us knew how many potential contributors to such a book existed or how many would be willing to exhibit their lives in print. We sent out a call for stories to Lesbian/

feminist/gay journals, newspapers, and newsletters; we distributed announcements at professional conferences and sent them to women's bookstores to be posted. Letters and phone calls came pouring in almost immediately. Not having been active in the Catholic Church since about 1968, I was surprised to receive responses from present nuns, so we widened our scope to include the stories of Lesbians still in religious communities.

During the past two years Nancy and I have been in touch with several hundred Lesbian nuns and ex-nuns. We have arranged gatherings and panels at bookstores, conferences, and festivals and given interviews around the country. During Winter 1982–1983, Nancy took a leave-of-absence from her English teaching at Napa College to travel across the country with her partner Barbara Evans and visit the nuns and ex-nuns who had written to us about their lives. Without taking a leave I have been able to meet authors on the route of my professional trips for research and conferences.

Gradually I discovered many common threads in our stories and conversations. From a questionnaire which I designed in June 1983 I learned about family background and attitudes; consciousness of sexuality before, during, and after religious life; the evolution of spirituality and religious practice; recent work, lifestyle, and political commitments. Despite our colorful diversity, I doubt that the women who wrote to us represent a random sample of the Lesbian nun population: we are perhaps more articulate and courageous than our Sisters who are not yet ready to tell their stories to the world.

The women whose lives break silence in this book range in age from late twenties to mid-sixties. About half of the contributors cluster within an eight-year span from age thirty-eight to forty-five (precisely the ages of the editors). Those of us who left the convent spent an average of eight years in religious life — that is, from one to twenty-nine years. Present nuns have spent from seven to forty-five years in religious communities.

More than half of us entered the convent in our late teens between 1955 and 1965. During that period the population in American convents reached an all-time high of approximately 183,000. However, during the next two decades in the wake of Vatican II — the period during which almost all of the former nuns in this book left the convent — the population declined by one-third. We were then in our mid-twenties to late thirties.

Most of us are white and come from Irish, German, and Italian working-class families in the Northeast and Midwest and from large cities. Four of us are Black, and three are Hispanic. Three of us are Canadian.

Growing up, we generally perceived ourselves as different from our families and friends, as adventurous or athletic tomboys resisting feminine passivity. We remember being both fun-loving and guilt-ridden, religious and rebellious, feeling split or confused. Of her adolescence, Jeanne Cordova writes: "Life was simple. I hung out in church and on the softball field."

Although a few of us were converts, most of us grew up in Roman Catholic families. We remember daily family rosary, strict Lenten penances, holy pictures, statues, crucifixes, holy water fonts, Advent wreaths, and May altars in our homes. We remember our mothers suffering daily from rigid rules about birth control, divorce, and wifely subservience. The Church condoned only procreative sex in Catholic marriage. Contraception, abortion, masturbation, homosexuality, and sexual pleasure itself were considered sins against nature. We learned to split hairs in moral theology and to practice daily penances. Kevyn Lutton summarizes her religious upbringing: "Catholic Girl Martyr!"

We were abysmally ignorant of our sexuality. So thick

was the blanket of homophobic silence that nuns and priests merely warned us about avoiding heterosexual occasions of sin and resisting impure thoughts. Only a handful of us knew we were Lesbians before entering religious life, but all of us intended to be celibate in the convent. About half of us had heard the words *queer, homosexual,* or *Lesbian* while growing up. Only now do we recognize that our devotion to our girlfriends and the nuns along with our discomfort on dates with boys was not, as we suspected at the time, an unmistakable sign of religious vocation, but a premonition of our late-blooming Lesbianism.

We entered religious life because we believed that God was calling us. Passionate attachments to nuns as intellectual, spiritual, and moral role models led many of us to choose religious life. Despite the frequent recruiting in Catholic schools and pulpit preaching that a religious vocation was a call to a higher life (an implied reserved seat at the head table of the heavenly banquet for all eternity), most of our families were not enthusiastic about our choice of religious life. Some were so horrified that they disowned us.

We were so eager to enter the convent that we counted the days until entrance. Some were permitted to enter an aspirancy during high school. We who were told to wait until we had finished high school or college felt frustrated by the delay. Several describe the experience of being refused acceptance or the soul-shattering fear of being sent home once we arrived. Some who were asked to leave, usually without any explanation, during the novitiate or before final profession, tried again and again to enter other religious communities.

Service to the needy constituted the work of our communities, but our convent occupations were far more diverse and challenging than the jobs our mothers performed while we were growing up. Religious life offered us better education than most of our parents could provide. The majority of us entered the convent during or after high school. Only a dozen of us came with academic degrees. During our one to forty years in religious life we earned ten master's degrees and twenty bachelor's degrees. Half of us took college courses without earning a degree, although most of us who left religious life continued our formal education. Almost all of the authors in this book have at least one degree. More than twenty have master's degrees, and twelve of us have doctorates.

In many ways religious life offered us a learning and growing beyond our parents' aspirations for themselves or perhaps for us. In addition to formal eduction, degrees, and job experience, religious life enabled us to develop positive personality traits: greater self-knowledge, ability to lead and to take risks, greater sense of community and belonging, personal power, poise, independence, creativity, integration, finesse with authority.

Unfortunately we also developed the less desirable traits fostered by our religious rule and superiors: blind obedience, self-denial, discipline, custody of the senses, and perfect self-control. We became more solitary, ascetic, studious, mystical, scrupulous, and introspective, as well as angry, rebellious, revolutionary. A few felt scared, confused, lonely, guilt-ridden, or crazy. Women who remain in religious life are more likely to report having developed healthy traits. Many who stayed less than three years found the life personally disabling.

Eager to enter religious life, most of us blissfully embraced our new family when we were safely behind the novitiate walls. The initial joy beyond belief of finding ourselves gathered into a family of loving and generous, beautiful and brilliant women often contributed to our first and major trial: constant struggle against particular friendship. Many of us mention discovering the taboo against

p.f.'s, as we and our peers called them, by unwittingly violating it. Our superiors described particular friendships as exclusive intimacy with another sister, drawing us away from
total dedication to God and community. Ideally we were
expected to love all of our sisters equally and to show no preferences. As a safeguard we were advised to recreate in groups
of three or more and with as many different sisters as possible. Although our superiors did not state that particular
friendships left unchecked might become Lesbian love
affairs, the official caveats were so cloaked with an aura
of forbidden, dangerous, and vague evil that we feared them
as serious violations of the religious rule and probable
grounds for dismissal.

Despite the solemnity of the prohibitions, several stories
relate the innocent exuberance of our particular attachments
in aspirancy and novitiate nipped in the bud by watchful
superiors. Our superiors and confessors, while preaching the
prohibitions, often trivialized our consuming passions. Re-
pression of our affectionate feelings and sexual desires led
many of us to work ourselves to exhaustion while suffering
through chronic debilitating illnesses and pains, which our
superiors often called psychosomatic in an effort to deny
their reality or our need for treatment or rest.

Falling in love with another sister, in some cases with
the sister with whom we became sexual after months or
years of repressing our desires, led many of us to leave
religious life. Some sisters, after acknowledging Lesbian
inclinations have chosen to remain in religious life and
forego sexual activity. Other present nuns whose particular
friendships have evolved into loving relationships do not
consider sexuality incompatible with the vow of chastity.

Those of us who left religious life five, ten, twenty
years ago, after experiencing sexual intimacy behind convent walls, remember our lovers and our bruised or vibrant
hearts as sharply as if it all happened yesterday. Not only

was every experience unique, but some of us imagined ourselves the only sisters who had ever dared to traverse the chasm from consecrated virginity to passionate sexuality.

Leaving religious life was usually filled with anguish. The longer we had been in the convent and the more cloistered from worldly commerce, such as looking for a job, opening a bank account, finding a place to live, and buying clothes, the more difficult was our adjustment to secular life. To be no longer protected by convent walls and the religious habit, to be without material resources, to be alienated from our religious family and, in some cases, from the whole Catholic Church left most of us devastated with grief. If we left the convent more than ten years ago, we were probably shuffled out the back door in shame, after being instructed not to tell anyone about our leaving. If our sense of guilt in failing at our vocation to a higher life had also the stigma of the incurable sickness of homosexuality, then our emotional survival was indeed precarious.

Strangely enough, the question most often asked by strangers and friends on first learning about our convent past is "Why did you leave?" Many of us felt lonely, exhausted, unsuited for religious life, unable to resolve the conflict between our vow of chastity and sexual desire and/or activity. Before the changes prompted by Vatican II, which encouraged personal independence and creativity among religious women, many of us left when religious life offered us no further growth. One former nun said, "I needed the unsafety of lay life." When liberal theology and philosophy in the sixties opened us to radical thinking, some of us left raging at the rigidity of Church hierarchy.

Those of us who were asked to leave found departure most excruciating. Our superiors usually did not explain why it had been decided that it was "God's will" for us not to continue in religious life or who made such decisions. Official pronouncements reached us in the passive voice as *faits accomplis.* A few of us knew but most did not, whether the discovery or suspicion that we had particular friend-ships, lovers, or homosexual tendencies triggered our superiors' decisions to abort us. We observed convent treat-ment of other suspected deviants: incarceration in mental hospitals, drug and electro-shock therapy, which eventually led some nuns to suicide. Nuns who sought or were coerced into psychotherapy or psychiatric care found it difficult to distinguish between depression and a dark night of the soul. Many of us resisted therapy. We felt embarrassed and outraged that our superiors considered us crazy, sick, deviant, unfit for religious life, or physically malingering.

Most of us have not been sexually involved with men. The men to whom a minority of us were attracted were often gentle, sensitive, intellectual, and nun-like. One former nun whose story appears here calls herself bisexual. Very few of us married, and few of us have children. Chris and Sheila are co-mothering a son conceived by artificial insemi-nation. I am the only divorced single mother.

The ages at which we began identifying ourselves as Lesbian vary widely, from age ten to the late forties. On the average, we discovered ourselves as Lesbians in our thirties — usually only after we had several intimate rela-tionships with women either in or out of the convent. The majority of contributors to this book are living with lovers in committed relationships of up to eighteen years' dura-tion.

As women struggling to change and save our world, most of us have been political activists. We have been active in the feminist or women's liberation movement. Seven of us have been officers in the National Organization for Women at local and national levels. The current and a former Executive Director of the National Gay Task Force, Virginia Appuzo and Jean O'Leary, are ex-nuns. Lesbian former nuns have chaired numerous gay rights organizations, and written, edited, and published Lesbian journals. Many of us have been involved in peace and nuclear freeze efforts, and in civil rights or anti-racism movements. We have participated in political parties, teachers unions, labor movements, shelters for battered women, efforts to end violence against women, women's health centers, feminist press movements, Women's Pentagon Action, environmental movements, credit unions, food cooperatives, prison rights, Students for a Democratic Society, women's ordination, educational awareness of Central America, civil disobedience, and leftist, anarchist, Marxist, Communist, and socialist organizations.

In addition to donating our time and talents for causes we support, we also hold full-time jobs. Among us we have attorneys, social workers, college professors, elementary and secondary school teachers, owners of businesses, administrators, musicians, artists, writers, editors, psychologists, massage therapists, secretaries, nurses. We also have a photographer, actor, dancer, media producer, environmental engineer, word processor, publisher, graphics designer, cabinetmaker/draftsperson, chiropractor, woodworker, custodial supervisor, waitress, bakery worker, acupressurist, herbalist, and bird consultant. Several of us are currently at work on advanced degrees in graduate or law school.

Spirituality remains at the center of most of our lives. Many of the former nuns lament the loss of a spiritual community of sisters, although most of us who have left the convent have also left the Church. Only five of us who are no longer nuns have remained active in the Catholic Church. Two of us are active in Judaism. Twelve of us now practice Wicca (witchcraft) as feminist spirituality. We are discovering pagan feminism through astrology, goddess imagery, tarot, dreamwork, I Ching, herbal healing, meditation, massage and body work. We are creating communal rituals for solstices, equinoxes, and full moons. Many of us are practicing meditation and psychic work in order to ground our solitary spirituality.

Editing the stories and interviews with Nancy Manahan, I have been amazed at our strength to survive patriarchal oppression, gender stereotyping, and pervasive homophobia. Reading these stories of my sisters has been both painful and cleansing. I have been choked by tears for myself and all of us as waves of our collective suffering sweep over me. At times in my present radical feminism I feel ashamed that I could ever have given myself wholly into the hands of the patriarchy. And yet even though the outer structure of religious life was the cloak of male dominance, the inner reality of convents is genuine sisterhood.

Just as coming out as a Lesbian to certain family members and friends requires courage, so does coming out as an ex-nun (or present nun) to our Lesbian and feminist friends. Those who describe religious life as against nature recognize that developing habits of denying personal desires and spontaneous emotions requires constant struggle. Externally we practiced custody of the senses: we kept our eyes lowered and our hands folded under our scapulars. We learned to curtail exuberance and to walk up and down stairs at a slow measured pace. Internally we denied our impulses. We learned not to assert our own wishes, ideas, or opinions. On a deeper level we developed a belief that anything that came from ourselves was suspect and unworthy. Blind obedience was our highest goal. We were encouraged to remain childishly dependent, told that our superiors would make all decisions for us. Such habits of denial do not easily disappear when feminism ignites us.

Whereas all women under patriarchy find it difficult to assert ourselves against the docility and dependence we are taught to emulate as feminine, we who were trained in religious life find it particularly difficult to be strong and to take our power. My own healing fusion of my past as dutiful daughter of the Church with my present revolutionary fervor comes from reading these stories, meeting and corresponding with many of the authors. Yes, we do carry the scars and pain of old wounds, but we are visionaries who believe fiercely in the power of the spirit to heal and transform ourselves and the world.

I cannot predict how the silence broken by this book will affect religious communities. Some nuns may feel exposed or suspect. This book does not assert that all or even most nuns are Lesbians, nor does it condemn or condone sexual activity in convents. Rather it simply cracks open some crusty old prejudices to voice the truth that daughters and sisters have always resisted the rigidity of the fathers.

Nancy Manahan, 1967

WHAT SILENCE DOES THIS BOOK BREAK?

Nancy Manahan
(Sister Nancy Manahan, 1966-1967)

"Breaking silence" has a double meaning. The first is the breaking of the historic silence about erotic love between women in religious life. This is the first book published on the subject. The second meaning is probably familiar only to those who have been in religious life. Before the radical changes in the Catholic Church prompted by the Second Vatican Council (1962-1965), silence was the rule of convent living, especially during the novitiate years.[1] Nuns could speak only at specified times, usually in groups. We worked, studied, and ate in silence. Speaking at other times was a grave infraction of the rule. I remember confessing to my sisters and superiors at Chapter of Faults, "I broke silence five times." All five were probably with

Sister Johanna, my particular friend at the Maryknoll Missionary Sisters' Novitiate near St. Louis.

I entered the convent after two years in college. Maryknoll required only one year of post-high school study or work, but I was not ready to leave the world after my first year. I was troubled by my growing scepticism of Catholic doctrine, including belief in a Christian God. Yet I felt called to a life of service. I had worked at a camp for ghetto children and had marched with Martin Luther King, Jr. in Chicago. I felt appalled by my middle class rural Minnesota family's big Buick, Fostoria crystal, and baby grand piano when so many were starving. My boyfriends struck a response in me like the flame of one paper match. Yet none of the leaping fires of my high school and college girlfriend crushes had developed into satisfying relationships; we were all trying to be heterosexual. I made the rational decision: I could give myself most completely to a life of service by joining a missionary order. I hoped either that my atheism wouldn't matter, or that once I devoted myself to studying the great mystics and doctors of the Church, I would see the light.

At the Maryknoll novitiate, I confessed my religious doubts to my postulant mistress, Sister Rita Anne. She suggested I talk to Johanna, an older postulant and an articulate convert to Catholicism. Johanna and I debated the creation story, original sin, indulgences, and papal infallibility. Perhaps I never saw the light because I didn't want our meetings to end. I didn't know I was in love with her. I only knew that the chapel vibrated when she walked in, and my stomach lurched when she knelt soundlessly behind me. I longed for her touch.

As assistant infirmarian, Johanna visited me when I was hospitalized for spastic colon and ulcer symptoms. In my misery, I held to the end of her long grey scapular for comfort. Even then, I was afraid that others would see us and KNOW. I knew that what I felt for her was wrong. Home from the hospital, I remember lying on my stomach after the Profound Silence bell, my pajama tops unbuttoned down the back, waiting for her. She came in silence, warmed the cream in her hands, and touched me. I hardly breathed through the whole backrub.

Several weeks into my second year at Maryknoll, I heard Robert McAfee Brown speak. I was in a room full of people working for social justice, and most of them weren't nuns. That night I realized that I didn't have to be in the convent to do good. During the fifty-minute drive back to the novitiate with my sisters, I held Johanna's hand under her scapular and sobbed silently. I didn't want to leave. I loved singing "Salve" with a hundred women, praising a woman, celebrating the cosmos, as light streamed through the chapel windows. I loved cutting apples in the big kitchen while Sister Belinda next to me rolled out pie crust. I especially loved having time to meditate every morning, to read each afternoon, and to study in the evening.

But that night I knew I had to leave. Despite my efforts to believe in the Church, some stubborn part of me refused to swallow. Unless I believed, I would always be an outsider, a pretender. My body was telling me in every way it knew how that it was not happy in the convent. And Maryknoll itself had not lived up to my ideal of "Sell all you have, give it to the poor, and come, follow me." It did not occur to me that being in love with a woman was contributing to my decision.

I left two weeks later. Sister Johanna left six months later. We were lovers for seven years. I didn't talk much about the convent with her or anyone else. It was too painful and too private. In leaving, I had cut off the spiritual dimension of my life. Like an amputated arm, the emptiness ached. But each time I yearned for that missing limb, I would ask, "What do you want? The convent?" The answer was always, *"No."*

Then in 1981, during bodywork therapy, I realized that my body held deep feelings about my life at Maryknoll and that in suppressing those feelings I was blocking powerful sexual and spiritual energy. I couldn't speak about the convent to my therapist, my friends, or my lover. None of them had been in religious life. I needed other Lesbian ex-nuns. The search for those sisters was the beginning of the book you now hold in your hands. Since that time, I have reclaimed the spiritual dimension of my life. I can now speak about religious life with people who have not lived it. I no longer feel a sheet of iron, where my diaphragm should be, preventing me from taking a good deep breath. I have helped create a community I could not have imagined when I hugged Sister Johanna goodbye on the day I left Maryknoll: a community of Lesbian nuns and former nuns.

This book breaks a many-layered taboo: the first, an internal one. I was not the only nun unable to acknowledge that she was in love with another woman. We had no language with which to think about our feelings and actions. We had no name.

The second taboo is interpersonal. We did not speak to anyone, not even to our special friends or lovers, about what we were feeling and doing with each other. Our religious communities, too, were silent on the subject, except for vague warnings about the evils of "particular friendships." Even today, most Lesbian nuns, including those who are celibate, dare not tell their religious communities.

These layers of silence rest upon a centuries-long historical silence. Even sources that discuss sexuality, pregnancy, leaving religious orders, and other forms of convent "deviance," are silent on the subject of same-sex relationships.

Boccacio, for example, satirizes only heterosexual licentiousness in Italian religious houses. Scipio de Ricci, a Roman Catholic bishop, investigated monastic corruption in the last half of the eighteenth century in a book entitled *Female Convents: Secrets of Nunneries Disclosed.* According to de Ricci, sexual activity between priests or monks and nuns was common, and many nuns were pregnant. But de Ricci does not mention sexual relationships between the nuns.[2]

In our own century, Eileen Power, author of *Medieval English Nunneries,* discusses the great problem of nuns' lapses from chastity, but never hints that from the thirteenth to the sixteenth centuries, some British nuns might have lapsed with each other.[3] More recently, Helen Rose Fuchs Ebaugh, an ex-nun and sociologist, published a scholarly study of nuns who remained in and those who left three religious orders after Vatican II. Ebaugh never mentions Lesbians nor suggests that loving a woman might have contributed to any nun's decision to leave or stay.[4] Even a promising 1975 title like *A Nun in the Closet* is merely a mystery novel starring two nun sleuths among a cast of heterosexual characters.

However, a few historical clues have survived. Most of these were written by outsiders rather than by Lesbian nuns themselves. Just what evidence of our existence is there? The following fragments provide a sketchy survey of some uncommon nuns of the past.

An early hint of erotic love between women in religious life is in the fifth century when St. Augustine warned a community of nuns over whom his sister had been superior that the love which they bore to one another "ought not to be carnal, but spiritual," and that "those things which are practiced by immodest women, even with other females . . . ought not to be done even by married women . . . much less by the widows or chaste virgins dedicated by a holy vow to be handmaids of Christ."[5]

Another hint is in Medieval and Renaissance penetentials (books used by the clergy, which prescribed punishments for sins). They dealt at great length with homosexual acts between men and included provisions for lay women and nuns engaging in homosexual behavior. According to Anglican theologian Derrick Sherwin Bailey, the penetentials generally prescribed more severe punishments for religious than for lay offenders. Secular women who confessed to homosexual behavior were assigned a penance of three years, while nuns received seven years.[6] Bailey mentions the Church councils at Paris in 1212 and at Rouen in 1214 which prohibited nuns from sleeping together. Founders of religious orders were also concerned about sleeping arrangements; their rules for convent living go into some detail about the matter.

In the sixteenth century, jurist Antonio Gomez records that two nuns were burned for using "material instruments."[7] Louis Crompton believes that the term refers to dildoes employed during lovemaking since using instruments for masturbation would not have incurred so severe a sentence.[8]

Judith Brown has discovered what she believes is the first documented case of a Lesbian relationship between nuns. Her archival note, "Lesbian Sexuality in Renaissance Italy: The Case of Sister Benedetta Carlini," describes the ecclesiastical investigation of a young abbess who made extraordinary mystical claims. The investigation revealed that she was having a sexual relationship with another nun. The trial transcripts contain explicit information about their lovemaking. Brown provides a historical context for the transcripts and a sensitive interpretation of them.[9]

A strange case in seventeenth-century Spain involved a woman who reportedly escaped from a convent, disguised herself as a man, and lived as an adventurer and soldier for twenty years. According to her biographers, Catalina De

Eranso was engaged to be married to women several times, although "fighting, one imagines, presented more delights to her than making love to young ladies or rich widows."[10]

To save her neck after a bloody duel, Catalina revealed her sex and was returned to a Poor Clare convent. Upon her release two years later, she was greeted as a celebrity and, in an audience with the Pope, was granted permission to wear male attire for the rest of her life. When she died in 1650, she was buried in the Church "with ceremonies befitting a pious ecclesiastic."[11]

A few hints of Lesbian experience may be found in the writings of nuns themselves. John Boswell has translated what he terms "the outstanding example of medieval lesbian literature," written from one twelfth-century Bavarian nun to another. It begins, "To G., her singular rose/From A. — the bonds of precious love," and continues, "When I recall the kisses you gave me/And how with tender words you caressed my little breasts/I want to die." The poem goes on to urge the friend to come home quickly.[12]

A seventeenth century Mexican nun, Sor Juana Inez de la Cruz, known as "the Seventh Muse," corresponded with the intellectuals and artists of her day, wrote feminist tracts, and composed love poems to women. Sor Juana entered religious life for the same reasons many of the contributors to *Lesbian Nuns: Breaking Silence* did: to escape marriage, to receive an education, and to live in a community of women.[13]

Biographies of founders of women's religious orders may also provide clues to romantic friendships behind convent walls. For example, *Frances Ward* by Kathleen Healey depicts the intense relationship between Ward, the founder of the Sisters of Mercy in America, and Catherine McAuley, who founded the Sisters of Mercy in Ireland. Their letters and journals express the fierce love for each other which fueled their work. Unlike earlier biographers,

Healey deals with their devotion more openly, revealing, for example, that Frances was not called to Catherine's deathbed because the nun in attendance was jealous of their intimacy.[14]

Whether such women ever had physical contact is not the issue. As Lillian Faderman states, " 'Lesbian' describes a relationship in which two women's strongest emotions and affections are directed toward each other. Sexual contact may be a part of the relationship to a greater or lesser degree, or it may be entirely absent."[15]

Much less circumspect than biographies and autobiographies are the handful of articles, stories, and plays written in the 1980s which deal openly with Lesbian nuns and former nuns. (See Additional Reading.)

Mary Gilligan Wong, in her 1983 autobiography *Nun: A Memoir*, includes descriptions of two convent friendships, one frighteningly intense, and an account of a recent conversation with a gay priest.[16] She admits her error at having assumed that there was very little incidence of homosexuality in the convent and that "those who had demonstrated such tendencies had been promptly asked to leave." Wong concludes that she will probably never know the truth because "the emotion surrounding the whole issue, both inside and outside the convent, remains intense, and lesbian sisters, as long as the intensity persists, will undoubtedly continue to be very, very discreet."[17]

We have been suffocated by discretion. But inside and outside the convent, we are finally telling our stories — in this book, in newsletters and journals, at conferences and workshops, and in small groups across the country. We are finding each other and acknowledging ourselves. After centuries of invisibility, we are at last breaking silence.

Notes
[1] See the Glossary for religious and convent terms.

[2] Scipio de Ricci, *Female Convents: Secrets of Nunneries Disclosed*, ed. Thomas Rosco (New York: D. Appleton, 1834).

[3] Eileen Power, *Medieval English Nunneries* (Cambridge, England: The University Press, 1922).

[4] Helen Rose Fuchs Ebaugh, *Out of the Cloister: A Study of Organizational Dilemmas* (Austin: University of Texas Press, 1977).

[5] Quoted in Derrick Sherwin Bailey, *Homosexuality and the Western Christian Tradition* (London: Longmans, Green Co., 1956), p. 85.

[6] Bailey, pp. 120–123.

[7] Louis Crompton, "The Myth of Lesbian Impunity: Capital Laws from 1270 to 1791," *Journal of Homosexuality*, 6:1/2 (Fall/Winter 1980/81), 17.

[8] Crompton in conversation, May 22, 1984.

[9] Judith C. Brown, "The Case of Sister Benedetta Carlini," *Signs: Journal of Women in Culture and Society*, 9:4 (Summer 1984), 751–758.

[10] Edmund B. D'Auvergne, *The Nun Ensign* (London: Hutchinson, n.d.), p. 26.

[11] D'Auvergne, p. 43.

[12] John Boswell, *Christianity, Social Tolerance, and Homosexuality: Gay People in Western Europe from the Beginning of the Christian Era to the Fourteenth Century* (Chicago: University of Chicago Press, 1980), p. 220.

[13] Octavio Paz, "Juana Ramirez: Her Life and Writings," *Signs: Journal of Women in Culture and Society*, Autumn 1979, pp. 80–97.

[14] Kathleen Healey, *Frances Ward* (New York: Seabury, 1973).

[15] Lillian Faderman, *Surpassing the Love of Men: Romantic Friendship and Love between Women from the Renaissance to the Present* (New York: William Morrow, 1981), pp. 17–18.

[16] Mary Gilligan Wong, *Nun: A Memoir* (San Diego: Harcourt Brace Jovanovich, 1983), pp. 119–125 and 224–226.

[17] Wong, p. 382.

Section I

VOICES FROM GHOSTS

What was it like to live in a convent? How did we discover that we were Lesbians? Decades after leaving our religious communities, we discover convent ghosts still haunting our dreams. Tenderly we recall our fumbling naivete. Our memories of emotional struggle and stifled desires empower our present lives as political activists and spiritual leaders.

Jeanne Cordova, 1983

MY IMMACULATE HEART

Jeanne Cordova
(1966–1967)

Distorted by the eerie winter fog, the red light atop the Los Angeles City Hall blinked on and off thirty-four times per minute. Should I stay or should I go? My heart beat with it as I lay there in my cell for five months. Should I stay or must I go?

They promised me monastic robes, glorious Latin liturgy, the protection of the three sacred vows, the peace of saints in a quiet cell, the sisterhood of a holy family. But I entered religious life the year John XXIII was taking it apart: 1966. The fathers of the Holy Roman Catholic and Apostolic Church were sitting in the Vatican Council destroying, in the name of CHANGE, my dreams. Delete Latin ritual. Dump the habit. Damn holy obedience. Send nuns and

priests out into the REAL world. If I had wanted the real
world, I'd have stayed in it!

My seventh floor "cell" in St. Joseph's Immaculate
Heart of Mary Convent in downtown L.A. at the corner of
Second Street and Skid Row (Los Angeles Street) was
degenerately REAL. Mother Superior had aptly described
it as "missionary work." I was much too young to comprehend the world of the drunks who lived below me, outside
the walled gates, but my soul felt the loneliness I had no
experience to describe. My view of the real world was the
top five floors of City Hall with its blinking red light to
ward off airplanes and folks who might have strayed into
forbidden territory. Should I stay or should I go? All I ever
wanted to be was a nun. Now I was, and it was hell.

When non-Catholics ask, as they ALWAYS do, "Why
did you become a nun?" what they really mean is "Jesus
Christ, why the hell did you do that? Did your parents
brainwash you? Were you too ugly to catch a man? Guilt?
Couldn't get a job? Wanted a free college education?" Even
ordinary Catholics cannot understand the sweet madness
of hearing the voice of God compelling the chosen one to
love.

My parents were strong Catholics. "Devout" was the
description used by their friends. "Fanatic" was the expression used by mine when I told them I had eleven brothers
and sisters. Mom was a sheltered, upper-class, convent-raised
Irish Catholic from Queens, Long Island, who probably
first read about birth control in the L.A. Times between
her ninth and tenth kid. My father was a volatile Mexican
("Spanish" in his words) military man, who took to
Catholicism on his deathbed at age twenty-six, was
miraculously cured, married UP (luckily the woman of his
passionate choice), and raised his "troops" with military
discipline.

It would be easy to credit or blame this background to

explain why I became a nun. But the happy secular careers
of my sibling troop disprove this easy theory. I have a baby
brother, swish as they come, who recently dropped into
monkdom; but the other ten apparently never gave religious
life any consideration. My extremist nature, inherited from
my father, probably has more to do with why I went all the
way with Catholicism but not on my obligatory Saturday
night dates!

Perhaps I became a nun because in my day little girls
had two options: grow up and marry a daddy facsimile or
become a nun. Being a bright child and knowing subconsciously that I was gay, what could I do?! Dozens of other
Catholic friends managed to find their Sapphic selves without going into the convent, but for me it was LOVE.

At seven, I made my master plan for life. I made a vow
to the Infant of Prague to enter the convent when I grew up
and give my life to the service of God. Just like in the movies
where the star falls in love and gets married, so it would be
with me and Jesus. Falling in love with Jesus and Mary was
a simple, irrational and inexplicable obsession. Jesus gave
his life for me. Who could ask a lover for more? Mary, sweet
mother, gentle protectress, never-ending font of nurturing,
was anyone's perfect mother lover. Big Daddy God himself
promised rewards like immortality if you just went along
with his program for your entire mortal life. For twelve
years I was in the throes of a forever commitment to my
first lover — God.

Between the ages of seven and nineteen I went to Mass
and Communion every morning seven days a week. When
my doctor recently asked if I had eaten a lot of eggs in my
lifetime, I had to use a calculator to add up how many
times I'd been to Mass. Each morning Mom put two hard-
boiled eggs in my lunch box to eat after Mass. That's close
to a quarter million eggs. Monday through Friday, month
after month, year after year, we kids sat at our desks during

first period spelling class chewing on our hard-boiled eggs. Crackling egg shells and buttered toast crumbs on the floor would have gotten us thrown out of any public school, but the nuns just smiled indulgently if I couldn't spell because my mouth was full. To this day I blame Christianity for my notoriously poor spelling.

Running back to class every day from recess, I stopped to say hello to Jesus. When all the other kids were busy eating lunch, I went to my special place in Church to talk to Jesus, even though sometimes it was hard to stop playing baseball. I liked to pray at the little side altar with the Infant of Prague baby Jesus statue. At certain times of year the priest changed the clothes on my own private statue: purple for sorrow during Lent, bright orange to celebrate Christmas, white with flashy gold trim for Easter. I wondered if baby Jesus noticed that I was sometimes real, real late during baseball season. All year round he stood there smiling vacantly in that same little gold crown with the red rubies.

Things went smoothly — religiously speaking — for the next four years. From age seven to eleven, I learned the art of contemplation, kneeling for four hours at a time and never feeling a thing. In the summer when it hit 104, some kids would faint in their seats because they couldn't make it through the Stations of the Cross. For Jesus' trek up Calvary every Friday afternoon in Lent, the nuns could pack 800 kids into that Church. Southern California temperatures could soar over 100, but I never fainted because I was a Cordova, and Dad said we never give up. Besides everyone knew I was going into the convent, and nuns didn't faint when praying. Life was simple: I hung out in Church and on the softball field. That was all I needed. Life was good.

Then things got complicated. I tried out for varsity softball in sixth grade and met Miss Trujillo. With the onset of puberty, which coincided with the onset of Miss Trujillo,

I began a double life: to my life as aspiring nun was added my life as latent baby butch.

By high school it was time to get down to the practical aspects of entering the convent. When an ex-nun meets another ex-nun she never says anything dumb like "Oh, really! You don't look like a nun." Or "Not YOU. I don't believe it!" Her first words are, "What order?"

In grammar school we had Benedictines. So in addition to thinking that the whole world was Catholic, I also thought there were only Benedictine nuns. In high school it was big news to discover Carmelites, St. Louis of France nuns, and, yes, Immaculate Heart of Mary (I.H.M.) nuns. The easiest way to keep the crucial differences clear is by colors. Carmelites wore brown habits. Benedictines wore brown and black. St. Louis of France nuns wore all black with a ridiculous box affair right out of the 1700s around their faces. And the IHM's — be still, my heart — wore this beautiful royal blue and black. I hate to reduce the entire direction of my religious life to color schemes, but . . .

Sister Paul Francis and Sister Mary Anthony, both IHM's, finally tipped the balance. I was "crushed out" on Paul Francis since the day during my sophomore year when the loudspeaker broke into religion class to announce the death of Kennedy in Dallas, and I saw her collapse on her desk to cry. From that day on, I sat in the front row so I could "take care of her." Mary Anthony? What a butch! Of course, at the time I said, "What a coach!" It nearly broke my heart when Kathy O'Brien got to drive her home from baseball practice instead of me.

In addition to my latent lust for a couple of IHM's, I loved the exquisite novitiate in Montecito, just south of Santa Barbara. Not only Clara, my camp counselor, was joining the IHM's, but everyone who was anyone was going to Montecito. The IHM's had zip and a zest for life and intensity of spirit that I later recognized as akin to my own. I counted the last three years of high school by days until I too could join the IHM's in Montecito as a postulant.

On the hot California summer afternoon of September 6, 1966, Dad and Mom and four of my older siblings made the two-hour drive north to Santa Barbara. Dad rolled down the convertible top, and we were all singing and laughing. I cannot say what my parents were thinking or feeling. They never said, and I never asked. I assumed what others said: that they were proud to have a child entering the religious life. (I remember vividly the day I arrived home after leaving the convent. Mom was sitting there quietly reading in our darkened living room. I tried to explain why I had left, stumbling over my words. I couldn't say, "I WAS MISER-ABLE!" So I said, "I'm sorry, Mom. It didn't work out." She never asked about it.) Anyway, on that September day when Dad and Mom deposited me at the Motherhouse, I was home.

The next day things started going poorly — like getting Patti for a roommate. As one of twelve, I wasn't brought up to be particular about who didn't put the toothpaste cap back on. But Patti picked away at my sloppy "character" from morning till dusk. Some of the girls made fun of my dark sunglasses. I'd worn them since second grade when Sister Mary Vincent said, "I can see everything you feel in your eyes, Jeanne. Don't look at me like that." So I never looked at her or anyone else without my dark glasses.

Then I met Michelle. Her blue eyes made me feel all confused as hell. I lay awake wondering how come she wasn't my cellmate. I could hear Michelle laughing down the hall and having fun with her rommate Donna. When Mother Humility called Michelle and me into her office and bawled us out for walking in the garden and being "particular friends," I didn't understand — just like I didn't understand when Mom brought me into her bedroom that day in my sophomore year and showed me Kathy O'Brien's Valentine card and asked, "What does this mean?" I looked at the little ten cent card — a big lion with a fake ruby nose and the scrawled message "You're a beast, but I love you anyway! Always, Kathy." I said, "What does what mean, Mom?" She told me I couldn't spend any more weekends at Kathy's.

Mother Humility told Michelle and me that we couldn't walk in the garden anymore and that "particular friendships" were not "God's way." A month later Michelle slipped in the kitchen while doing the dishes, had a mild concussion, and was sent over to live at the Motherhouse in a special private sickroom where Sister Agnes Marie, a novice, took care of her. One day Patti whispered to me that Michelle and Agnes Marie were "particular friends," and I was sad. Years later in friendship and in bed, Michelle was to tell me that she "got sick" very conveniently and quite often back in those days.

I was sad and lonely when I met Sister Anne Marie, a novice who played the guitar and sang like an angel. She taught me "Puff, the Magic Dragon," which I played for two months because I couldn't see her often enough to learn another song. I don't remember how I could fall in love in twenty minutes, but I did — with Sister Louise and her blue eyes. She was sent away after three weeks. Everyone was leaving me, and I had no one to talk to except Jesus and Mary.

In the middle of these earthquakes of my latent sexuality, the Vatican council changed the course of this little dyke's life. The whole Catholic United States was soon to hear about Sister Corita and the IHM's: "that crazy order in California that's going too far." I was buried in the core of the hurricane just going to theology classes like a good (albeit miserable and confused) little postulant, when the Catholic Church made its leap into the twentieth century.

We stopped saying prayers in Latin. There was talk of

"dropping" the habit. Visiting priests named Berrigan, Elliot, Duran, and other famous people taught seminars or passed through and stayed for dinner. Our teachers were reinterpreting the sacraments, concepts I'd lived by since birth. We could eat meat on Fridays. We were told that non-Catholics could be just as good as Catholics. We couldn't sing Gregorian chant much anymore. And by the time we took first vows the order probably wouldn't be wearing the habit.

The sixties had come inside the wall. The times they were a-changing, and I was alone with my guitar and another song: "Hello, darkness, my old friend." And as my vision began to fade in my own silence, we were all called into Mother Superior's office on January 1, 1967, and told we were being sent down to Los Angeles to live in convents in the real world and go to Immaculate Heart College.

Home for me became a five by ten foot cell in nine stories of gray cement inside a fourteen foot chain link fence, erected to protect the grammar school kids from the bums. Home was a tenement they called a convent perched at Second Street and Skid Row. Home was getting up to teach grammar school kids and going to bed sometimes with no one having spoken my name because the fourteen other nuns spoke only Spanish. Home was abysmal loneliness and confusion.

I stopped getting up for 6:30 Mass in the cold dark chapel. Nuns weren't "required" to go to daily Mass anymore. Over at the college, nuns were changing their names from Sister Charles Borromeo to Jane Smith. Very little mattered anymore. Except stopping my pain. I wondered if God was trying to tell me something.

Michelle's convent had a rep as "the swinging house." When I saw her in class at the college, she said she was getting to be buddies with her Mother Superior. I was sure that my Mother Superior didn't even know my first name.

Sometimes I'd laugh to myself way into the night: thank God ol' Patti wasn't sent to this God-forsaken skid row "convent" with me. Mostly I didn't laugh.

The college campus, however, was a whole new beautiful world. Famous people like Sister Corita were teaching us to appreciate art. One great "exercise" was running along the tops of the classroom desks dabbing on canvasses and "expressing ourselves." Sister Richard, a great brain in philosophy, tied the sacrament of baptism in with the order of the cosmos. I heard older nuns talking and arguing about big changes coming down from Montecito. Even though no one had much to say to us lowly postulants, it should have been an exciting time for a nineteen year old college fresh-man. Years later when friends asked me what I thought of The Doors vs. The Grateful Dead or LSD vs. mescaline, I would greet their queries with a blank stare. My lover used to marvel at how someone my age managed to miss the most important events (rock and drugs) of the most im-portant decade in our important generation. On the edge of adulthood when life should have been opening up, I was sinking into the quagmire of broken dreams.

One rare night the phone broke the silence. It was Patti calling to tell me to stop being friends with Sally Jacobs. My new friend Sally was one of the few girls at college who would talk to me. I was convinced that she was the smartest girl on campus. Everyone said that she was a genius. And she was a junior (which made her a big shot to me). She was so interesting that even some of the young nuns went up to her room to hang out and talk. I was happy to have found a friend at last. Patti's warning was the first of many. Other postulants said I shouldn't be friends with Sally.

Sister Rose, the superior in charge of us postulants, called me into her office. She wanted to know about my family and my background. Was I happy? Did I feel sure convent life was what I wanted? Did I understand about

poverty, chastity, and obedience? Ridiculous! I hadn't seen
any poverty since the day I arrived at Montecito. I thought
chastity mean not kissing men. And of course I obeyed. I
didn't know what the hell else to do, so I just did what I
was told. She wanted to know about Michelle. She told
me that particular friends could be people who weren't
nuns. That meant Sally.

By that time, I didn't give a damn about what Sister
Rose said. Maybe it was because I was skipping Mass or
because I was just so goddamn lonely that I would have
talked to the Devil with a nametag if he'd been willing. I
stayed friends with Sally and tried to talk to her about
being lonely in the convent. She said it was just hard getting used to a new way of life, and I should stick it out,
be tough, and I'd probably get sent to a more friendly
convent in summer. Sally was signed up to join the IHM's.
She thought the whole order walked on water. But when
she tried to join, she was told to wait a year. She didn't
know why. Sally told me not to worry about particular
friendships because she knew some of the older nuns were
real close "friends." As I hung around Sally I could see
that other nuns were particular friends of hers, or so it
seemed. But I didn't understand.

One day I asked Michelle how come she could have
particular friends but I, it seemed, couldn't. That day her
answer made me adult. "You're not doing it right," Michelle
said. "You're not subtle about it. You wear socks instead
of stockings. You cut your hair too short. You wear those
dark sunglasses. You're too obvious about it."

"Too obvious about what?" I demanded.

"About particular friends!" Michelle dashed off to
her last Friday class.

Too obvious about friends? That's the dumbest bullshit
I ever heard, I told my blinking light. In high school I had
lots of friends. What do my socks have to do with particular

friendships anyway? What difference does it make how often I go up to see Sally and if I'm subtle about it?

Then the light dawned: Michelle is trying to tell me to be a sneak. Obedience means lying and saying, "Yes, Sister," and then doing what you want. Hypocrisy.

That spring of 1967 I watched Michelle and Sally and the other nuns. I saw lots of not going to Mass, lots of particular friendships, a whole sub-culture of in-group and out-group, who they were and how they did it and how you could just lie your way out of anything. To a lonely postulant in a miserable friendless world, it was an absurd outrage. I fell out of love with Jesus and the IHM's who betrayed and mocked my innocence.

On a warm May night I got out of bed and closed the blinds and never looked again at the blinking light. I opened the little suitcase I had carried to Montecito and put in the two towels Mom had sent with me in September, the heavy steel gray cross Anne Marie had given me at Montecito, my songbook, a picture of my family, my underwear, my one uniform skirt and blazer, one white shirt, and my socks.

I sat down and tried to write a letter explaining to Sister Rose why I was leaving, but I couldn't find words to express my rage and betrayal. The next morning I just marched into her office and said, "I quit."

Let me finish my story with an epilogue, which is also Michelle's story, as she remains a most particular close Lesbian friend to this day. I don't remember those traumatic days immediately following. One goes into emotional shock at the death of a lover. Silly as it may sound to those who have never loved spiritually, I had built my life around being in love with God and becoming a nun. That life ended that night. Persuasive Michelle talked her mother superior into allowing me to stay at her convent house with her. She explained that I had no place to go, nothing to my name, no car, no job, no education, no money, no clothes. Perhaps

she also mentioned that I was naive as hell and shouldn't be
forced out into the cold cruel world.

So after I had joined the convent and left the convent, I
went to live in the convent. I shacked up with my former
sisters for two months, taught fifth graders how to distinguish Africa from South America, and got my first job
mailing envelopes for the Beverly Hills Social Register at
75 cents an hour.

With Michelle I made plans for my future and tried to
figure out what to do with the next sixty years of my life.
During my second month, Kate, a "dear friend" of Mother
Superior, dropped in late one evening. Finding Mother
Superior out, she stayed to talk to me. In the wee hours
of the morning I realized that a woman was FLIRTING
with me. Kate took me to "her place" as we say. All I
remember of that evening were two whiskey sours and my
first orgasm.

Two weeks later I left Michele's convent house with
Kate. Three years later Michelle left with Sister Sebastian!
Patti left with some unfortunate male on a date I have
chosen to forget. Anne Marie left with a sweet Franciscan
monk two years later. Michelle's mother superior, the loving
woman who offered me my first adult home, left shortly
after Michelle to join the political movements of the mid-
70s. We left each in her own way.

I left with anger and bitterness towards sanctified
hypocrisy, believing this my reason for "quitting." When
leaving a lover, we construct lies as well as admitting truths
just to get the guts to walk out the door. Any excuse helps
us survive. I harnessed my anger into love for gays as an
oppressed people. My bitterness demands the straight world
to move over and accept our rights. I have learned that my
anger takes me where others are afraid to go and that outrage is good in the eyes of whatever Higher Power gives us
righteous, if misguided, anger to protect us.

I wonder what my mother would say now, seventeen years later, if I told her the real reason I was called to leave the convent. Would she sit in shock, as she has so often this last decade when she hears about my exploits on behalf of gay liberation, if I told her "god" needed me in the world because he had a shortage of gay activists? My Lesbianism is more than my sexuality. It is my vocation!

Michelle left to pursue her real vocation as social worker. She touches people's real lives with food and housing. Michelle's mother superior works in Guatemala. The movements for social justice in the 70s and 80s are replete with ex-nun Lesbian leadership. I have come to see the convent as Boot Camp for all of us, our alma mater of the soul.

If my story sounds cute or witty, I want those who read it, Catholic or non-Catholic, nun or priest, outside or in, today and last year, to know that being a nun, especially a latent Lesbian nun, is not funny. We must educate our young, in high school, college, or the convent, so that the celebration of being gay is not destroyed by any authority's hypocrisy.

I left the convent in 1967 to join another sisterhood: the Daughters of Bilitis. I founded and published The Lesbian Tide, *the national feminist newsmagazine, 1971–80. I now publish* The Community Yellow Pages, *Southern California's Gay and Lesbian telephone book. I live in Hollywood, four blocks from the former Immaculate Heart of Mary Motherhouse.*

Sr. John Michael, 1965

Barbara MacKenna, 1980

JOURNAL OF A NOVICE

Barbara MacKenna
(1964–1966)

December 25, 1964. J.M.J. I'm seventeen. It's my first, wonderful Christmas in the convent. On my bed last night there were gifts from the novices and the Mistress of Postulants, Sister Helen. Under my pillow I found a note from Sister Claire. At 11:30 the novices carolled us. It was so beautiful I felt like crying. I loved Midnight Mass. After breakfast and dishes, about 3:00 a.m., Sister Claire and I went out on the porch even though it was raining. We talked about our families, our lives and how much we care for one another. The sky was beautiful. It felt so good to be able to talk to Claire after waiting all Advent. I always feel excited when I am with her. It was 4:00 a.m. before I got to bed!

After the 8:00 a.m. rising bell we had hot chocolate and toast before Mass. Sister St. Peter, the Mistress of Novices, gave us all the kiss of peace. I hardly saw Claire all day.

January 7, 1965. The holidays flew by. I saw Sister Claire every day. We walked down past the bridge and over to the pond. We talked about ourselves — how we want to be good sisters and how hard that is sometimes. I love being around her because she makes me feel happy. Sister Claire is so good. I know she wouldn't do anything to hurt anyone. I feel that our friendship is a good one and a true one. We have talked about our feelings. Sister Helen noticed I've been with Claire quite a bit and told me I should be sharing all the love I have with others. I felt sad because I do love others.

One night Father Roland, the retreat master, spoke on friendship. He said, "Only an unholy love militates against God. All else contributes to it." Sister Helen was upset that I missed one of his talks to be with Claire, but I can't say I feel guilty. God has given me a good friend in Claire, and I hope He blesses our friendship. If she is such a wonderful person, then how much more so is Christ, who is infinitely lovable. She will lead me to Him.

January 21, 1965. Today was really hard. I saw Claire several times in passing, but we couldn't talk. After supper I helped her carry the garbage down. I told her I was ready to crack. I just can't stand it not being able to talk with her. She says she feels as I do. I'm glad she understands. There must be a reason why novices and postulants are separated, and I know it's probably a good one.

January 22, 1965. I'm trying not to want to be with Sister Claire, but I can't help it.

February 2, 1965. I was up today for the first time after almost a week in the infirmary following my toboggan accident. The postulants visited me every day. Sister Helen was concerned about my back, but I think she feels better now that I can walk around. I missed Claire terribly and would have given anything to see her, but she wasn't allowed to see me. I saw her this afternoon for a moment just after chapel.

February 6, 1965. Last night after everyone had gone to bed Claire and I met downstairs in the hall by the laundry room and talked for over an hour. I could have talked with her all night. It felt so good to see her that I didn't care about breaking the silence. Every so often we could hear Sister Helen looking for me, but I stayed where I was. Back in my room, while I was getting ready for bed, there was a knock at the door and Sister Helen came in. She didn't say a word. She just looked at me, turned her back and left. I felt so terrible I couldn't sleep.

This afternoon Sister St. Peter had Claire in her office for a long talk, and Sister Helen spoke to me. She told me it had been a deliberate act of disobedience to stand and talk with Claire. She'd been afraid that I had fallen down someplace. She said she understood how I felt, but she asked me to do something that I don't know if I'll be able to do. I am never to speak to Sister Claire unless at the proper times. But if I ever do, I'm to tell her. Right now, that seems utterly impossible. I felt terrible when I left Sister's office because I had disappointed her. Doing the right thing seems so hard, and I feel very weak and small. I was even tempted to leave the convent but that wouldn't have solved a thing. Tonight I feel very miserable and very tired. Please help me.

February 7, 1965. Today was visiting Sunday. I had a chance to see Claire this afternoon during recreation. We decided that with one another's help we can do what's expected of us. She said she'd leave tomorrow if she thought she would affect my vocation in any way. She told me about her talk with Sister St. Peter, and I related mine. We were told practically the same things. I'm trying very hard to be obedient and I know she is. She's so wonderful. I thank God for letting me know her.

February 27, 1965. Sister St. Peter's feast today was wonderful. It has snowed and everything is covered. I was with Claire, and it felt good to talk with her without feeling guilty.

March 5, 1965. Lent has started. Six weeks seems like a long time. I made out my Lenten program with a stress on silence. It hasn't gone badly so far, but it's early in the season. I've broken it with Claire but not at times when I should be someplace else, so I don't know if I should count it or not. I just can't acknowledge that I've seen her. I know Sister Helen says she understands, but even so, she can't help but form an impression of Claire if I say I've spoken with her. She'd think that because Claire is a novice and older than I am that it's all her fault, and I couldn't stand that.

Today in class Sister spoke about the noon-day devil being those times during the silence when you feel you just have to talk to someone. Well, that's exactly the way I feel. Sometimes I just have to talk to Claire even if it's only in passing, or for a couple of minutes. That doesn't seem wrong and yet it really is because it's during silence, and I'm only supposed to talk with her at recreation anyway. In all honesty and humility I have to admit that we are more obedient than before that episode. I think our friendship is stronger now that we can't see one another so often, and yet I know she's there when I need her.

March 15, 1965. (During the Seniors' retreat). This afternoon Father's conference was on friendship — just when I needed it. He said that everyone needs someone who understands and sympathizes, someone who shares the same ideas. Loving one person more than another isn't wrong because, if it is, then Christ was imperfect. Friendship doesn't consist in merely a passing hello or how are you or working beside another, but in really loving someone. I wanted to stand up and cheer.

March 18, 1965. Today we were fitted for our second and third habits. It was so funny standing there in the long habit. Sister Maureen let me put on her rosary and cincture. She was fixing a guimpe, and I held it up to me. All I need are the linens.

March 24, 1965. Today I am 18. It was great. Last night when I came upstairs there was a card from the family and also from the postulants. This morning on my bed, Claire left me an envelope with holy cards and a book she made. She also wrote me a note which I loved most of all because she told me how much she cared for me. We all went for a walk tonight, and I was able to talk to Claire for a few minutes. It felt wonderful. We hardly see one another now except at recreation.

April 16, 1965. Lent is nearly over. I wonder how much I've progressed or regressed. I have a million faults. What are they? I can't pin them down. Tomorrow I'm going to try harder, but really, I just can't keep quiet. I'm proud of one thing, though. I didn't talk to Claire today. When we passed each other outside, neither of us said a word. It would have been so easy to find an excuse. I've been told I shouldn't recreate with the same novices and postulants all the time. I really have tried. I do love all my sisters, but some more than others. I've been trying not to have recreation with the same ones all the time. Loving everyone is so hard.

May 21, 1965. Yesterday at acknowledgements, Sister Helen got on the topic of giving myself to others. She says she doesn't know me even after living with me for eight months because I don't really give myself. I love Sister Helen and would do anything for her. I just don't know what to say when I go in to see her. She says that when I'm with Sister Claire I'm not conscious of anyone else around me and that others feel they can't intrude on us. I'm mixed up.

June 23, 1965. (Retreat: eight days before receiving the

habit.) Our band went away for a week to the summer place and it was wonderful. I got to know Sister Paulette, a second-year Junior Professed. She left me a book of poems and a note. She's here at the Motherhouse now, but we can't talk to Juniors here. Last night most of the sisters went to Lois Marshall's concert. I didn't see Claire right away, but I saw Paulette and went over because she'd said she wanted to see me before retreat opened. I sat with her and after a ridiculous mix-up, I ended up not seeing Claire at all. Now I won't be able to talk to her and explain what happened. I've been cry-ing and wish that I didn't have to start retreat this way. I pray that during retreat I can get a few things straight, par-ticularly concerning love. I know I harp on it all the time, but it's so much a part of my life that I can't help it. In a note she gave me, Paulette said that in religious life, friend-ship is a kind of poverty because we have to be detached and that we may get more graces from letting a friendship go, than if it continued. I think this is going to be the hardest thing in my religious life.

June 25, 1965. In one more week I'll no longer be Barbara MacKenna, but Sister??? If I become close to a postulant I want to be good for her, and I don't want her to find it difficult loving in religious life. I know it hurts very much becoming close to someone, especially here.

July 2, 1965. I am now Sister John Michael. About 8:30 a.m. we went downstairs to get dressed. I wore Mom's wedding dress. As we came upstairs and walked down the corridor, the sisters stood alongside. When we entered the chapel the organ started and the sisters sang as we walked up the aisle. I felt wonderful. When Mom saw me she cried. Then I started to cry. We stood in our places, and Bishop Grant intoned "Veni Creator Spiritus." Then he came down to bless our habits. Dom Josef Thomas (our retreat master) gave the sermon and mentioned again the vows (poverty: detachment from things; obedience: detachment from self;

and chastity: detachment from persons). When it was over Bishop Grant asked, "What do you ask, my children?" We asked to take the habit; then we renounced the vanities of the world and promised to live according to the rules of the community. Finally, the bishop said, "Go now, my children, and receive the holy habit." We flew downstairs. I couldn't believe it was all happening. Sisters Luke and Danielle helped me dress. I couldn't even do up my own stockings. Sister Regina came along to cut my hair. I felt I was being scalped but I didn't care. After an eternity we were dressed. I looked around and there stood my band. They looked so good. We walked up the aisle to our places and then what we had been waiting for — our names. "Miss Barbara MacKenna shall be known in religion as Sister John Michael." I was so happy. At communion time when I said the "Suscipe" I meant every word. I didn't say it during retreat so that I could say it with all my heart on reception day. After nearly a year I was ecstatic to see my family. After relatives left we sang our good-bye song for the second-year novices who leave for the Juniorate tomorrow. It was a happy sad day.

July 7, 1965. We started Chapter of Faults today. I felt strange listening to the second-year novices saying that they had failed at such and such. We didn't acknowledge our faults this week, but we will the next time.

July 22, 1965. Today was Chapter of Faults again. I felt funny. My voice caught. It's really humbling and it's what I need. I think I'm more vain and proud in the habit than I was before. I always have to have my linens just so, and my veil with just the right amount of peak. At least I don't spend half my time in front of the mirror like I did at first. For a couple of days before Chapter, Claire and I were really miserable to one another. I was sarcastic and teasing. I don't know why that happens. I love her so much, why do I hurt her? After our talk everything was wonderful. That's the part I like — being able to talk things

out when there's misunderstanding. Sometimes when she
and Sister Janice (a woman in my band) are together, I think
I'm jealous, and yet I love them both. Sometimes I feel ready
for a psychiatrist.

August 10, 1965. I'm really enjoying the conferences
during the second-year novices' retreat. Tonight Father
spoke on the love we should have in our "religious families."
True charity should be Christ first, others second, and me
last. That's what I want to do, and yet I think sometimes
when I do things for others, I'm really doing them so I will
look good in their eyes. I've been thinking too, how lucky
I am to be one of the people you chose, Lord. How do I
rate when so many other girls would make much better
sisters than I ever will? Father says that You must love
religious who make a dozen resolutions a day and fall
a dozen times, yet pick themselves up day after day to
"become perfect as your heavenly Father is perfect." We
started the discipline.

August 31, 1965. Lately I've felt terribly restless. I
feel I have to do something and I don't know what it is.
At times I even wonder what's the use of going on. Everything is such a drag. I know, Lord, that I have to go on
trusting and loving You and that this is part of the cross,
but half the time I don't think of that. I'm too wrapped up
in my own self. I'm so fond of Claire and feel so close to
her. I know I can't be with her every second. I've been
trying mortifications to help me overcome the temptation
to want to talk with her all the time. But when I see her
talking with others it hurts so much. I don't show it and
no one but me knows what's going on, thank goodness. I'm
so weak. Lord, I need your love to keep going. Don't leave
me alone.

November 18, 1965. The novitiate is certainly different
from the postulate, thank God. My life seems so much more
vital now. Claire and I are closer this year. I'm aware of her

all the time. I just can't help it. I can't help but think that my love for her is selfish because I like so much just to talk once in a while by ourselves. We both feel this way but often we don't talk to one another for days. Lord you know what's in my heart. You know how I feel about Claire. Please keep it a "selfless" love on my part. I do go out to others and no one else knows what's going on inside me — I don't think.

December 16, 1965. I need to grow up so much it's pathetic. I'm relying too much on Claire to govern my moods. I'm embarrassed to write that down, but that's it. Sister Catherine said she thought I was being governed by a force outside myself. She felt the same way last year with another novice. Even though they're in different houses now, that bond between them is growing stronger. That's the way it has to be with me. I'm trying hard, but it drives me nuts at times.

January 30, 1966. I've written this so often before that I begin to feel crazy. I love Claire so much, but we're never together. I just don't get it. I know I said I didn't want to depend on her too much and be running after her all the time, but this is ridiculous. I must be horribly selfish. I'm trying my best to make that total dedication to You, Lord, and to give myself completely to my sisters. Why is everything so muddled? Claire always seems to have time to spend with Sister Janice now, and I can't stand it. But I love them both. So why do I feel like this? Help me to be selfless and to keep my thoughts on other things. I feel like screaming. I need to think. Please help me.

April 21, 1966. I am nineteen now. Tonight, Lord, I'm really at peace for the first time since I entered. You gave me the grace to really follow you, to spend my life for You. I am finally able to say "yes" this is what I really want. I made the idea of the Resurrection my own during Lent, and it changed my outlook considerably. Please let this peace remain even on my down days. After a year and a half of indecision and uncertainty I can finally say "yes."

May 23, 1966. Last week Claire and Janice left the novitiate. I don't know what to say. They're happy, and I thank God for that. I miss them so much. Claire told me after we had seen the movie "Nobody Waved Good-bye." I was just beginning to comprehend that she was leaving when she told me that Janice was going also. I broke down completely. I have never cried like that. I couldn't help it. Oh Lord, it was such a blow, I don't really understand. I cried so hard on Saturday, Sunday, and at times Monday. I just couldn't hold it in. It hurts so much. I've never felt like this. I still expect to see her at table or walking down the hall. I am empty.

August 5, 1966. I don't think religious life is my vocation. I spoke to Sister St. Peter and she told me to wait . . . but how long? I know I'm not leaving because of Claire. I feel I would be a traitor letting the novitiate down. But I can't stay for others no matter how deeply I love them. I'm afraid. Maybe I'm making a mistake. Sister said to live this life day to day for a while to see if the decision becomes more definite or it it's just a temptation. Whatever I've learned here I'll never lose; it's too deep within me, too much a part of me. Love is the only answer and people outside need it so badly. Maybe someday I can give my love to a man who feels as deeply as I do.

September 10, 1966. Today I'm aware of myself as a woman, and that awareness brings a deep responsiblity. When I leave, if that's what You want, Lord, I won't be a child anymore, and I won't be able to live the same or look at people and events in the same light. To be a Christian really does mean to get yourself crucified. Let me accept Christianity in its fullest.

[I left the convent on October 9, 1966: Thanksgiving Day.]

*When I was with the Sisters of St. Joseph in Canada I
kept a journal, which remained mysteriously intact, although
I destroyed most letters and papers from that time. When I
was 31, I began coming out as a Lesbian; only then did I
understand the significance of my convent relationship with
Claire.*

I am a writer and a co-founder and former editor of The
Radical Reviewer, *a feminist journal of critical and creative
work. After several years as an editor with Canadian publishing houses, I currently work for wages as a social worker
in Vancouver's skid row. I dedicate this piece to Barbara,
my partner of four years; to Linda, also a Lesbian former
nun; and to Claire.*

NOT EVEN AN ALTAR GIRL

Diana T. Di Prima
(1960–1962)

When I was eight, I asked, "Why can't there be altar girls?" I was up against that crude, arrogant illogic of a sexist Church in which women's roles have been defined for years by tradition and convenience. Catholic women's roles, ordained by God or nature or evolution or other uncontrollable forces, are to be wives, mothers, and housekeepers.

These roles took on a different light in religious life. Being a wife of Christ meant being asexual. When I was in the convent, in the early 1960s, our clothing created the appearance of neuter beings. Yards of heavy cloth hid our female forms. Less shapely women had less to overcome than the more well-endowed. A buxom sister had to wear special bindings to flatten her. Our hair was shorn to further defeminize us. Our identical rooms were not to betray individual preferences in style or color. We readily accepted these rules of the order as freeing us from temporal concerns in order to spend more time in lofty contemplation of our Groom.

We were all spiritual mothers. Regardless of individual skills or preference we mothered children, the aged, sick and infirm as teachers or nurses. Needs of the community or requests of pastors of parish churches and the bishop of the diocese determined our "career" assignments. I was sent to college because teachers were needed. Fortunately, I was scholastically inclined and was able to maintain high grades while keeping up with all my chores.

Yes, chores. For in addition to our wife and mother roles, we were housekeepers as well. We performed servile, menial, repetitive tasks manually regardless of technological advances. Keeping our hands busy lessened our leisure time, the "occasion for sin." Free time was regulated for academic study and lesson planning.

Homophobia ran rampant. We recreated in groups: "Seldom one, never two, always three or more." I was surrounded by people, yet lived in isolation. I was to relate only to my spiritual Lord. We glorified Mary as the ideal Eternal Woman, in opposition to developing an authentic individual personality — unique, self-critical, active, searching. Shrouded in mystery rather than recognized as a genuine human person, the Eternal Woman is said to have a vocation for surrender and secrecy; hence, the symbol of the veil. Although in general society, women are increasingly recognized as persons with rights equal to those of men, stereotyped notions concerning their supposed nature continue within the confines of the cloister.

The blind obedience which our vows demanded implied that women couldn't think. Everything was done in a particular way or by a certain method, and once told

to do something, no questions asked! I recall having the
chore of washing and drying all the towels for the three
hundred-member community. I was told to hang them
outside to dry even though the community had an auto-
matic dryer. Since it was drizzling, I questioned the sense
of such action. Commanded to complete the job, I knew
that my obedience was being tested. Later in the day as
the increasingly wet towels hung on the line, I was repri-
manded for hanging towels in the rain. Having been imperfect that day, I was to confess my faults at the evening
meal and beg the community's forgiveness while kneeling
at the entrance to the refectory. Looking back at the incident now, I see only waste of human potential and energy.

The sister not suited for teaching or nursing became a
"lay sister," locked into performing demeaning female
chores. Sister Mary Housekeeper planned and prepared
the meals, purchased the groceries, washed and ironed the
clothes, and kept house while the rest of us taught or nursed.
Her special inclinations or artistic talents remained dormant.
In our communal "classless" society, everyone knew that
the lay sister role was ranked lower than the teacher or
nurse role.

In fact, we were disciplined by being assigned the hated
chores of starching and ironing the habits, thus emphasizing
the demeaning aspect of traditional female chores ordinarily
performed by lay sisters. In my religious house, Mary ranked
higher than her sister Martha as our role model.

In order to become malleable enough to fit the ideal
and be divested of all personal attitudes and preferences,
my sense of eighteen years of personal history had to be
erased. The self-effacing ethics of St. Matthew's Gospel
accomplished this spiritual lobotomy. I came and went,
passed from one part of the convent to another, went from
chore to chore, ate and tended to my basic human needs
only with the verbal permission granted to me by those

in charge of my spiritual growth and development. According to the spirit of Christ proclaimed in the Beatitudes, all aspects of human living were regulated by precepts and injunctions. As He was obedient unto death, so must be I!

Reconstructed as religious women, we were to look alike, talk alike, work alike, pray alike, and be alike. When likeness was the common denominator, we had become "Brides of Christ" in a totally male-oriented religion where God is male, priests are male, and all males are preferred over females. Only as a "consecrated virgin" was I permitted within the altar rail and in the sacristy. Yet any male, "consecrated" or not, could do the same. My eight-year old yearnings to be near the altar were resurrected. I began to realize the illogic of anti-female ideas surrounded with an aura of alleged divine approval.

I left before the last cord of Diana was severed. With that one last thread I tried to reweave myself and my place in the outside world once again. The eight-year-old girl, now a grown woman, has come through pain, anguish, and soul-searching to realize that the true spirit of Christianity has been lost within the institutionalized Church. Using the gospels of John and Matthew as my guides, I find that spirit in my daily encounters with people. Insofar as the Church stunted my growth and the potential strength of its women, it has diminished and warped its own life. Since the Church is a powerful cultural institution, this warping affects — and infects — the whole society.

At forty, I live with my lover and teach in New York City. We are active in the gay and Lesbian community, including the New York Gay Synagogue.

Sr. Mary Vianney, S.P., 1960   Sr. Mary Vianney, S.P., 1967

Judy Smith (self-portrait), 1983

EXAMEN OF CONSCIOUSNESS

Judy Smith
(1959-1968)

[*Editors' note:* Before the mid sixties, most nuns performed a nightly ritual of questioning ourselves to check our consciences for sins committed that day and for our infractions of the Rule.]

O Sisters, I think of you often and wonder where you are, my friends, band members, counterparts from other congregations. We lived the religious vocation as long and as well as we could, then left the convent to pick up the ragged pieces of life "in the world."

What happened to Sister Mary Vianney, S.P., after she wrote to the pope asking for dispensation from final vows, aware that this permission-begging was ludicrous, because even if he said no, she was still leaving? Did this person cease to exist? Did identity come off with the holy habit the morning she changed into secular clothes and got a hush-hush ride to the bus station? (1959–1968, *Requiescat In Pace.*) She (whom I used to call "I") got buried in my subconscious. Now she haunts my dreams.

What happened to your Sister Ann Brigid, Sister Fidelia, Sister Thomas Marie? Have you tried to ignore that persona as if "Sister" were merely a role you once played? Do you tell people you are an ex-nun, or do you conceal those years of your past? (Most people who are close to me find out soon enough. I can't stand the suspense, and I think if they know this about me it will explain my strangeness.) Was the convent necessary for your development, or do you see it as an embarrassing mistake? Do you mind my calling you "Sister"?

Do you get these questions: "Why did you enter? Why did you leave? What was it really like? Were there a lot of Lesbians?" Are you, like me, still refining your answers?

Have you been able to give up the vows without tormenting yourself with guilt and imagined failure? Do you still attempt to maintain the essence of that lifestyle? Does the "real world" seem alien to you?

Did middle class convent life leave you hungry for a fuller poverty? Are you still attached to poverty? Are you afraid of money? Has feminism helped you give yourself permission to prosper? Have you entered the patriarchal rat race? Is it worth the effort?

Has your divorce from Jesus made you an unfit lover for any mere human? What is your relationship with Jesus now? Were you in love with a woman when you left? Perhaps you left your woman-love at the convent gate. Have you acknowledged your love for another woman? Have you faced the social consequences of being Lesbian or bisexual? Do you find that honest love for a particular man or men prevents your becoming a Lesbian separatist despite your powerful attraction to an all-female environment and lifestyle? Have you been sexually promiscuous? Are you sometimes celibate? Is your loss of community a gaping wound?

Do you have problems with authority — vacillating between passive obedience and flaming rebellion? Do you sometimes find yourself paralyzed with indecision, afraid of doing the wrong thing with your time, longing for someone to give you a permission or an order? Do you feel guilty about setting your own career goals?

Do you feel emotionally damaged? Have you needed therapy to learn that your feelings count and that anger is a valid response to injustice? Do you get nostalgic, fantasizing your convent world as a safe, idyllic haven from which you have been exiled?

Do you painfully miss the old liturgy? Have you burst into tears singing "Veni, Sponsa Christi" to yourself? ["Come, Spouse of Christ" — Gregorian chant sung at profession of vows.] Are Christmas and Easter especially difficult for you? Do you crave silence?

Are you a perfectionist? Do you recall excruciating humiliations inflicted upon you by superiors in the name of training in virtue? Have you become cynical? Do you let yourself hate? Have you punished yourself instead of fighting repressive structures?

When you left the convent, did you also leave the Church? Do you still pray? Do you miss the status being a nun gave you? Have you adjusted to being just another human? Has your family forgiven you for entering? For leaving? Did your mother save your old possessions? Do your sisters who stayed in the convent have time for you now — or you for them? Are you friends with other ex-nuns?

Have you endured a crisis of faith? Have you explored diverse paths through theology, psychology, atheism, paganism, scientology, Buddhism, feminism, witchcraft, radical politics? Have you discovered a path into nurturing

connections with like-minded others? Has your creativity
somehow survived?

Examens traditionally end with an act of contrition,
but I am not sorry I entered, remained in or left religious
life. I am not sorry I rescued myself from a crushingly
oppressive system. Life out here is often rugged and lonely,
but at least I am no longer silent or invisible. I am here in
solid sisterhood with you.

*I am a bisexual feminist artist, writer, photographer,
and dramatist. I belong to the Women's Community Bakery
in Washington, D.C., and WATER (Women's Alliance for
Theology, Ethics, and Ritual). I have lived in eleven states,
attended thirteen schools, and had sixteen serious jobs. I
am a former member of the Sisters of Providence of Saint
Mary-of-the-Woods, Indiana.*

Sr. M. Danielle, C.P.P.S., 1965

Wendy Sequoia, 1983

VOICES FROM GHOSTS, INCLUDING
THE HOLY

Wendy Sequoia
(1958–1967)

Recently, as I meditated on the mysteries of Lesbians and nuns, I found myself calling forth ghosts. As my dusty convent memories stirred and resumed shape, images of who I am and have been mingled with images of others, past and present.

See the nun! That used to be me. How strange to see one so self-contained, untouchable, other-worldly. Are we really looking at me? *(god calls only a few. we know not why he chooses us from amongst our companions. he has given us the greatest privilege of all, a call to religious life.)*

See the Lesbian? That looks like me. How tense she stands, as though ready to spring for a quick exit. After all, many in this crowd view her as sinner, abomination, one who is dangerous to little girls. Do you suppose Jesus would wash her feet? *(homosexuals perform unnatural acts, disobedient to the laws of god, repulsive to normal persons.)*

How could I appear so madonna-like to some? So approved? So whore-like to others? So disapproved? I never planned to be unusual. In 1958, when I went into religious life, I was filled with idealism. At eighteen, I planned to be a nun until death.

I was a middle class city girl. Joining the Sisters of the Precious Blood, a modest community of 800 based in Dayton, Ohio, was a step into a different class and culture. I did not understand the older sisters' veneration of a large collection of saints' relics displayed in little brass monstrances at side chapels in the motherhouse. Each side chapel also served as a crypt. In one lay the remains of Mother Brunner. Her face and hands had been reconstructed in plaster, as if she were a statue; but she wore a habit with clear plastic panels over the arms and legs, through which her real bones showed. In the other crypt was a statue of the boy martyr St. Cruzier lying on his back with eyes transfixed. Partially decapitated, his bloody throat was slashed from ear to ear. At the time it did not occur to me to question the appropriateness of such models.

From the moment I walked into the Precious Blood Motherhouse, I embraced the religious life wholeheartedly, no questions asked *(give yourself completely to christ.)* I especially embraced the Rule of Silence *(god speaks in the silence of our hearts)*, mortification of the senses *(don't look out the windows, don't smell the flowers)*, and secret self denials *(offer up little inconveniences and disappointments)*. All of this was highly encouraged as the first step toward the life of perfection *(the lord notices your little sacrifices)*. For me it led to isolation, depression, and confusion *(you may break the rule of silence only for a Very*

Important Reason). I need interaction for sanity; these practices amounted to psychological solitary confinement.

The community, of course, assisted in this isolation. Severe restrictions were placed on our communications with the outside world as well as with each other. Our families could visit us only once a month for three hours *(you have turned your back on the world).* Unless there was a death in the immediate family, we were never allowed to go home. Our incoming and outgoing mail was censored. Telephone calls were forbidden. We had no money, no clothes other than our religious garb, no access to transportation except through our superiors *(god spoke to you directly to lead you to religious life, but now he speaks through your superior. the devil will tempt you to leave the community. your superior has the grace of office. she will decide whether you will stay or leave).*

When I was a junior sister, I received a letter from my mother describing my father's heart attack and his sojourn in the hospital's intensive care ward *(you have turned your back on the world).* Because it was Lent, we were not allowed to write letters *(you belong to God now).* I was confused because my mother had used the term coronary thrombosis, not heart attack. Even after looking it up in the dictionary, I was unsure of its meaning *(you are not to break the rule of silence except for a Very Important Reason).* I took my fears to my superior who had little patience with me *(you show your feelings too much).* By refusing my request for an exception to the letter writing rule, she showed she did not know the meaning of coronary thrombosis either *(the most important vow is obedience).* My mother wrote again, this time more plainly and more urgently. Then I was allowed a phone call, and my classmates signed a get well card. But I was allowed no visit and received no apology. God's instrument did not like to acknowledge fallibility.

By this time in my religious life, I had been ill for some time *(a sister who leaves her vocation commits a mortal sin and is condemned to everlasting hell)*. In my second year I had developed an ulcer which was not diagnosed or treated until my fifth year *(offer it up, sister. ask jesus for strength)*. Also in my second year I began to hyperventilate regularly. The hyperventilation was never diagnosed, treated or even named while I was a nun *(your desire to leave religious life is a temptation, sister. very intelligent girls seldom succeed in religious life)*. Following the Little Way of St. Therese, I offered it up, but the twice weekly attacks left me chronically fatigued, mentally disorganized, depressed and confused *(god first self last not worthy sickness in head temptation obedience)*.

Somehow I graduated *magna cum laude* from the University of Dayton in 1963. While my community and family were proud that I was the top achiever at that graduation, my stomach pains were excruciating. I would rather have been in bed. The self confidence with which I had walked into religious life was shattered by the time I completed my five years of postulancy, novitiate, and juniorate. In September, 1963, I went to teach eighth grade English in Falls Church, Virginia, with trepidation. Imagine my surprise when I turned out to be a good teacher. Slowly my ulcer healed. Slowly my hyperventilation attacks abated.

It was my great fortune at that time to have a friend, a slightly older and very wise sister who took me under her wing. She was mentor and comforter to me. My isolation was broken at last. Others were not pleased. *(you have come here to give yourself to god. you must guard against getting too close to another sister. you must treat all the same with the love of christ)*.

The possibility of sexual contact between us was not an issue. As well as being earnest about our vows, we were both homophobic. But we were secretly affectionate in platonic physical ways such as holding hands and hugging. We barely held to the line of convent propriety *(you must guard against Particular Friendships)*. I have never loved anyone more dearly. She was salvation for me at a critical time, and I ignored the voices where she was concerned.

I taught for four years. After my third year, the General Council made the community's first acknowledgement of my long-standing problems. They did not allow me to proceed on schedule with my class to make final vows. Rather, with their encouragement, I renewed temporary vows for a sixth year.

During that year I developed psychosomatic heart pains, which led me to seek psychiatric counseling. After six months of weekly visits, the psychiatrist pronounced me fit to continue in religious life. He wrote a letter to the Superior General, but to no avail. I still was not allowed to make final vows. Since I had reached the legal limit on temporary vows, the decision meant I had to leave the order. I asked for explanations but was told only that it was thought best I leave.

I did not understand the timing of the rejection. Expulsion in my second year, when I first reported my problems, I would have understood. I had even requested it. Expulsion in my ninth year was hard to bear. I walked away from religious life and did not look back. A year later I was filled with a rage so great that I left the Catholic Church never to return.

My coming into Lesbianism was indirect. On the assumption that I was heterosexual, I dated men, with various unsatisfactory results, for several years. After being raped by a blind date in 1970, I bought a copy of Kate Millet's *Sexual Politics* and discovered feminism. It opened my life. From there I read many of the wonderful feminist books that proliferated in the early 1970s, and I became active in the National Organization for Women *(ball busting women's libbers)*.

In 1972, I first said out loud to my best friend in NOW, "I'm afraid I might be a Lesbian" *(repulsive, loathsome)*. By 1975, however, I was running as an open Lesbian for my second term on the NOW board. By 1977, I was helping my lover organize the Lesbian Activist Bureau in Cincinnati. By 1978 I had become a featured speaker at Cincinnati's annual Lesbian/Gay Pride Day. During these activist days, my house was egged several times, obscenities were written on its sides *(lezzie sucks, bitch go to hell)*, and my car was doused with a corrosive substance that stripped its finish.

The ongoing harassment caused me pain and fear. Yet once I realized I was a Lesbian, I knew I would become a visible, activist Lesbian. My struggles as a nun had taught me how to be strong in the midst of fear. My feminism had led me to know my rights. I had become too much in touch with the core of my integrity to allow old voices — or new ones — to stop me.

Yet a new struggle waited. My parents cut me off *(we cannot condone your way of life)*. My public activism embarrassed them *(you are flaunting your lifestyle and flouting your parents' values)*. Their rejection was painful, but my integrity did not allow me to yield *(why are you doing this to us? where did we go wrong?)*. From 1977 to 1981 my parents and I did not see each other and maintained only minimal contact through mail. Our distance was facilitated by the fact that I lived in Ohio and they lived in Florida. I gave up on seeing them again. I said, "I have no parents." Then they shocked me by initiating a visit of a few hours during a trip where they passed through town. The politely positive visit seemed but a drop of reconciliation in an ocean of estrangement, but it was a beginning.

A year later my lover and I visited them in Florida at their warm invitation. It was as though there never had been an estrangement. The visit was wonderfully healing. We didn't talk much about what had happened between us but my mother did say, "Your father and I decided that we were being arrogant, intolerant, and unchristian."

I have allowed this sentence to ring in my mind over and over. By their reconciliation, my parents, who are in their 70s, give me hope and optimism in my deepest self. They have reached across many decades and levels of societal conditioning to say "You are our daughter and we love you." They have walked down strange paths with me, paths none of us anticipated when I was their bright, achieving child, full of promise for the fulfillment of their dreams. They have had to give up those dreams and accept who I have become instead. For this I applaud, thank and love them.

As for religious life, there are parts of it I miss, ghosts who are welcome in my heart. I miss the music and poetry of the liturgy, the soaring and moaning of Gregorian chant, the novice choir singing with one voice. I miss the summers at the Motherhouse with hundreds of sisters home for summer school, strolling the grounds in clusters of three or four, filling the chapel with their loving energy. I miss the feast days when rules were relaxed and we laughed and played. I miss being part of a whole that felt so worthwhile, the many role models, the concentration of so much caring and talent in one place.

I suppose it is not surprising that I continue to gravitate toward women. I like the energy of women who are striving to transform themselves, their relationships, and life on our mother earth. This description fits sisters I have known and loved both in the convent and in the world of Lesbians, feminists and witches.

Always with me are these good sisters, past, present, and to come — the sisters who loved me, the nun, in 1963; the sisters who love me, the Lesbian, in 1983; and the sisters who will love whoever I am in 1993. The power to hold these loves, apparently contradictory, always present, is

mine. As for my many ghosts and their voices, I simply enter-
tain those I like and exorcise the rest. That power also is
mine.

*I am a middle-aged, middle-class white Lesbian from
Cincinnati, Ohio, with many dreams for bringing more love
into the world. Feeling torn between an autonomous, free
spirit self and a traditional conformist self is my daily
struggle. I am currently concentrating on deep self-healing
and freeing up of my personal powers.*

Section II

RACE, CLASS, AND CULTURE

Are convents havens of multicultural freedom? Unfortunately not! Racism, anti-Semitism, and classism infect religious communities just as they do every sector of our society. Where we anticipated charity, those of us who are dark-skinned, foreign-born, or working class experienced condescension, silencing, or outright persecution. We were forced to whitewash our own culture and to adopt middle-class values and manners in the name of holy obedience.

GET RID OF THAT NUN

Marie Dennis
(1960–1968)

I was the first black to enter the Sisters of Notre Dame de Namur. The novitiate was in Reading, Ohio. At that time, Reading had an ordinance prohibiting black people from living there. Any black who came to that town had to be out by six at night. No one knew how the town would deal with my coming to live in the novitiate. The lawyers got ready, but the town decided not to create a fuss.

There was racial prejudice in the order. The older nuns were very direct about it. One told me, soon after I entered, "Yes, you'll make a good house sister; Negroes aren't smart enough to teach." I never dreamed I would be a teacher. I just assumed I'd be a house sister and do the physical work. I came from poverty. But the order recognized my intelligence and decided to train me in medical technology. Later

I took additional classes and was certified to teach math and science.

I encountered open hostility when I was sent out on missions. Convents would receive threatening phone calls: "Get rid of that nigger nun." In one town, a rock was thrown through our window. It was 1966 in Columbus, Ohio. I was scared. A cross had been burned outside the convent when word got around the parish that a black nun was arriving. The other nuns in that house were scared, too. Some wanted to leave; some wanted to take a stand. The superior was a wonderful woman. She tried to make me feel welcome and she instructed the other sisters to do the same.

I was assigned to teach in the high school. The first day my classes were boycotted by 50% of the students. The principal put his foot down: attend class or be expelled. They attended class. I got snide remarks at first, but my math class placed first that year. Remembering how I hated school, I always tried to teach the way I wish I'd been taught. The second year I got the math teacher of the year award. Kids were fighting to get into my classes by then.

In the convent, I didn't know I was a Lesbian. But I fell in love with another nun when we were teaching together. I was on cloud nine all the time. Sister George Ann and I were co-awarded Freshman Teacher of the Year Award. The students said it was nice to have teachers who liked each other and were so warm; they wished the other nuns felt that way about one another. But Sister George Ann and I were separated after that year. Our superior reminded us that particular friendships were destructive to the community; they encouraged the breaking of the rules. She transferred Sister George Ann to another city.

I left the community for two reasons. One was the discovery that I could have such deep feelings for another person. The other was my growing disillusionment with the Church; I could no longer support the Catholic position especially on sexual and social issues.

My belief now is in ultimate evolution toward love: love oneself, other people and the earth. That includes practical concerns like disarmament and saving the land from pollution.

I don't regret my eight years in the convent. Religious life gave me the tools I've used ever since for thinking, living, loving, and growing. I'm a better person for having been a nun.

I was born in 1942 and grew up in the Cincinnati ghetto called West End. I presently work as a lab technician at the University of Cincinnati Medical School. I have served as a deacon in the Metropolitan Community Church, was co-founder of Labyris, a radical Lesbian group, and have spoken on Lesbian and gay rights on television and radio.

This story is based on an interview with Nancy Manahan in February 1983.

Sr. Kevin, Ad.P.P.S., 1962

Kevyn Lutton, 1984

FROM CONVENT TO COVEN —
A WORKING LIFE

Kevyn Lutton
(1960-1967)

(This 1983 interview by Donna Warnock took place in San Francisco.)

Donna: What was your family background?

Kevyn: I was born in 1942 in Granite City, Illinois, a steel mill town northeast of St. Louis. I was the eighth child of nine — working class. My father was a railroad engineer. My mother cleaned offices, took in laundry, and, for a while, was a bookkeeper at a doctor's office. She also ran a household for eleven people. I have white skin and wish I knew more about my ethnicity. I feel a loss. I suspect that my paternal grandmother might have been Native American. My grandfather was French-speaking with a German-sounding name.

Donna: What was your religious upbringing?

Kevyn: Catholic Girl Martyr! I was very religious. From the time I was nine years old I was obsessed with figuring out why life was so hard. The Catholic ritual, symbolic paraphernalia, music and mysterious language took a hold on my heart. It comforted me, as rhythms and seasons dramatized always do, and it gave me a place to figure out mysteries.

Donna: What images of women were you raised with?

Kevyn: God, so much suffering! So much misery! The daily cross — you bear it! When my mother was in the fifth or sixth month of pregnancy with her ninth child at age forty-six, she was in an automobile accident and suffered a broken pelvis. The doctors urged her to allow them to abort the baby; otherwise there was a strong likelihood she would never walk again. When the parish priest heard this he forbade her to abort because of the Church's stance. My oldest sister, who was my mother's confidante and knew that this was an unwanted pregnancy in the first place, "lost her faith" and left the Church. This grieved my mother more than her own plight. As it turned out my youngest sister was born with Down's Syndrome. The reactions of the adults to my sister's disability brought a permanent state of crisis into the family that shaped my childhood, since I was expected to be the caretaker, not my brothers. I learned that women sacrifice and take care of others.

My mother also taught me about passing for middle class. Our house was not just clean, but VERY CLEAN all the time. It was a matter of pride to look good. My mother prayed constantly — still does. It's her way of accepting a hard life. My mother won the All-American Mother contest just after Granite City, Illinois, was named All-American City of the Year. In 1957 the steel mills were buzzing with pollution and violent working conditions — but high employment. My mother had nine children, including a disabled baby and three sons in the military during the Korean War.

Donna: What are your memories about sexuality?

Kevyn: Catechism lessons about sexuality being the major sin really got to me. I remember the first time I masturbated, when I was twelve. It was a hot summer day and there was nobody in the house, which was rare. I had just taken a bath and was standing naked in front of the mirror. I started feeling myself and got totally aroused and had my first orgasm. Then I was overwhelmed with the realization: "This is IT — the ultimate sin! Now I have to go to confession before I do anything else because if I die I'll burn in hell for all eternity." That confession was a nightmare. There was this long line of people down the aisle of the Church waiting to be forgiven. It was hotter than hell, but every time my turn came to enter the confessional, my courage failed and I went to the back of the line. I stayed in that stuffy Church for three hours. I was so ashamed.

Donna: Can you remember your first thoughts about being a nun?

Kevyn: By the third year of high school I was convinced that I wanted to go into the convent where I could live and work with women and no men. It would end all my problems. I was working peeling potatoes at Hullings Cafeteria in St. Louis from 4 to 8 a.m. before going to school. I didn't want to do that for the rest of my life. The privilege and status of nuns were flattering in my imagination.

Donna: What did you expect would happen when you joined the convent?

Kevyn: There was something very seductive about contemplative life for me. It meant total freedom from having to relate to the world at all. I thought I would get into this state, like Teresa of Avila, the mystic who wrote books on spiritual love and was reported to levitate.

Donna: What order did you join?

Kevyn: Sister Adorers of the Most Precious Blood of Jesus Christ. They ran my high school. Every year they sent Sister Timothy to recruit. I fell in love with her. I still love her.

Donna: What's unique about Sister Adorers — as opposed to other teaching orders?

Kevyn: Sister Timothy!

Donna: How did you like convent life?

Kevyn: I liked it. The first three years were a real high. Order, cleanliness, peace, living in the country, wonderful food, fresh bread baking in the oven. Here I had taken the vow of poverty, and I had never eaten so well in my entire life! Of course, we worked to create it all, but not nearly as hard as I had at home. There was total security. I had what I needed. My family didn't have to provide for me. I gained access to a lot of privilege, particularly education. I felt so protected from crisis. My favorite sister postulant was from Chicago. She grew up poor. There was this heart-bonding crush between us, but we were living a strict monastic lifestyle. We had only two periods of the day, totalling one hour and fifteen minutes, when we could speak to one another. My friend had been there almost a full year when I woke one morning to find her gone. She was sent home because of her health. She had never had such good food. She overate and got an ulcer.

Donna: What were relationships like in the convent?

Kevyn: There was a lot of deep affection, interest, and caring. But class divisions were especially obvious between the maintenance women and the academics. I think there was class oppression directed at me and some others. I was required to take workshops on parlor manners: how to set out for tea and what not to say. I resented that.

Donna: How about the issue of race?

Kevyn: There was only one woman of color in our

convent of about five hundred. This reflected the racism in the larger community the parish served. People of color were invisible to them.

Donna: Describe your own sexuality when you were a nun.

Kevyn: I was sexually closed down. All that energy was rerouted through my analytical mind. I was striving for an altered state of spiritual consciousness.

Donna: Were you aware of any Lesbian activity in the convent?

Kevyn: No — except for nuances. There was one teacher I really loved. She became my special mentor, and she was the first person to make me think about classism. She was raised poor, Irish Catholic, and had spent much of her childhood in an orphanage. As my English teacher, she encouraged me to write about growing up in Granite City. One summer back at the motherhouse when I was feeling blue about lack of allies in the midst of the political struggles, she came to me late at night, and we hugged and cuddled. That was quite sexual and daring. Her affection and support were really beautiful.

Donna: How did Vatican II change things?

Kevyn: All over sisters were breaking solemn silence talking about Vietnam and the exploitation of Third World countries. Pierre Teilhard de Chardin's books were being smuggled into the convent. They were blacklisted in the Church. Chardin was excommunicated for saying things like the earth is the Body of Christ and sacred, and Christians are required to take responsibility for its evolution. This sacrilegious talk created an internal split. Many nuns wanted to be more politically involved in the world and felt we had no right to sit around in comfort and security. Those of us who were speaking out were intentionally isolated from each other and sent to remote parishes where rigid superiors were in charge. Sister Esther, a brilliant woman

I loved, vanished for a time. She was given shock therapy. Mother Superior would tell me that my spirituality was flawed because I spoke out on these issues. I had been receiving her disciplinary lectures for about a year when my father fell ill with cancer. I got permission to go home to help my mother nurse him. It was a nightmare. He screamed in pain. I gave him morphine injections, but then he became poisoned by the drug and screamed in terror from hallucinations. My mother and I had very little support from my community. After my father died, I was very depressed, but I was not allowed to grieve. We nuns were well schooled in the art of detachment. I returned to the parish where I was teaching forty-seven seventh graders subjects like geography, which I hadn't studied since I'd been in seventh grade.

After three weeks back, Mother Superior took me late at night to a mental hospital in St. Louis. The admissions clerk asked, "Why are you here?"

"I don't know. She brought me. Ask her," I answered pointing to Mother Superior. They gave each other knowing looks. I was committed and heavily drugged. The doctor told me he was considering giving me shock treatments. Thank goodness he didn't.

After three weeks I was sent back to the same school to teach, but the parishioners had learned of my incarceration and circulated a petition to have me removed. I was depressed anyway, not allowed to process what had happened to my father during his long and violent death. To find myself labeled mentally ill really undermined my inner resources. Then I was sent to an even more remote parish where the superior demanded strict obedience and made the nuns kneel before her to take orders.

Donna: How did you leave the convent?

Kevyn: I was asked to leave, but I refused. "No, I'm going to stay in here and struggle." I wrote to the provincial motherhouse in Rome and was allowed to continue. But after another year I wanted to leave and did. I was driven to my mother's house by another nun. I went in, took off my habit, put on street clothes my sister had gotten for me, gave the habit to the nun, and she left. It was a sharp cutting off of my whole life. Feelings of being a stranger and alien in the secular world were so painful. Relating to my body again after all those years was difficult. It took some time looking at my face in the mirror with my hair showing and my head bare and round before I could deal with the freedom of choosing a "look." I was befuddled by clothing and fashion and style.

That first month out I was very depressed and still seeing the shrink from the hospital and taking drugs. Giving up the convent struggles was a dream dying. I had no community outside — only my family. Although they were affectionate and helpful in a material way, they couldn't relate to my radical ideas about how the Church needed to change. Art classes at Southern Illinois University were very healing. I also studied theology and became a "whiz" on the "death of God" theme and the secularization of religion — hot topics in theological circles in those days. That year others left, including my postulant mistress and Sister Timothy. I helped her re-entry process, realizing all along I had a crush on her. But she fell in love with an ex-monk.

Donna: Do you have any regrets about having been in the convent?

Kevyn: Not now. Given the circumstances of my life, it was a fortuitous thing to do. But for ten years after I came out, I regretted the time I had spent there. I felt that I had been exploited from childhood by the Catholic Church, that I had spent seven meaningless years as a nun. At first I was so angry that the sight of a nun brought up a lot of resentment. I thought all nuns and priests were

stupid and that all the smart ones had left. But now I consider myself a religious person again and have respect for
anyone engaged with spiritual issues connected to taking
responsibility for our earth. Many Catholic priests and
nuns are deeply committed to political struggle. Now I
see nuns as just working women, different among themselves.

Donna: I work for a peace organization which has a
counter-military recruitment program for people thinking
about entering the armed forces. We counsel them on alternatives and provide referrals for job placement, training,
and educational opportunities, especially for low-income
people. Do you think there should be a counter-recruitment
program in the women's community for young women
considering the convent?

Kevyn: Yes, definitely. I would also like to see support
structures in the women's community to facilitate ex-nuns'
re-entry into secular society. We need consciousness raising
about ex-nuns. It's oppressive when people smirk at women
who have spent time in the convent. It invalidates the person
herself, her choices, her background; and it reinforces the
internalized oppression of ex-nuns. I would like to see
Catholics stop putting nuns on pedestals. I would like more
of a sense of community between nuns and women outside the convent. Anti-psychiatry information would have
helped me see my psychiatric treatment as the oppressive
silencing it was. I hope that at least grief counseling is available now. I also fantasize about networking between Lesbian
witches and nuns. It would be wonderful for both groups.

Donna: What about your first sexual relationship?

Kevyn: After I came out of the convent, I got my degree
and taught art in St. Louis inner city schools, scattered
about the projects among this maze of poorly constructed,
overcrowded high-rise buildings for poor, urban black people.
I had a wonderful relationship with another teacher, a black

man. When I was twenty-seven, I got married and moved to Florida, where I taught art and worked against segregation in Florida schools. When I returned to art school I was really attracted to women, but homophobia was so acute that I chose to remain in the closet.

Donna: How did your spiritual beliefs evolve after you came out of the convent?

Kevyn: At first, I gave up all spiritual practices. I considered myself an ex-Catholic and did a lot of writing and reading about the secularization of spirit, as I called it. God was dead. I mourned that loss and comforted myself by making art. I was frightened. I pushed myself from time to time into political struggle but found myself morbidly aware of my powerlessness and oppression from sexism and classism. The final clincher came in 1975 when my inability to find employment landed me on welfare. Welfare sent me to Vocational Rehabilitation which sent me to a psychiatrist. I spent the next five years being drugged and exploited.

But during this time a young Jewish woman befriended me and admired my art. She was researching and teaching classes in witchcraft. She wanted me to join the coven she was forming. My depressed, drugged, withdrawn state kept me resisting for two years, but I finally joined. A year later my rage at the psychiatrists who had been abusing me emotionally and sexually began to surface. I was hospitalized in a psych ward, drugged more, and put in restraints. My coven visited me every day, pacified the keepers, and got me out. I began to take more seriously the witch's belief in her ability to TAKE her power. I was formally initiated as a witch and a priestess by my coven and committed myself to a passionate relationship to the goddess, the female spirit, as I find her immanent in the Earth and all her natural creatures and in women.

Donna: When did you come out as a Lesbian?

Kevyn: I identified as a political Lesbian about three or four years before I came out to my sexuality, which was about three years ago.

Donna: Can you draw parallels between your expectations in becoming a nun and in becoming a Lesbian?

Kevyn: There was the expectation of being able to live and work outside male privilege and dominance. The convent presented that illusion, but our powerlessness in the patriarchal Church was brought home to us daily. When I thought about becoming a nun, I dreamed of spiritual ecstasy, and when I thought about becoming a Lesbian my dream was sexual ecstasy. Now both expectations are satisfied because I'm open to my sexual feelings in a satisfying way. Working with another woman who turns me on sexually is the ultimate. To have work carry a conscious erotic charge energizes me. There are other parallels between Lesbians and nuns: the ways we work together, the ways we communicate, the ways we shape our goals, the ways we go about achieving them, the ways we look after each other. In groups I work with there's a commitment to feminist spirituality, community building, and taking responsibility for the earth.

Kevyn's note: I am grateful to my working class sister and political activist partner, Donna Warnock, for forcing me to submit this story despite all my resistance. It was painful to recall so many buried hurts. However, a lot of pain was caused by the stubborn belief that my life was not normal. Then I realized that "normal" is what those with too much power want us to be and the way oppressed people never are. As it turns out, I'm happy to have shared my story.

WHAT WAS A NICE JEWISH GIRL LIKE ME DOING IN A CONVENT?

Ayyelet Hashachar
(1962–1968)

Dear Shoshi,

Your letter has been sitting on my desk for weeks. I promised myself that I would answer your question before I did another thing, but every time I faced this blank page, I could not begin. What was a nice Jewish girl like me doing in a convent? I had no idea it would be so painful for me to remember. Yet I must write this story, not so much for you as for myself. You know the rabbinic saying: "If I myself am not for me, then who will be for me? And if not now, when?"

No wonder my former life as a nun surprises you. Glossing by biography is a reflex response. I have camouflaged an entire period of my life to avoid answering questions

about my convent years. When I met you, I had been living
as a Jew for ten years. Not that you would have questioned
my credentials as a Jew or held my Christian past against
me. But there was a time, after I had returned to the States
from Israel, and before my conversion was official, when
I was denied jobs, when my support of Israel was held
suspect, and when a few students even challenged my professional competence. Imagine the reaction if such people
had known that I had been a nun!

So I became a dissembler, attempting to cover the six-
year gap in the passport of my Jewish identity. To make
those years intelligible to Jews, I would have had to por-
tray the chilling atmosphere of Catholicism which Mary
Gordon evokes so well in her novels. When I finished *Final
Payments*, I felt that I too, like the protagonist, had been
saved from the quicksand only by the force of self-perserving
rage.

Since I left the convent, I have searched for something
worth salvaging from my days there. I did receive an excellent liberal arts education and I made some good friends.
No one discouraged me from studying any subject because
I was a woman; on the contrary, I was encouraged to excel.
In high school, too, I was attracted to nuns because they
were such independent women. I especially remember the
nun who taught me literature and creative writing: she
was bright, witty, strong, non-conformist, athletic, and had
a man's name. I wanted to be like her.

I entered the convent when I was seventeen, although
I had never been "religious" and had never experienced a
"call" (vocation), only a sense of guilt induced by the nuns
because I was making plans for my life after high school
graduation without taking God into account. The other
young women who joined with me were no different. The
sisters skimmed the "creme de la creme" off the top of
each graduating class: the officers of every school organiza-

tion, the brightest, most creative students, the best athletes. I remember only one misfit: she was sent home from the convent after reporting a vision of the Blessed Virgin Mary.

My ambivalence about entering the convent should have become obvious when I got an ulcer during the summer after graduation from high school, but I did not perceive the connection at the time. My parents were more resigned to my decision than happy about their only child leaving them for a life of service in the Church. Some people have suggested that I entered religious life to get away from home; but the community I joined, like my family, was Irish Catholic, authoritarian, and conservative. When I realized that the convent wasn't all I had hoped for, I didn't leave right away. I chose to stay and to try to conform. From my family, which had always been involved in politics, I learned to fight the system from within — but only from within. I put up with what I didn't like and suppressed my anger. Each year I thought that the next one would be better: things were bound to change. I would have more freedom later on. Although each work or teaching assignment seemed worse than the previous one, I believed that a decision as important as this one should not be based on one particular set of circumstances. I had professed vows with the intention of keeping them for life. If I were to leave the convent, maybe I would be incapable of any kind of final commitment again.

I never did adjust to the regimen of long prayer services at dawn, mass, the rosary, confession, lectures on the religious life, readings from spiritual books during meals, chapter of faults, days and nights of silence, wearing a crew-cut to keep on headgear fashioned after medieval armor, and kneeling to ask permission for everything from soap and sanitary napkins to my academic schedule. I did what was expected of me when omission would have been obvious. Each year I did less and less. I substituted yoga at night for meditation, which I slept through each morning. Gradually, I lost everything, not only confidence in institutionalized religion but also spirituality and belief in God.

I also developed an allergy to the communal life which had become both a benefit and a burden to an only child. I couldn't be lonely since I was surrounded by people; I couldn't have solitude on my own terms either. I was a walking representative of the Church twenty-four hours a day, at the service of laity and religious alike.

At first I was able to look up to women ten to fifteen years older who seemed to share my values. As long as they were making it, there was hope for me too. But the community failed to implement changes in religious life proposed by the Second Vatican Council. The women in power chose to "stay the course." Many Sisters abandoned hope of changing the system from within, and between 1966 and 1968, women between ages twenty-five and fifty left in droves. With my role models gone, I had nothing to look forward to except working to pay medical bills for the elderly Sisters. When one of those recipients of my salary reported me for wearing bermuda shorts one Saturday morning, instead of my habit, my rage erupted. I quit.

Looking back, I see now that the convent was an early version of the women's separatist movement. We were women who left behind the world in which women were given to men by men. We were all Lesbians, to varying degrees, depending on our awareness of ourselves as women-identified women. The convent, however, fell far short of being a utopian, all-women society. The very setting which could have fostered women loving women prohibited its strongest bonding force. We could have had power as women together, but the flaw in the scenario, what prevented the convent from the fullest realization of its potential as a separatist society, was sex. Homophobia operated in the convent with even more force than in society at large.

My first night, as we prepared for bed, in silence and semi-darkness, I began to be afraid of Lesbianism. That seems humorous now. My first dormitory slept eighteen. The only breach of Grand Silence came from three women around me talking in their sleep. Grand Silence, group bedrooms, sheets hung around beds, dorms being off limits during the daytime — all these prevented physical intimacy.

We were lectured on the dangers of "particular friendships." No one used the word Lesbian. The prohibition of close friendship between two women was based on the ideology of community life: if you restricted your time and attention too much to one person, it limited your availability to the community as a whole. I didn't understand that this prohibition was also designed to prevent the development of physical intimacy. One was supposed to sublimate "the stirrings of the flesh," but I never felt any because I had never explored my own body. We were even forbidden to use tampons. Chastity, a vow perceived only in heterosexual terms, was easy: I didn't miss what I didn't know and couldn't imagine.

Nevertheless, rules and regulations could not prevent people from falling in love. And I fell hard during my first year — the first love of my adult life. We thought it was a sublime friendship. We discovered in each other an affinity of the inner self. Gradually, during that year, our emotional closeness led to a desire to be physically close and to touch each other. Finally, the intensity of our feelings alarmed us. My friend decided that for the sake of the common good, we would have to part ways. Because she didn't trust herself to maintain a sensible balance by dividing her time and attention, she gave me up entirely. Although we lived in the same college, she did not speak to me for three years. Had the renunciation been mutual, I wouldn't have been so hurt. But I was not ready to let go.

The end of this friendship-love had consequences later. Like Berenice in *The Member of the Wedding* who married "pieces" of her first love in other men, after I left the convent, I met, fell passionately in love with, and almost married my friend's brother. I should have been suspicious that he, more than any other man, evoked so intense a response in me. At eighteen, however, the intensity of my feelings and my anger at the loss of his sister's love had led me to try to stifle my emotions. I almost succeeded in blotting out my capacity to love along with my anger.

Eventually I became involved with another woman before I left the convent. When I learned that my mother was terminally ill, my roommate tried to comfort me. The relative privacy of our dorm room allowed us to be physically close and tender, but we didn't dare sleep in the same bed for fear of discovery. Our natural curiosity led us to experiment kissing each other's lips and breasts. We went no further since neither of us suspected the power of sexual arousal which lay dormant between our legs. What we did felt good and answered needs in each of us. Even when we were assigned to teach in different places, we continued our physical involvement during visits. Then she too broke off the relationship before the renewal of her vows. When I told her a few months later that I was leaving the convent, she told me to go to hell.

After I left the convent, I immediately began dating men again to find out what I had missed in heterosexual society. I engaged in short-term relationships, gained some experience sexually, read books on sex, and learned how to masturbate. I became active in the civil rights, women's liberation, and anti-war movements. My feminist friends in graduate school dragged my consciousness out of medieval Catholicism into the twentieth century. They discussed freely any issue that touched them as women, including Lesbianism. I fell in love with one of these friends and later had an affair with another. That was my real sexual awakening, and the beginning of accepting myself as a Lesbian.

One of the characters in Djuna Barnes' *Nightwood* claims that "the contemplative life is an effort to hide the body so the feet won't stick out."

I like that image. During those convent years, I did attempt a form of self-murder through my efforts to conform, but my sexuality kept sticking out no matter how hard I tried to suppress it. Later, I tried to blot out those six years of my life and pick up where I had left myself at eighteen, perhaps from a sense of guilt: I was complicit in the process of killing off my *self*. Neither the Church nor the convent could have done that to me unaided.

Remember the Meg Christian song about her Southern home: "No longer to blame for the pain that I could have found anywhere?" It is time I stopped blaming the convent for the pain of those years; it could have happened to me anywhere. It is time I stopped using laughter and forgetting as the numbing endorphines of my past. I'm ready to "embrace what I've loved and turn over the rest," as Meg says.

Shoshi, it has been difficult to write this letter, but I'm glad I did. I will save the story of how I became a Jew for another time. Write soon. I miss you.

Love,
Ayyelet.

Ayyelet Hashachar, Dawn's Strong Gazelle or Morning Star, is a Jewish Lesbian who teaches Judaic literature at a university, lives with her lover near the country, is writing a Lesbian novel, lifts weights, feeds birds, and wishes she could have a cat named Balagan — disorder, mess.

Sr. Mary Agnita, M.M. (r) and Sr. Bernard Damien,
M.M. (l), 1966

Jessie (r) and Fran (l), 1981

SO GOOD, SO RIGHT

Jessie
(1959-1967)

I was born in the United States, and so by an accident of birth am said to be an American. I am statistically classified as Negro, but I am actually a multi-racial mix.

I was born to Catholic parents and grew up in a very Catholic atmosphere. My family was poor. My introduction to middle-class values and living came with my convent years. Upon leaving the convent I continued a middle-class lifestyle for five years. Now I am poor by choice.

When I was growing up, my attitudes toward sexuality were based on the Catholic Church's teaching that sex was a necessary evil, a function to be performed in marriage blessed by the Church and only for the perpetuation of the species. Like many Catholics, I was confused and guilt-ridden.

73

I can place my first conscious interest in females — other than as friends — at age ten when I stayed overnight at my friend's home. Luna and I shared a bed. I felt drawn to be physically close to her, to touch and fondle her. I recall the immense exhilaration I felt in close body contact with Luna when she wrestled free of my "capture" of her on the playground.

Sexuality was a rare topic of conversation in my family. I vaguely recall occasional references to men who were "funny," meaning their effeminate behavior. Some women in my neighborhood were called "mannish," but there was no sexual inference. "Mannish" meant dress: the then uncommon practice of women wearing pants and keeping their hair short, their "unusual" physical strength, or their taking jobs usually identified with male workers. "Homosexuality" was not part of my vocabulary until age twenty-five. "Lesbian" entered my vocabulary at age thirty-two. I had been in love with a woman emotionally, romantically and sexually for six years at that point.

As I grew up, I never considered entering college. Marriage, a family, and work were the only options I knew. But I sensed I had a religious vocation. I began dating boys to test my vocation. I, of course, had predetermined the outcome of this test. Dating also helped me appear normal so that when I entered religious life it would appear that I had enjoyed all the things normal girls enjoyed and was giving them up for a higher calling.

In 1958, I entered a foreign missionary community in the northern United States. Before this I had not travelled farther than one hundred miles from my home in the South. Among some two thousand missionary sisters in this community I was only the second black to be accepted for training. The convent represented drastic changes on every level of my life. But my conformity served to make me a model religious for most of the eight and a half years I spent there.

For most of my convent life my emotional and sexual needs were either repressed or redirected into prayer, work, or other acceptable activities. As a young professed sister, I formed deep, true friendships with women in my community, many of which continue today. One of these friendships was my first falling in love with a woman. I did not identify my feelings as romantic emotion. I simply felt, reeled, glowed in her presence. I wept for days at her departure for other community pursuits and reveled in our reunion. Our times together were intense but never overtly sexual. We hugged in greeting and touched hands frequently, but a deep fear of admitting what might be stirring in us prevented expression of our desires. In addition to social taboos, our vows prohibited entertaining even thoughts of sexual behavior. Had we met outside the convent, one can only guess what might have developed. We are still close friends.

Overt sexual involvement came several years later with another sister who was a close friend. Fran's first impression of me was that I had few opinions on anything of substance. She was an activist ready for change. To her, I seemed quiet and spiritual. Gradually our understanding of each other grew as we shared joys and disappointments, tense and carefree moments. We had discussions on changes inside our community and outside and how these changes affected us. As our relationship deepened, Fran became threatened by our closeness and tried to push me away. Knowing her better than she suspected, I chipped away at her defenses, and she became less threatened, more trusting.

One evening during a violent Pentecost Sunday windstorm, we realized that we were on the verge of crossing the line that would lead to romantic involvement. That evening, spent in clothed and seated physical closeness and ending with a kiss planted by me on her forehead, was intense with emotion. The next day we left for different summer schools, and the miles between us gave us time to make sense of our feelings. We exchanged many letters. By summer's end, we were prepared to share more than a friendship. What that meant, neither of us knew. The taboos and prohibitions of my earlier life had begun to lose relevance. My choices became more inner directed and responsible, less outwardly motivated and reactionary.

After months of fumblings, bunglings, and emotional pain, we realized we were deeply in love. Our relationship evolved as so good and right, so growth-producing for us individually and together that it never occurred to us that it could be wrong or sinful. In our sexual naivete, both of us experienced confusion over the exact nature of this new dimension we were exploring, but we did not feel guilt or anguish. Self-denial had been the path taught by our superiors. Giving, self-affirmation, and receiving in abundance became our experience in loving each other.

One and a half years after we became lovers, Fran left religious life. Five months later, I left too. Neither of us was asked to leave, but we both felt that we had outgrown religious life because it had outlived its usefulness.

After we left the convent, we participated in Catholic ritual at a local parish (a disaster), then at a university Newman center (less than uplifting), and then at avant-garde, in-home Eucharistic celebrations. Within a year of leaving the convent, we stopped participating in such rituals.

For the first eight years of our relationship, we had absolutely no contact with any Lesbian community. We had no support system, no outside affirmation of our lifestyle, and no models for reference. We had no name or definition for what we shared, and perhaps that absence had a positive effect on our relationship. During those early and sometimes stormy periods, we were forced to confront each other and resolve our difficulties together. Later, connections with Lesbian communities provided the opportunity to share our experiences with other Lesbians and receive that long-awaited outside affirmation of our Lesbian identity.

We consider ourselves moral and spiritual persons using the golden rule as our moral measure. We strive to live in communion and minimize conflict with the natural order of things. We experience communication within our immediate environment extending to sentient and non-sentient beings on our planet and to the moons, planets, and stars in our galaxy and beyond. We are opening closed doors, drawing on untapped energies within ourselves, taking previously inconceivable risks. We daily discover new powers, new capacities for healing, new dimensions for our loving and caring for each other and others.

We feel that goddesses and gods are creations of humans out of a need to explain the unexplainable, to achieve some selfish power over other persons or objects, or to avoid responsibility for action or inaction. We are content to wonder at the unexplainable and do not desire power over persons or objects. We take full responsibility for our actions or inaction. For example, we strive to use only energy and materials we need, never to abuse or waste, to live simple lives uncluttered by possessions. For seven years we have lived in a two-room cabin half a mile into the woods. After sunset our home is lighted by kerosene lanterns. Our water source is a hand-pumped well a few feet from the cabin. We heat and cook with wood. We elected not to have a phone when we learned it would be necessary to install several poles to re-attach existing wires. The prohibitive cost, heavy equipment scarring our natural landscape, and removing trees were all incompatible with our lifestyle.

Politically we are striving anarchists. We earn our living

as self-employed carpenters/painters/remodelers/repairers, charging fees commensurate with our needs. We take great pride in doing a job well, our rate of pay being in no way related to the value we place on our work. Many people, including some feminists, perceive us as undervaluing ourselves because they continue in the male tradition of equating work value with the price tag. We reject that tradition.

For sixteen years we have been searching for new ways of living. Some things we have tried have not worked, or at least not perfectly; some have been good for only certain periods of our lives; some remain integral parts of us; and many have yet to be tried. Together, as two women in love, committed to each other and to our way of life, we have come to where we are; and together we are moving on. Individually neither of us could have come half this distance.

Jessie and Fran live and love in Maine.

Section III

THEY SHALL NOT TOUCH

Our superiors encouraged blind obedience, self-denial, custody of the senses, mortification of the flesh, and avoidance of particular friendship. We were forbidden to touch each other. We were told that we were sick, evil, dangerous, unforgivable. Confused and guilt-ridden, we worked ourselves to exhaustion to purge and punish our wayward desires. We were advised to pray harder for the grace not to feel what we were feeling.

THEY SHALL NOT TOUCH, EVEN IN JEST

Margaret
(1963-1965)

I graduated from high school in June 1963. I didn't want to get married, and I did want to do something good for the world. I was idealistic. When I told my mother I wanted to enter the order of nuns that taught in my school, she cried and said she had been praying for years that one of us would have a vocation. She thought it best for her to tell my father, so I went out one evening. When I got home my father was lying on the living room floor crying in the dark. He never cried and never lay on the floor. He asked me why I was doing this and pleaded with me not to go. He said he would send me to any college I wanted to study anything I wanted for as long as I wanted. I told him the convent was what I wanted. He just cried more and said he didn't understand. We never talked about it again. After I entered he somehow decided to be proud of me and had my picture on his desk at the office and bragged about me to coworkers.

Entering the convent was my first experience away from home, and it was two thousand miles. I loved the community I entered for its spirit. I loved the feeling that we were all united in a common goal. The "we" experience was new to me and very liberating. We were there for something larger than ourselves, and there was union, community, a framework that allowed and accepted individuality. I loved the singing too. Oh, the beauty of all those women's voices singing harmonies and chants. Sometimes I would stop singing for a few seconds and just let the sounds flood my being. It was like a declaration of life. The sounds and colors and feelings filled me so that I thought I would burst.

One of the first rules we learned was "They shall not touch one another, even in jest, except when going out or returning from a journey, and then only according to custom." We were warned not to form particular friendships, even though we didn't know what that meant.

One day we had fittings for our Sunday postulant dresses. Mine was too large in the bust. I was a 34B and it was at least a 38D. I met my postulant mistress in the hallway, and I asked her if I could get it altered. I opened my cape to show her it was too big. She looked at me, then my breasts, then reached out with both hands and stroked my breasts several times with her index fingers from the side to the nipples. "Oh no, dear, it fits fine. It fits fine." I was aghast. I could not believe she was touching my breasts. Not once, but two or three times, and in public. No one had ever touched my breasts. It sent chills through me. I couldn't speak. I never got my dress altered.

When John Kennedy was killed in November 1963,

it was an emotional trauma for me. In 1964, as novices, we were watching a TV program commemorating the anniversary of his death. Most of us cried. Sister Barbara, another novice, put her arm around me as I cried. After everyone else left the room, Sister Barbara and I stayed. She held me, and it was such a relief. I had felt lonely, and this holding, this softness, took that away. Being held seemed like heaven. We soon developed a neurotic relationship. I played needy, and she played nurturing.

We began meeting privately, usually just before the afternoon recreation, sometimes in the trunk room, but most often in the tub room. One of us would sit on the chair and the other on the tub ledge. We'd hug. Then we began holding each other's breasts, cupping but not fondling. We didn't speak much. The echoes would have been noticed in the hallway. When we'd leave, one would remain behind for a few moments.

One night, after small silence, Sister Barbara was in my cubicle. There were eight people in that dorm, with each cubicle separated by a curtain or a partition. The privacy was strictly visual. At 9 p.m. the bell rang for profound silence. Sister Barbara did not leave. The next thing I knew she had me laid flat on the bed. She was on top of me, kissing me on the mouth. Her tongue darted in and out. I had never been kissed on the mouth. A lot of thoughts surfaced in those few seconds: "What the hell is this? What's she doing? What's this tongue business? There are seven other people in the dorm! Oh, I like this!" As I started responding and letting my tongue slide in and out alternately with hers, she shoved off me and whispered fiercely, "We must never do that again." In a daze I asked naively, "Why not?"

We were reported, of course. The next day, while I was waiting for classes to begin, Sister Barbara came out of the novice mistress' office. All her coyness was gone.

She grimly told me that Mother wanted to see me. She told me to deny that she had been with me after profound silence because she had denied it. I went in and told Mother that she had left my cubicle at 9 p.m. Mother asked me if I was sure, and I said that I was. There were no other questions. Sister Barbara and I began sleeping together, just sleeping spoon fashion on the cot size beds. I was always the one who went to her cubicle. Sometimes I would go to the bathroom before "lights out" and sit there till the night sister went by calling, "Laudetur Jesus Christus," turning off the lights.

At first we slept in our nightgowns. Then we slept nude. Once, I let my hand brush across her pubic hair (accidentally on purpose) and excused myself. She said it was OK. We never kissed after that first time. We never stroked or petted. We got into our spoon position and talked and went to sleep, waking before the morning bell.

For a time, I passed off what we were doing as "creature comfort." Then one day after being with Sister Barbara in the tub room, I went to my cubicle and masturbated. I went to Sister Barbara and told her we had to stop because I had masturbated after being with her. She asked me how I had done it! She, who never would kiss me again, wanted to know how to masturbate! I felt angry, confused, and help-less.

Once Sister Barbara and I and some other novices were in the noviceship for a short recreation before class. The novice mistress was expected momentarily, and we were all standing around talking and laughing. Sister Barbara grabbed my cincture and started pulling me around by it. She was laughing and teasing me and wouldn't let go. I was so embarrassed. She was exposing me and our rela-tionship. All I could do was grit my teeth and say over and over, "Let me go!" She was flaunting her power over me. After an eternity she let me go, still laughing.

Going to confession was hell. The priest was old, retired, barely shuffling in each morning to mumble through
Mass. If I had to go to confession before Mass, I stuck out
like a sore thumb. At one point I received permission to
talk to an outside priest. I wanted permission to do a physical
penance, thinking that my body's yearnings could only be
curbed by physical discipline. I had in mind something like
sleeping on the floor. I felt somewhat constrained because
this priest was a family friend of Sister Barbara's. He said
that this sort of thing sometimes happened in a confined
environment and not to worry or do any extra penance. I
was simply to follow the rule and that would keep me from
these occasions. I tried and failed a number of times, letting
the need for warmth and comfort prevail until the guilt set
in. Then the need would grow again.

I asked Mother to switch me to the dorm which ad-
joined her office/bedroom because it was rumored that she
was a light sleeper. She accused me of trying to be nearer
Sister Barbara's dorm. I told her I wanted to be next to
her office, not Sister Barbara's dorm, which was on the
same floor, and she gave me permission. After a week or
two I was slipping off in the night, despite the chance of
being caught by the novice mistress herself.

Finally, I couldn't stand it. The emotional upheaval,
the guilt and torment, the isolation and the loneliness. I
felt it in my body, my chest, my being. I was being ripped
apart. I went to Mother and asked to speak to Sister
Barbara privately. She gave me a long disgusted look before
granting permission.

The Rule was not enough. Even God was not enough.
Truth was my one last hope. If only Sister Barbara and I
could speak its name, while looking one another in the
eye, it would change the situation. I mustered up all my
courage, looked Sister Barbara in the eyes, and asked her
if she knew the word for what we had been doing.

She turned away and I knew I was lost. She kept saying, "Don't! Don't!"

I said, "Say it! Don't you see we can face this if we name it?" I was cold and scared and grim.

She kept saying, "Don't!" until I finally walked out. We didn't sleep together anymore.

The time between our talk and my decision was probably a week. I had to wait a few weeks until my hair grew. I had cut it to the scalp to keep myself in. Mother set a date for my departure with no "Are you sure, dear?" No talk about problems. Nothing.

Good-byes were forbidden. No one was to know before anyone left. The usual procedure was that Mother would announce the day after a person left before the morning lecture, "The Lord gives and the Lord takes away, praise be the name of the Lord. Sister So-and-So went home last night. The lecture for today is. . . ."

I walked out the front door the day I left. I turned for one last look at the immense grey stone abbey. My eyes swept up to the bell tower, my face contorted with rage and bitterness. I had one hand on the car door, and the other was raised in a fist. My anger was seething in me when my eyes came to rest on the doorway. There stood my novice mistress. Her mouth and eyes were open in shock at what she was seeing in my face and gesture. Our eyes locked for the brief moment. At last! At last I had communicated with someone. I turned, covered my anger, and got in the car.

I live on the West Coast with my lover.

CERTIFIED STRAIGHT

Kate Quigley
(1961-1966)

Born in a prairie city in Canada in 1940, I was adopted as the only child of a couple in their 30s and raised in a middle-class suburb which was slowly but surely inching its way out over the prairies. My father was of Scottish Presbyterian descent and my mother of Irish Roman Catholic stock. Although adopted, I identified strongly with their origins, helped by the fact that I had the "Celtic look," dark hair with fair skin and high coloring.

My father dominated my early and somewhat lonely childhood, explaining such diverse subjects as Napoleon Bonaparte's exile or the origin of volcanoes. At our summer camp we worked in the toolhouse on outboard motors so that by the age of ten I could change a spark plug or a shear pin. When my aunt lamented that my father didn't have a little lad to take fishing with him, my mother tartly replied that he didn't need one — he had me. My mother drummed into me very early that my behavior and appearance reflected on her. Our neighbors laughed at my disgust when, in my eleventh summer, my mother refused to let me appear in public shirtless, because I now was a young lady. I learned that boys had more freedom and that freedom equaled fun.

When I was six, I fell madly in love with the beautiful nun who prepared me for my First Holy Communion. In junior high school, I remember standing behind Sister Coleen, the current object of my affections, during a baseball game, when she ducked to avoid a fly ball which hit me instead, right in the middle of my forehead. With a rush of adolescent chivalry, I bent over her, groggily asking if she was all right. My devotion to the nuns in junior high school knew no bounds. I hung about the school every night, singing in the Glee Club under the direction of a brilliant nun for whom I developed a passion that lasted ten years.

My behavior was typical of most students of that era. We felt the nuns loved us, and we loved them back. As a teacher myself, I now marvel at the amount of time the nuns spent with us in spite of their enormously crowded schedules. Given this mutual affection, it was not surprising that many of us considered entering the community.

My path to the convent was by no means easy. I had wanted to enter after twelfth grade, but my homeroom teacher convinced me that I should study for a B.A. first. Reluctantly I agreed, sensing on the one hand that my application might not be accepted and, on the other hand, that my motives were perhaps not the purest. What if God didn't want me to become a nun? What if my attraction to religious life was based on my emotional involvement with the nuns? Worse still, what if my attractions were based on sensuality or, horror of horrors, on sexuality? My basic honesty forced me to discuss my doubts with my confessors. One priest told me that I had the makings of a saint. Another cheerfully allowed that I might be lesbian, but that I could offset any tendencies in that direction by being completely open with my superiors.

When I applied to the local superior in my last year of university, I was told to wait another year. My roof fell in. I listened in stunned silence while this nun, built like a six-foot policewoman herself, suggested that I was very "masculine" and that it would be better if I were to take a bachelor's degree in education and mature a bit more. I was shattered, angry, and in a panic.

My history professor, a remarkable woman and a nun in the community immediately took me in hand. For several months she counselled and supported me and at the same time went to bat with the superiors for me. In March, word came that my application was being considered. I learned later that my confessor had threatened to go over the heads of the local superiors in Montreal if action wasn't taken immediately. When at last accepted for entrance in July, I felt the old doubts once more, as well as new fears of rejection as a novice or before first or final vows. This fear was to remain with me during my religious life and finally to bring about its own fulfillment.

The novitiate schedule left us little time for ourselves. For reasons connected with the next morning's meditation, we were not permitted to read in bed, not even a meditation book. Accustomed as I was to reading myself to sleep, I lay awake long into the night, wondering how I would survive in the physical misery and homesickness that washed over me in dismal waves. Standing on the long gallery overlooking Dorval, I watched the planes take off, heartily wishing myself aboard one of them. Hot and humid summers in the Montreal novitiate while I was swathed in yards of

French serge made my mild childhood allergy to wool
and a new one to ragweed blossom into what seemed an
incurable succession of colds. I missed my city, my home,
the climate, and most of all, the nuns who had taught me.
Perhaps that superior had been right about staying out a
year to mature.

Why did I stay? I had convinced myself that it was God's
will for me to choose what was then considered the most
perfect way, the surest path to sanctity. I was probably too
proud, moreover, to admit defeat to my mother. Furthermore, I eventually found companionship living with a group
of bright, idealistic young women. Leaving the convent
then would have been like leaving the womb.

During the novitiate, warned against the famous
particular friendships (how could a friendship not be particular?), we kept physical distance, but the intense emotional
bonding was a source of both strength and anxiety to me.
What if one person began to dominate my consciousness,
crowding out God during times of prayer? Why was I so
disturbed if I couldn't talk to her during recreation? Later
on, as a young professed sister, I experienced these conflicts
with a greater intensity. In confession I worried about in-
ordinate attachments (never named as sexual sins) interfering
in my prayer life. During the eight days of retreat before
first profession of vows, I began once more to experience
the old doubts and fears. My superiors did their best to
calm my fears. But as I made my vows, I felt as if I were
committing a mortal sin.

The celebrations and the trip West were an agony for
me. I couldn't discuss my state of mind with anyone at
the Motherhouse and certainly not with my mother, who
travelled back with me on the train. At home, I sought out
my history professor as soon as I decently could and poured
out my fears that religious life was not God's will for me.
She was sober but reassuring. She lamented that my scruples

had cheated me out of the joy that I should have felt on giving my life to God.

That first year of teaching grade 10 in a remote mining town over 500 miles north of home taxed all my mental, emotional and physical energies to their limit. By October one of the nuns had indicated her preference for me. After my initial reluctance (I'll never get mixed up with Sister Genevieve!), I found myself enmeshed. I would have done well to have heeded my inner warnings and to have avoided her like the plague. But how does one avoid someone in a house of six people with practically no social outlets? We ate together, prayed together, recreated together. Her bedroom was next to mine. I could follow her every move whether I wanted to or not. The attraction became an obsession fuelled by her flattery and attention.

Although there had been no sexual contact, I brought up my obsession in confession. The priest was compassionate and good-humored. He advised backing off a bit. I tried, but by Christmas I was quite hopelessly in love. The superior, a wise and gentle woman who, I dimly realized, had been living a platonic relationship with another nun for many years, said at one point with great urgency: "Don't give your heart away!" Sister Pauline also tried to warn me that I meant nothing to Sister Genevieve. This was too difficult to accept at the time, but later I realized that she was right.

Things came to a head at the end of January when Sister Pauline and Sister Genevieve made a trip to the provincial house, ostensibly on community business. I sensed that community finances weren't the only item on the agenda. After their return, Sister Genevieve was cold and distant, bereft of the old intimacy and affection. I was out in the cold. The temperatures of fifty-six degrees below zero outside were nothing to the chill that crept into my spirit, leaving me in almost unmitigated misery. I tried to do things for my friend, but my services were refused, even

scorned. The friendship, if it can be called that, continued
for five years, even after I had left the community. The
superiors saw to it that we were separated for the next
two years of my teaching.

When the time came for me to renew my vows, the
provincial advised me to leave. The tensions had worn down
my health and made me irritable and hard to live with.
She had concluded I needed the support and companionship of one person, a man. Being refused permission to make
my vows gave me a feeing of *deja vu.* I had gone through
this five years before. The feeling of rejection that settled
on me lifted temporarily the day my vows expired. Some
of the accumulated tension of the last five years dissolved.

Regarding these years in religious life, I must clarify
one thing. I never saw, nor heard of, any overt sexual activity
among the nuns. Their vow of chastity was taken seriously.
My observations were confirmed by my history professor
who had lived in community for more than twenty-five
years. To be sure, the famous particular friendships
fluorished and were remarked upon, not without humor.
Most of the nuns seemed to take the phenomenon in stride
either in their own lives or the lives of others. Perhaps the
most striking example of this grassroots sanity was the
remark of an elderly provincial, speaking at a community
gathering in the twenties, who exclaimed regarding P.F.'s:
"Let them go to it! Thank God somebody loves somebody!"

After a disastrous year of living on the West Coast with
my mother and working on a M.A. in history, what little
confidence I had left had been undermined by my mother,
who was ashamed of me, thinking I had done something
awful to get myself thrown out of the community. After
all, hadn't she accused me of being a "queer" just before
I entered? The superiors (bless them!) had assured her
that I had indeed been a conscientious nun, but that the
life was too hard on my health.

Feeling physically and mentally drained after finishing my M.A., I took a job teaching at a large public high school for two years, while becoming more and more lonely and depressed. I missed my friends in community and lacked an outlet for my main interest, church history. My mother had reinforced my feelings of worthlessness. The depression worsened and began to manifest itself in gastro-intestinal upsets. My physician insisted that I seek psychiatric help. For more than a year I saw a kind doctor who didn't just fling pills at me. We discussed history, religion, and the possibility of my being lesbian. He was ready to certify me straight. When I moved East to begin my doctorate, I went to the university's psychological services to seek help for depression. A psychiatrist to whom they referred me assured me that I wasn't gay and sent me home saying he didn't like treating healthy people.

During summers at home I became acquainted with an ecumenical charismatic prayer group and a house of prayer run by sisters from my former community, with whom I discussed my loneliness and depression. When I still experienced nothing but dryness, one woman suggested that the way to open myself to God's action in my life was to thank Him, not just for the good things in my life, but for the hard things. Her insight proved to be a major breakthrough in my emotional and spiritual life. The house of prayer became a centre of hope for me. I loved the Friday night liturgies, the shared prayer, and the conversations with the sisters, some of whom were my contemporaries in the religious life.

I developed a friendship with Maura, a nun I had known before entering. We had studied together at the university. Finally here was someone who seemed to enjoy being with me as much as I desired her company. Our shared experiences in community created a bond between us. Each knew what the other was about to say before we spoke. After a particularly bitter visit with my mother, I turned to Maura for comfort, and she responded generously and warmly. I felt grateful, then frightened. Had I awakened in her needs that she couldn't satisfy in the religious life? Although nothing sexual had happened between us, I began to fear that I was corrupting a nun. Fortunately, we were able to discuss my scruples, and she did her best to reassure me that I was not leading her down the garden path.

I asked my spiritual director about the possibility of my re-entering the community. At the risk of sounding masochistic, I must report that my old longings for religious life began to reassert themselves. Both my community and I had undergone radical upheavals.

Just as I was considering re-entering, Maura wrote that she had been advised by a counselor either to re-dedicate herself or leave. I was shattered. She was the ideal religious: serious, intelligent, warm, prayerful, dedicated. In the months that followed, I tried to help and support her as she cast about for a job or place to study. At one point it looked as if she were going to settle in the city I was studying in, but surprisingly she wasn't interested in sharing an apartment with me. My desire for religious life was on the wane. I was forced to face the fact that it was my friend's presence I had wanted, not community life.

I remained in close touch with Maura by lengthy long-distance phone calls and by 4000-mile round trips, twice by car and three times by plane. During these visits, we discussed the possibility of my being lesbian. Her acceptance and the support of a Jesuit friend in the East helped me to acknowledge finally at the age of thirty-five that I was indeed gay. At this time, Maura told me gently but firmly that she preferred men. There followed a painful period of distancing, complicated by my perception of an ambiguity in her manner towards me.

When she moved to within a hundred and twenty miles from me, a mere nothing in comparison with the two thousand miles I had pounded through each summer in my aging car, she was alarmed by the prospect of having me on her doorstep every weekend, interfering with her work and her social life. She said that she was not ready to share as great a part of her life with me as she had and, in fact, wished to share only a small part of it with me.

For the first time in my life I became genuinely suicidal. Her rejection came close to convincing me that no one would want to have a relationship with me. If what I had considered to be the best relationship in my life had ended like this, what sort of person was I? I despaired of finding someone.

I still had friends who cared. A counselor with Gay Social Services arranged for me to meet a volunteer peer group counselor. With encouragement from the counselor, I met a woman with my interests and arranged to go skiing. When I learned that the woman was married, although her relationship with her husband was platonic, I had misgivings. What I didn't know was that my new ski buddy, immediately sizing me up as a former nun, and recalling her unhappy experiences in convent schools, decided not to go with me again.

About six weeks later we became lovers, and for the past six years I have lived a compromise, sharing in her family celebrations as a friend of the family, deferring at times to their needs. Louise now sees much more of her husband than before she met me. Her lifestyle has become quieter, more reflective. Her presence remains my stability, reassurance, warmth, a gift of God for me.

Looking back on my journey toward self-acceptance, I marvel at the eagerness of my counselors to reassure me that I was not gay. They failed to discover my interior life. My thoughts and affectivity were directed towards women long before I came out. Even at the age of eleven, I knew that I would never marry a man. Had not the Jesuit priest and Maura taken my feelings seriously, I would probably still be in the closet today.

Shortly after coming out, I joined the local chapter of Dignity. After a few months, the president, overtaxed by his own work, dumped the presidency into my lap until a former seminarian took over so that I could continue to work on my doctorate.

My experience with Dignity has convinced me that we need an organization of Catholic or Christian lesbians. Women are struggling, not just against a hostile society, but against a Chruch which has fairly consistently discriminated against women for two thousand years. Some of us have been so oppressed as to have lost faith in all men. I believe that the experience of men as oppressors, not a scarcity of Catholic lesbians, accounts for the relatively few women in Dignity.

We need a theology that deals with human freedom and respects our ability to choose the objects of our love responsibly. As a lesbian I refuse to accept a theology which robs us of our freedom in order to absolve us of our "guilt." We are called to love. How dare we not love?

I make my home in eastern Canada where I teach history, geography and English in a private high school. I have a doctorate in medieval studies and am currently working on a M.A. in pastoral theology. My hobbies include skiing, gardening and caring for my pet rabbits, Vita Sackville-West and Virginia Woolf.

Sr. Robert Mary, 1966

Betsy Snider, 1979

FRESH STARTS

Betsy Snider
(1964-1967)

My decision in 1964 to enter the convent was a gesture of despair and rebellion. I knew that I would never marry and that I did not want to go to the Catholic women's college my mother and sister had attended. I wanted to serve God and follow in the footsteps of Sister Redempta, my high school civics teacher, with whom I was in love. I would finally have the ultimate freedom of the choice-less.

The order I chose was among the most progressive in Cleveland, but it was still bound within certain tradi-tions; we wore habits (two years after I left, the habit be-came a suit, and than all restrictions disappeared); our only career choices were nursing and teaching (within five years of my leaving, complete career choice was allowed); we had daily silence hours, sacred silence and weekly chapter; we attended daily Mass and evening Compline. The atmosphere was a mixture of the vaguely progressive (we could visit home while we were novices) and the traditional (no mingling between professed nuns and novices or between novices and postulants).

I believe the primary satisfactions of the religious life for me were two: it fulfilled my need for solitude and introspection, and it gave me a deep sense of belonging and closeness. I was part of a community, involved with sisters who had a grand mission in life.

Although I was not consciously aware of my Lesbianism in the convent, I was constantly warned against developing particular friendships with fellow postulants and novices. I never knew that the term referred to Lesbian relationships. Although I had been warned about my friendship with another postulant, it was not until I took the habit that I formed a genuine particular friendship.

Gina was a year older. During my postulant year, I was frightened of her and avoided her as much as possible. However, when I became a novice, she and I were in charge of a group of children during summer day camp. We spent much of the summer together. We began giving each other massages. During my postulancy, I gave frequent massages to other postulants. It was all fairly innocent. However, Gina liked to give naked back rubs, using oil and powder. I found it exciting and terribly disturbing. Throughout the winter, we continued to meet alone, go for long walks together, eat together, and spend much of our free time in each other's company.

During this entire time, I was overwhelmed by confusing emotions. In hindsight, it's clear that I was in love with Gina. I was jealous when she began spending time with a postulant. I felt guilty whenever we would snatch a few minutes alone. I thought about her whenever we weren't together. Torn between my desire for her, which I couldn't acknowledge, and my need to be a good nun, I continually promised myself that I wouldn't see her alone and just as continually broke the promise. Finally, in the spring, our novice director (my ideal) called me into her office and told me I had to stop spending so much time with Gina. I was unhappy and yet relieved, and I promised that while the director was away for the summer, I would not see Gina alone. However, Gina was not part of the agreement and was outraged at being treated like a child. Since it was to be our last summer together — Gina would be professed and move to another state in the fall — all promises were soon forgotten, and we spent even more time together. With our director gone, we were more open about ignoring all restrictions. I recall that summer as idyllic, yet laden with tension and apprehension.

On the eve of our novice director's return, my former postulant director called me to her office to read me the riot act. She said that she would inform my novice director that I had spent the entire summer breaking my promise. I came out of that meeting devastated. My novice director's disappointment in me the next day hurt more than any tongue-lashing. As in the spring, she spoke only to me and not Gina.

We met in the cemetery where I told her the bad news. Gina was outraged. I told her that I couldn't stand breaking the rules anymore. And so two weeks before Gina left for the juniorate, I broke off all contact. I felt as though a part of me had been ripped out. What made it so difficult was our inability to acknowledge the truth of our relationship. The words Lesbian or homosexual were never mentioned by anyone during this entire period.

My final break came six months later — five months

before taking my vows. I felt emptiness inside. After intense soul-searching, I decided to leave the convent, not really knowing why, only knowing that I could not stay.

Since that time, I have been involved in traditional Catholicism, which I can no longer tolerate, and in the Catholic Pentecostal Movement, which finally killed all traditional religious impulses. I have felt no need to replace God with Goddess, although I still believe firmly in our spiritual roots and vaguely in some universal (divine?) force. Matriarchal rituals and celebrations of sun and moon cycles make me uncomfortable. My own spiritual inclinations are remotely pantheistic, and I continue to be intrigued by mysticism.

My experiences in the convent have left indelible marks: refusal to accept the status quo and profound isolation from suburban society. The combination of spirituality and collective womanhood allowed me to continue my own non-traditional lifestyle no longer bound by societal expectations. Those three years gave me a time out from my family and my future, enough for me to realize that life is constantly filled with fresh starts.

I am a corporate attorney living in an older house in Hartford, Connecticut, with two dogs and two cats. I enjoy cross-country skiing, biking, hiking, and especially marathon running.

FINDING MYSELF IN HARLEM

Marie
(1952–1970)

Even though I left my religious order twelve years ago and survived the break-up of a ten-year closeted (entombed) relationship, I still felt not okay until just recently. Do you know how it feels to have searched so long for something I didn't even know I was looking for and to find it at last? To feel okay about loving a woman? To allow bottled-up passions which I had held back for most of my life to nourish instead of suffocate me?

I was born in 1938 in a town of eight hundred people in Wisconsin, the third of ten children of good German–American Catholic parents. Since childhood, I've empathized with those who "ain't got it so good." I was deeply moved by missionary stories about China and about such dedicated spiritual people as St. Therese of Lisieux, Tom Dooley, Anne

Morrow Lindbergh, and Francis Liberman. I felt my
mother's compassion towards others as I watched her help
out neighbors in need. Although Mom did not object to
my older sister's and my entering the convent, she now
blames the convent for my Lesbianism. She believes that
sex is for procreation and that we were not put here to
be happy.

Actually, my first gay feelings date back to age six
when I fell in love with the nun who was my first, second,
and fourth grade teacher, a marvelous women who made
learning fun. She told my mother that I had a happy,
wonderful personality. I trusted her with my deepest family
secrets, much to the chagrin of my mother and sister. She
taught us not only to pray to God but to listen to what
God had to say. Fifteen years later, when a back injury
caused the order to take me from nursing, she said, "I know
you're going to be angry, but I'm glad you were taken out
of nursing. You're a natural-born teacher." (She was so
right, but I didn't appreciate it at the time!).

I entered a teaching-nursing order at fourteen and came
into contact with some fine young women. In the high
school aspirancy I looked up to the "old girls" (fifteen
and sixteen). I liked Edna for her gentleness, sense of humor,
and caring. Serious-minded Jean helped me find my way
through the vast two-block convent, told me where to
sit at table and morning prayer, showed me how to get to
classes, and warned me to be dressed in fifteeen minutes.
I felt it keenly when Edna left to take care of younger
brothers and sisters after her mother's nervous breakdown.
Jean was so kind the night Lee and I were told that our
Dad was sick and it was "God's will that we go home and
help." What a cold and lonely midnight train ride!

When Dad was better, Lee and I re-entered the convent
and became "old girls" assigned to help the "new girls."
Fourteen-year-old Darlene, with her black hair, dimples,

FINDING MYSELF IN HARLEM

and joyous dancing of the Irish jig, drew me to her immediately. We held hands under the table until the aspirants' mistress separated us. Not to be defeated, we held feet across the table until marks were noticed on the hem lines of our black skirts.

At seventeen I came under the regime of the postulant mistress, one of the most neurotic nuns I have ever met. Her screaming so terrified me that I used to run and duck into a room or the lavatory when I heard the sound of her Rosary beads. She was so cruel to those she disliked that she force-fed my sister oatmeal, yelling at her to eat faster in front of all eighty of us during the Great Silence at breakfast.

Sharon, another postulant, and I were punished for standing too near the geometry teacher's desk. The postulant mistress said we had infringed on the teacher's authority. After her "hell and damnation" instructions, I'd go to chapel and say, "God, you're not like that, are you?" The answer came back: "No," and I'd say, "I didn't think so."

As a senior novice at age nineteen, I met Sister Francis Ann, a junior novice who had a drunken father. Her stories of his drunken beatings of her mother, his destruction of the furniture, and the car accident death of her brother Ted, brought us close. We held hands occasionally. That was all. I knew I thought of her a lot; and when we'd meet in the hall, where silence was kept, we'd both nod and smile with all the love and understanding we could give.

I also liked Sister Nathan a great deal. Whatever I did wrong in asking her about her mother's death I don't know; but I sure did catch hell from the novice mistress, who said, "You're like a puppy dog. You never give up. Do you know how much you hurt Sister Nathan?" Surprise and hurt choked me into silence. After twenty-three years, I realize that Sister Nathan was probably a pet of the novice mistress. I was to leave "hands off," figuratively, of course, as nothing was going on. Since I looked up to the novice mistress, her accusation intensified my guilt and negative self-esteem.

I examined my conscience endlessly about "particular friendships." I always wanted to be hugged and held and rest my head against a woman's breast, but I sublimated these feelings into a very maternal picture of God. We were told that sexual temptations were to be stopped immediately, since they came from perverse, fallen nature. To let this temptation linger, after becoming aware of it, was a sin. We were told to use cold showers or a cold washcloth on the genital area. Since I couldn't stand cold, this was pure torture. "Sexual dreams" weren't sinful as long as "when you became aware of them you sought to get rid of them." Personally, I hoped I'd have them and not become aware of them too quickly when I awakened.

My first year as a professed sister and student nurse at age twenty was one of my happiest ones. I loved my clinical instructor in nursing, Sister Olga. I found a warm, caring woman concealed under her cold manner. Unfortunately, her over-strict melancholic, mercilessly guilt-ridden conscience probably led to her suicide at age fifty-three. During my nurse's training, I talked to her about my family and my feelings. I knew she really cared about me. At Christmas she gave me her watch, which I still have. As instructed, I never told anybody until four years after I left the convent and then only my lover. I always thought she was a Lesbian from the way she interacted with another nun, but she asked nothing of me. When I got taken out of nursing because of my back injury, she was furious at the way I was treated. Is it any wonder I never forgot her loyalty and sense of justice?

I injured my back as a student nurse when I was twenty-one. I felt devastated because nursing had been the dream of a lifetime. Obediently, I finished college and became a teacher, but I was angry at Sister James who said, "Your back injury is all in your head. The x-rays show nothing. Perhaps you should get into a different environment such as teaching." She was responsible for my six years of excruciating back pain. Later, car accidents and deterioration were to set it off into permanent daily pain. I learned a lot from Sister James about who not to be.

During the next six years of teaching with incredible back pain I was supported by Sister Bertha's concern and medical insight. She told me, "You can't be bitter." During this time the Mother General repeatedly threatened to send me home or to a shrink. I wanted neither and won.

During this period I met Sister Annunciata at summer school. She was an instant and faithful friend. She couldn't understand how my order refused help for my back. Once she asked me to kiss her. I said, "No, I want to keep our friendship and give it back to God." She agreed. We remained friends for over fourteen years.

Now that I'm out of the closet, she has dropped my friendship. However, her loyalty, love, and support are unforgettable. I often turned to her through correspondence even though my superior, suspicious of P.F.'s, censored my letters and even searched my drawers. I wrote a daily log — more like a diary — and hand delivered it to Sister Annunciata on our visits. When years later she told me she had cleaned out her trunk and, in a spirit of detachment, had discarded my writing, I felt as if a part of me had been thrown away. The spirit of detachment felt so cruel!

I questioned a lot in the years of renewal — the sixties — both in the Church, religious life and society. My back forced me to go a monetarily unprofitable route. Unless one is constantly producing, working, one is of no value. I have suffered from this greatly all my life. So much unnecessary guilt.

I decided not to let the hate of Sister James and a few

others cause me to leave a life I loved. I made perpetual vows, knowing I might never walk again because of my back. This possibility was confirmed by the orthopedist and surgical table during my first year in Harlem.

The next six years teaching and working in the inner city were filled with struggle, satisfaction, and pain. Work with those who "ain't got it so good" was draining, satisfying and ever painful. During this time, I had several close friends and corresponded with Sister Annunciata. I called my strong sexual drives loneliness. I ached, so I thought, from being bombarded by many different cultures in New York City and being away from my roots. I drowned myself in work, teaching in the parochial school, teaching also religious instruction on evenings and Saturdays.

One summer a Puerto Rican teenager and I visited two hundred families. We went up and down stifling, smelly, hot tenement halls to find the heart, the soul, the suffering, and the beauty of the ghetto. When the riots broke out in 1967, after watching people die needlessly, I began a block association, knowing I was initiating "an apostolate not sanctioned by the Mother General." But their suffering, despair, and loneliness were overpowering. Later, when my superior announced my transfer to Michigan in order to curtail my "disobedience" and "sinful apostolate" among the poor, I feared I would break mentally. I had seen the needs of the poor. Accepting the transfer away from my work would lead me to become as unthinking and inhuman as some nuns I knew. I left the order at age 32.

Several nun friends wrote telling me how wrong I was. Although I didn't write back, I missed them. It was another painful closing of a door. I had wanted to be a nun since the age of twelve. I had found much peace in the convent. The times I spent in chapel, outside walking alone, doing spiritual reading, chanting, saying the office, attending Mass, and meditating frequently offered me comfort and

incredible insights into life. I gave all in those twelve years
as a professed nun, first as a student nurse, then as a teacher
in the Midwest and New York City.

When I did leave, it was good not to have a superior
and others judging everything I did. I became very close
to Ruby, a parent and community organizer. During our
ten year closeted relationship, I (white, mid-western) learned
much from Ruby (black, Harlem-bred). I leaned on her more
than I had anybody in my life. Ruby helped me overcome
the shame and sense of failure I felt when telling people I
was a former nun. I felt no guilt about loving Ruby. Even
though mystical experiences with God have been my real
life-sustaining force both in and out of the convent, I never
knew love so deep and special until I made love with Ruby.
It didn't take long, however, before we had an S and M
relationship. I was the masochist. My low self-esteem and
lack of experience caused me to succumb and adjust to
her confusing demands. She constantly told me to date
men but became angry when I did. Because I felt ill at
ease with men I thought there was something wrong with
me. She even saved me from three Lesbian women we met.
"It's you I love," I kept telling her.

Ten years later, after more spinal surgery, Ruby walked
off saying, "I don't want to see you anymore." I was
devastated. After Ruby left, I remained pretty much alone
for over a year, trying to heal, to find out who I was. One
day, I was walking by the park and thought, "I guess I'm
bi-sexual; I've tried men and that didn't work. Well, I loved
Ruby. I bet I could find a woman."

Gay Teachers and Dignity were my first two places of
welcome. I had mixed feelings about being Lesbian for the
next three months. One day I'd feel fine; the next day I
had feelings of shame and fear at being found out. I had
trouble calling myself a Lesbian in the beginning. On a
Catholic Lesbian Retreat, in the twilight moments, I said,

"I wish some day I'd wake up and all this (homosexuality) would go away." Finally I came to my senses and realized that my sexuality comes from God. My job is to accept myself.

Entering the convent was leaving all and following Christ. "Coming out" as Lesbian was for me an even more honest following of God. With other gay people, I am reclaiming my lost world with untold peace and fulfillment. Standing up for what I believe is right summarizes my life's search. Being who I am — Lesbian — is an integral part of my quest.

I am 45 and live alone. I have a Masters of Education and the equivalent of a doctorate in graduate credit hours. A school accident cut my teaching career short, and further spinal injuries have permanently inhibited my daily activities.

During the many hours flat on my back in traction, I use the talking book service. I can also pray.

Sr. Theresa Stephen, 1969

Sonja Meidell, 1983

MY ART AND MY SPIRIT

Sonja Meidell
(1965-1970)

In seventh grade I announced to Mom that I'd decided to go into the convent. She was appalled. "I won't have any grandchildren. How could you do this to me? You don't love me. You're just trying to run away." Dad said it was my life to choose, but he wasn't thrilled about convent life. Nor did they think much of the Air Force. And they couldn't afford to send me to college to become a physical education teacher, although my younger brother went. Girls studied typing, boys went to college. At least, if I went to the convent, I would get to go to college.

I entered in 1965 for life. Life ended five years later when my ideals were not the same as my community's. I was anxious to go to Africa, work with the poor and be Christ-like. I chose the Bernardines, Third Order of St.

Francis, both because their habit was practical and because of my admiration for St. Francis. I worked hard and enjoyed the first two years. Once I left the novitiate, I realized that what the order taught and what it practiced were not always the same. My ideals of sisters loving one another were shattered by bitter, jealous women arguing and lying. So much pettiness. The final straw came for me when my mom died of cancer and my father was not allowed to see me or have me come home.

While in the convent, I successfully fought my need for masturbation. It was harder fighting PF's. I never knew they meant "queer." If I knew then what I know now, I probably wouldn't have lasted a year.

After I left the convent, it took me three years to deprogram myself. I moved to Connecticut to join forces with another ex-Bernardine to start our own community. Maria and I were very close. I trusted her so much. But then she married in our fifth year together. It was hard for me when I realized that she did not really want a community.

For another two years, I remained involved with the church. I did homilies, started folk masses, created visual slide presentations, and involved the parish priests with the community. I was also married for nine months — bah, humbug. I had a miscarriage and almost died. I gave up on marriage and the Church. Change in the Church was too slow. Women were really left out in the cold. Dignity was like the Church — okay for men, but women still on the outside, playing games to participate. My fight was over. I left the Church. I missed the singing but not the hypocrisy.

It was after my disastrous marriage and my disillusionment with Church that I began to explore my own sexual drive. My friend Dolores confided that she was gay but afraid I'd be upset to hang around her friends. I thought that was crazy — everyone to her own thing.

Since I had never seen any gay people (or so I thought),
I went to Provincetown with Dolores. I figured, what the
hell. Well, my mouth was open all the time. Matter of fact,
Dolores left me alone for a while, and I was approached.
Egads! Now what? Soon I was hitting the gay bars alone,
too dressed and too naive. A few drinks and some interesting women (I love to dance) brought me home to myself.
I still desire to make a better world for women. I touch
myself and others with my art and my spirit.

*I work in the Reader's Feast, a bookstore in Hartford,
Connecticut. I put my energy into my stained glass art
and watercolors, my music, and my poetry. My latest poster
is on equal rights for pregnant workers. I just became an
American Softball Association Umpire.*

DISSOLVING MY MASCULINE ALTER EGO

Jane E. McLarson
(1964–1970)

I grew up post-World War II with Irish-Italian middle class parents. My mother maintained the housewife role, while my father worked three jobs to support us and his venture into chiropractic school. My brother, born when I was ten, was the answer to my six-year novena to Our Lady.

Already an active little girl with a tomboy strain, as they described it in the forties, I was unhappy with the backseat that women and girls had in the Catholic Church. I memorized all the Latin altar boy prayers and accompanying rituals in preparation for the day when girls would ascend the altar with the priest. Although I was fond of playing nun, it was much more exciting to play priest. I dispensed Necco wafer candy for communion to curious

Protestant friends and amused relatives who were "required to attend Mass" while visiting. Playing church usher as well, I picked up a few dollars in the make-shift french-fry collection basket and split the proceeds between baseball cards and the purchase of another pagan baby.

At age nine, I wanted to be a filling station attendant. I did well in sports in school, but being best as a girl never seemed totally kosher. Therefore, I created a fantasy world in which my alter ego *michael* took risks and loved women in high adventures. It was a creative way to survive, although I instinctively knew that I wasn't like other little girls my age. My feelings for other girls were more like what I understood boy-girl feelings to be. I prayed that St. Bernadette would appear with a bottle of Lourdes water to pour over my head and make my alienation go away forever. I promised to erect a statue in her honor if she would come through for me.

Happiness, joy, contentment, and safety were not emotional states connected with God. To suffer was the chief means of merit, I learned, and that gave meaning to a lot of my early experiences. But meritorious pain, loneliness, and confusion made no real sense to me as a child. I longed for normal feelings of love and protection. I feared that I would be deserted by Mom or Dad if I was bad. My most vivid memory was waking suddenly in the night, hearing the familiar sound of anger coming from my parents' room, and being terrified of ending up alone. I remember shutting my eyes tightly and holding out my hand to a God I believed would be there to comfort me and take care of me. It was my first Act of Faith. It transcended gold stars or the blessings of conformity to ritual. It was a personal pact with God.

During adolescence I enjoyed many games including ones that involved touching other girls. My best friend and I spent some moments practicing how we would hug and kiss the boys. How I passionately loved practice more than the real thing. In my all-girl high school, I rose quickly to class president, all-star this, best that, most likely to win. On happy days I accepted the crushes of younger girls with great pleasure, but I hated the dreaded dances and proms, feeling alienated while pretending to enjoy. My alter ego *michael* lived all the feelings which I could not reconcile in myself. But his existence was terrifying and unspeakable.

Public models for service and adventure among women were scarce at the time. Nuns seemed to exemplify best what I wanted to do. Vaguely I was aware that entering the convent was a way of putting off facing the inevitable question of my sexuality, of continuing the good life of high school, and of giving my life some meaning. Believing that service and commitment to God would squelch the passionate desire I felt for women, I jumped into religious life at eighteen with seventy women my age. But my increasing alienation created deeper pain and fear. I felt split from who I was.

I hated visiting days especially. Not that anything was unpleasant, but I felt expected to feel a certain way. I kept my aversion a secret from the others who seemed to count the days. Although my family was supportive and they missed me, I always felt different from what I thought was expected.

During my religious life I always felt an attachment to someone, but I played it cool, never wanting to seem vulnerable or exclusive while longing for the love, warmth, and touch of another woman. Only by continuing my *michael* identity, sometimes separately, sometimes symbiotically, could I cope with my homosexuality, although I couldn't identify it as such. I was confused about the male person I had merged with. I believed that I had inherited some mental illness from my mother.

In my first year of religious life, I sought counsel from a priest, who advised, "You need to change your feelings now, or you'll have some problems later." But he offered no suggestion about how to change my feelings. I tried to mimic the emotional afflictions of my peers: homesickness and boyfriend separation crises. When I convinced myself and my postulant mistress that my distress was missing a boyfriend, my letters from home were censored, while my heart went on consumed by feelings for women.

In my second year my novice mistress informed me that two novices were upset because they were experiencing strong feelings for me. This German matriarch instructed me to stop whatever it was I was doing. I was unaware of doing anything but became terrified that *michael* was showing and that my sick feelings were coming out again.

Soon after, we took our first vows. As part of the ceremony we were to prostrate under the long black pall, professing celibacy, poverty, and obedience. I promised God never to feel again, never to be visible, to continue my path toward greatness that everyone told me I was destined for. With this blessing of vows surely my disturbing desires would go away.

I went into the third year of college and convent life committed to doing well and being the person who made everyone else feel good. I reached out to no one special, though I felt a painful attachment to one of my novitiate "betrayers." Another sister, a year older than I, beautiful in body and spirit, lovable, popular, emanating an unforgettable love, touched my heart and dissolved my stiff reserve. This remains one of my most vivid experiences of love conquering fear. I felt joy for the first time. For a few months I began to feel loved for as much of me as I was capable of seeing. I believed everyone loved only the *michael* in me. Sister Sarah and I never spoke of the intimacy we felt, and we were careful to avoid rumors of a particular friendship. We were both rising stars. I enjoyed the fantasy of two women loving each other and being the best we could be because of that support: loving the one and the many. After a few months I withdrew. In later relationships I felt a similar closing down. I avoided women I was attracted to because it was painful for everyone. It makes me sad now that such good feelings were so cloaked with confusion and fear.

I cannot remember dealing with my pain and guilt at this time. I did confess my sexual feelings for Sister Sarah. My confessor told me to change my feelings and sin no more. I wish now that I could have talked to some sensitive women. My spiritual life didn't seem to grow much during those years. I relied on the same simple faith in God that I had felt that night I reached out in the dark as a child.

By the end of my fourth year I was sent to practice teach. I was panicked and frightened. It felt like leaving home for the first time. I aced the teaching right away, but I felt shockingly alienated in the heterosexual community all around me. I finished my last weeks of formation with terror inside me. I feigned stomach problems in order to see a doctor to whom I confided my problem. I felt vulnerable and desperate. I left out the *michael* part but told him about my feelings for women. He responded, "You'll be a saint in heaven, Sister," but offered no earthly advice.

During the next year I got physically involved with a slightly older sister; this was my first sexual exploration. It was confined to nightly trips to each other's rooms to hold each other and kiss. It lacked the joy and spontaneity of the non-sexual love in the juniorate. Now added to my alienation and confusion was the guilt about breaking my vows. Like an alcoholic I promised myself one more time — and that would be the last. Even though I was the youngest member of the community elected to an official position,

my feelings of failure continued. And through the year I
thought more and more of suicide.

I told my superior I needed help. She told me I wasn't
the kind of person who needed help, but her love helped
me make it. I was sent to a doctor who suggested that I be
given special permission to leave for two years to get
"straight" before returning to make a better vow of
chastity. At our first post-convent session he suggested
that I join the army where there are lots of men! But where
were the good women I needed?

During my last convent days, while buying clothes
and preparing for my new life, I did the untimely thing
of falling in love with a sister my own age. Knowing that
I was disobeying doctor's orders, I continued to see Marcella for years. Eventually Marcella left the convent and
came to live with me.

During those first post-convent years, *michael* was
still a part of me, although fading some. I went to church
less often and then only for the Eucharist. During these
dark ages of my spiritual development, I was taking no
official stance against the Church but needing religious
practice less. As my need for *michael* was diminishing,
I began recognizing my feelings as my own. At twenty-
nine, I began an intense period of meditation asking to
be freed and healed and to be given peace of mind.

A year later walking on a beach in Hawaii during a
rare enlightened moment, I decided to explore the gay
world. I found someone who knew someone, and I spoke
with her. From that moment on, I have been out. As soon
as I claimed my own gay identity, *michael* dissolved. I
felt joy and control over my life, even when my relationship with Marcella ended.

My spiritual growth has been solidly linked with the
process of becoming me. I am no longer aligned with the
Catholic Church even though I claim being raised in its

traditions. It leaves me no room to profess my full identity. I will no longer put myself in a position of being judged. There has been too much agony to come to where I am. And this pain has formed my philosophy, one which is growing and changing and simplifying. I am drawn to thinking which combines Eastern philosophies with the teaching of Jesus. I am a Christian, for I believe that Jesus did what we are all meant to do: conquer fears which keep us from loving ourselves and others and becoming one with our true christ-god selves within. I walk the planet, the universe with all creation as part of one being.

I am glad to say that I am a Lesbian Christian, but mostly I'm glad to say I am whole. I am glad to have had my religious life experience. I am doubly at home with other Lesbians who have been nuns. In my idealism I expected the Lesbian community to be like the juniorate: women loving and caring about other women, creating their destinies alone and together. I have felt deep sadness watching my ideals dissolve. Even so, no disappointment, no heart-hurts over relationships begun and ended can ever match the pain of not being me, of believing I was sick and guilty, of feeling so split from myself.

Because of my involvement in the educational community as teacher and consultant since leaving religious life, I am using a pseudonym. I reside in the Midwest and pursue an active life of travel, hobbies, and professional growth.

Section IV

DON'T BE TOO RIGID IN YOUR
UNDERSTANDING OF CHASTITY

Can one be a celibate Lesbian? Is it legitimate to be an active member of a religious community and an active Lesbian? What is the purpose of the vow of chastity? Five present nuns analyze the connections and contradictions between love and celibacy, between sexuality and the vow of chastity.

DON'T BE TOO RIGID IN YOUR UNDERSTANDING OF CHASTITY

Sister Agatha
(1957-present)

I am in my mid-fifties, and for about twenty-five years have been in a community which is small, closely knit, traditional, yet open to change and renewal. During my first ten years in community, issues of sexuality did not arise. I had no close relationships. Such were not encouraged at that time.

My first relationship, a friendship with a sister I greatly admired, was never explicitly sexual, though later I came to realize that sexual undertones were present. My second relationship, which lasted more than five years, involved acknowledged sexual feelings on both sides and some physical expression, limited by inhibitions, and the sense of what was appropriate for celibates. It was a good relationship, leading to personal growth for both of us. It came to an end because my friend became more and more unhappy in community and eventually left. As she drew away from me, becoming increasingly preoccupied with her own difficulties, I withdrew psychologically from her. I was not ready at that time to work through a conflict between vocation and a love relationship which might lead me out of community.

The next few years were a time of establishing my gay identity. I struggled with guilt, self-acceptance, and religious doubt. I saw that I had internalized the negative judgements of Church and society, and eventually, as I came to accept my sexual orientation as good and potentially creative, I began to develop a more real and personal faith. I learned about the gay community and its aspirations; I read everything I could; I talked to knowledgeable people; I tried to influence people's thinking; and I even came out to a few trusted friends. I began to look toward some form of ministry with the gay community. I gradually made contacts, and eventually, I linked up with a network of gay priests and religious.

I also tried to understand my celibate vocation in the light of my new-found sexual awareness. At this time, I did not expect to have another relationship, though I was not altogether closed to the possibility. I thought I had come to terms with an element of loneliness and restlessness as something I'd simply have to put up with all my life.

However, last year I began my third relationship. I had been aware that another sister and I were reaching out to each other, and finally we declared our love. Our relationship deepened rapidly and for about a month we enjoyed it to the full, not worrying about how it fitted into our lives as a whole. It was a glorious, fulfilling and unforgettable time.

Before long, however, a severe conflict developed, as

the desire for a home of our own grew stronger every day. It was an agonizing experience, since my sense of commitment to the community was strong and I was very much aware of my sisters' love and respect. To leave, I felt, would wrench me apart. I would be betraying my sisters' trust. I was in a cruel dilemma, an impossible situation from which I could see no exit.

We remained in this state of acute conflict for four months, knowing only that we must give our religious vocations a fair test. Neither of us felt called out of community. Yet, we kept experiencing the need to express our love in ways which seemed impossible to reconcile with celibacy as we understood it. It was like walking a tightrope. How could we find a way which would do justice both to our love and also to our vocation? We were in a morally ambiguous region where we could only act in good faith and take responsibility for our decisions moment by moment, learning to live with the uncertainty and doubt which seem inevitable in such grey areas.

Finally the balance began to tip. Our sense of vocation had persisted, and at last it became strong enough to form the basis for a decision. After much struggle, trial and error, we decided that we must avoid expressions of our love which so intensified the desire for a home that the conflict became intolerable. This decision brought a measure of peace, though there was still much conflict and regret for "the road not taken." Moreover, it was only as we learned the necessity of claiming the grace given with our vocation that we succeeded in implementing our decision at all.

It is a measure of strength of the attraction between us that we finally came to a wholehearted acceptance of a celibate lifestyle as the only possible way for us. This is not in any way to deny the goodness and creative potential of alternatives. Indeed, for me, celibacy takes on meaning precisely in the context of religious community. It seems to me that just as genital intimacy forges powerful bonds between two individuals, so celibacy enables and expresses a bonding equally real among women who have committed themselves to God and to one another by common vows.

My understanding of celibacy has also changed. Whereas I used to think it meant keeping the lid on and trying to feel nothing, now, for me, it means experiencing the emotions and sexual feelings which love evokes but expressing them in ways compatible with my vocation. I see our sexuality as a strong deep current flowing out from God through our lives, renewing our creative powers, enlivening our ministry, and adding warmth and reality to our human relationships, within our community and beyond it. Our part is to do nothing we feel would divert or block the flow. This is particularly true regarding my friend and myself: our love has become even deeper and surer than before, and, at the same time, we have learned how important it is for each to give the other space to be and grow.

There is no doubt in my mind that our relationship has been a blessing and a means of grace to us both. To give love and to know myself loved has added a new dimension to my life. In a real sense, I have received my womanhood. I am aware that the desire for God which first brought me to religious life has persisted, and that the pain and conflict I have known during the past year have somehow opened me to God at a deeper level than before and perhaps made me gentler and more compassionate toward my fellow-humans.

Throughout the whole process — indeed, since I first broached the matter of my sexual orientation some twelve years ago — my superior has been most supportive. I recall that once when I was struggling with guilt in those early days, she said to me, "Don't be too rigid in your understanding of chastity." My friend and I have been able to be completely frank with her. Without her wise and accepting guidance, I do not think we could have survived in community. I urge any superior who may read this to extend the same trust, affirmation and non-judgmental attitude to a sister in like circumstances. It could make all the difference between saving or losing a vocation. I am convinced that a sister who is helped to live creatively through this kind of experience will ultimately become a happier, more human person with more to give her community.

I have also received support (explicit from my superior, tacit from several others) for my gay-related ministry, which has opened out during the past few months. Perhaps it could not have developed until I had fully faced my own sexuality, joyfully accepted it, and begun the process of integrating it into my vocation.

Looking back over the past year, surely one of the most significant in my life, I have felt myself guided by a wisdom greater than my own. I have had to live by faith as never before. I have lost some of my self-sufficiency, my need to understand, categorize and control. As I have pondered how our vocation and our love, both gifts of God, can fit together, I have come to see it not so much a problem to be solved, but as a mystery to be lived.

My experience in community has included pastoral, administrative, and literary work. For several years I have been engaged in gay-related ministry in a quiet way. My own Lesbian identity is known only to a few trusted persons.

GAY AND CELIBATE AT SIXTY-FIVE

Sister Marla
(1935–present)

(At the time of this interview with Nancy Manahan in December 1982, Sister Marla was sixty-five and retired.)

Nancy: Do you think of yourself as a Lesbian?

Sister Marla: I know that I'm gay. I love women. I adore women — in and out of the convent. At the same time, I am celibate.

Nancy: Are you happy?

Sister Marla: I'm extremely happy. My work — being a teacher and an administrator — has been satisfying. My personal life is also rewarding. I have dear friends, and I've lived with another sister, whom I love, for twenty years. We've never been physically intimate. Oh, I kissed her once, many years ago, when I woke her to go bowling. In those days we had to bowl early so no one would see us with our skirts up, having fun. Yes, I kissed her right on the mouth. She looked surprised.

Nancy: What do you feel toward men?

Sister Marla: I don't really like men at all. Not at all. Oh, there are some who are nice; I don't even mind if they put their arms around me in a playful manner.

Nancy: How did you discover you were gay?

Sister Marla: I've always loved women. I grew up surrounded by strong, wonderful women. My grandmother taught me half of what I know. I was polishing brass and carrying my own gun at eleven. I learned to hunt and fish and drive a car when I was very young.

Nancy: Did you have Lesbian relationships in the convent?

Sister Marla: In the novitiate, particular friends were forbidden. No one ever told us why. But uppermost in our minds, aside from the fact that we were having so much fun, was a fear that they might just send us home. So if they didn't want us to have particular friends, well then, we wouldn't. But it hurt a little bit. I had my ups and downs because of my volatile nature. I was chastised once for having a particular friend, but actual love relationships didn't occur to any degree in the novitiate.

Nancy: What about after the novitiate?

Sister Marla: Oh, yes. My first mission was as a second grade teacher. Immediately, I felt a bond with the sister who taught sixth grade, and we began having a little particular friendship. It went on for four years. Then other nuns came whom I felt pulled toward. One I thought was just the most stupendous person in the world. She was — I don't want to say ugly — the most unhandsome person I've ever met. But she was a genius, a universal genius. She knew everything about everything. This is what attracted me to her. I really love this lady. She had terrible headaches, and I used to massage her head and neck and shoulders. Then came along a little sister who gave me problems. She wanted to be the only person in my life. I had been in high school with her and had thought she was very homely and didn't have much of a personality. But she came to the convent, received the veil, and immediately became a glamorous person with gorgeous brown eyes. She suddenly sparkled all over with a personality that people fell for. I didn't have that much interest in her, but she did in me. It was uncomfortable for the five years that we were in the same house.

Then in 1965, I was sent to be principal of a school in Nevada. Immediately, I set eyes on a woman who had been the provincial superior. I was thirty-eight. I began to adore that lady with all my heart. I spent two years thinking continually — aside from running the school — what can I do to make her happy? What can I do to benefit the community and thereby help her?

When I think about a total giving of myself, physically and emotionally, it was to that lady. When I was transferred to Minneapolis and was no longer able to spend every bit of my being for her, I was the most unhappy I've ever been in my life. It was awful. I hope I never reach that nadir again.

Nancy: Was your relationship sexual?

Sister Marla: There was never anything physical. If I got to hold her hand as she stepped off the curb, that was wonderful. I would have loved her to kiss me and hug me, but it just wasn't done, and I didn't want to jeopardize everything by being forward.

Nancy: Did you feel guilty about your attractions to women?

Sister Marla: Goodness no! I was glad I got away with as much as I did.

Nancy: You felt no qualms about your particular friendships?

Sister Marla: No, you see, I never thought about kissing in a romantic way or embracing in a sexual manner. I didn't want to violate . . . well, of course, sometimes I had longings for closer physical intimacy, but it wasn't necessary. We were so disciplined.

Nancy: What happened when you were transferred to Minneapolis?

Sister Marla: I was superior and principal of a school there. It was a hard situation. Then Sister Mary Ellen arrived. She was thirty-two. I was forty. She is a supportive, warm, kind person, and she immediately began to think, "What can I do to help Sister Marla?" I began to delegate jobs to her and to feel a great deal of tenderness and gratitude toward her.

I have loved Sister Mary Ellen for twenty-five years and she reciprocates. She says she is straight, and I'm sure she is to a certain extent. People are gay to a certain extent: ten percent, fifty percent, or [pointing to herself] one hundred percent.

Nancy: How do you see homosexuality in the Church?

Sister Marla: Homosexuals belong to the soul of the Church. Women who are homosexuals — the Lesbian community — are a vital part of the Church. They are more loving, more kind, more giving of themselves and, I believe, very much loved by God. I'll never understand people who want to ostracize them from the mystical body of Christ. As a religious who's been involved in the workings of the Church for several decades, I totally support and identify with Lesbian and gay people.

Nancy: If your story is included in the book, could you use your own name?

Sister Marla: For the sake of Mary Ellen and for the sake of some of my friends, I would not want my name to be mentioned. I am sure you will do everything in your power to make the piece as honest as I have attempted to be with you. But because of my commitments to friends in my community, whom I love and who love me, but who don't even know what homosexuality is, I would prefer that you not use my name.

Nancy: So you are not out in your community as a celibate gay sister?

Sister Marla: No, I'm not.

THE GIFT OF SEXUALITY IN THE
SPIRIT OF CELIBACY

Sister Hana Zarinah
(1963–present)

Three years ago, when I discovered I was a Lesbian, it felt like coming home. I had found the edge that held the puzzle pieces of my life together.

Even as a child, I'd always felt close to The Source. As far back as I can remember, I trusted a Presence greater than I to make my life work. I entered religious life at eighteen. I did not want to get married, and in those days my only alternative was religious life. I chose my order because I felt called to be with the poor, and this group of sisters was founded especially to teach the poor. When I look back, I realize that I did have a deep spirituality than needed channeling, but I also think I wanted on some conscious or unconscious level to live my life with a group of women.

In 1963, in our European, pre-Vatican, semi-cloistered order, we received a hard, rigorous, but loving training. Even with its flaws, it helped me grow. Although in the novitiate I was not aware of my sexual needs, on my first mission I fell in love with my principal-superior. She loved me as well, even though we were not sexually involved. She helped me to know that it was OK to be in love and that all of us are a mixture of homosexual and heterosexual feelings. Through her, "homosexual" began to seep into my consciousness as more than a vague word connected with sick people. I have a wonderful relationship with this woman now; she is one of the few people I am out to. I am very grateful to her.

Later, I became interested in the parish priest. We became friends and slightly sexually involved. For a year I was preoccupied with sex. I prayed for continence, a Gift of the Holy Spirit for control of sexual feelings. By the end of the year, I'd received the gift and, much to my relief, had myself under control. My emotional needs were somewhat fulfilled during this time by great friends and nonsexual loves. Emotionally, I was always involved with someone, but even with close friends, I felt something was missing. We weren't supposed to have particular friends. I think we did anyhow. Today, I realize that what was missing was touch, physical closeness, and intimacy.

About five years ago, I fell in love with another sister. Gradually, thanks to her assertiveness, our relationship became sexual. To me it was a beautiful relationship, because I knew it was good to love anyone. I was now just deciding to be more free in my expression of that love. I could touch, be affectionate, be giving and loving. I felt myself opening up, becoming a more loving human being with everyone.

Even though I didn't feel any guilt, I knew others would think that what we were doing was wrong. When I did confess our relationship to a priest friend, I told him I didn't think it was a sin, but I was confessing it "just in case." The "just in case" came from "shoulds" implanted in my consciousness from the Church's code, the taboos of society, and my vow of chastity. The priest was very understanding and affirming. I felt relieved, as though someone from on high had sanctioned me. Although I felt OK about our relationship, it was a struggle for the sister I loved. She decided we would not be sexual. I agreed because I wanted her friendship. We were intimate off and on for about a year. But she couldn't be close and not be sexual, so she finally broke it off completely. I was heartbroken.

I still didn't think of myself as a Lesbian; I had just been expressing my love for a particular woman. Because of our painful separation and my need for self-awareness, I began going to a feminist Jungian analyst. It was there that I got in touch with many aspects of myself including my sexuality. At the same time, I took a self-defense course with many Lesbians. I felt both at home with them and like a stranger in their midst. I was woman-identified, but I could not identify with their culture or with their labels.

Finally, I met Rachel. We were drawn to each other even though she was a Lesbian and I was a nun. She saw my Lesbian self better than I did and accepted my nun self too. I went to a Meg Christian concert with Rachel and some of her Lesbian friends. It was here that I realized I didn't have to change to fit the Lesbian culture. I was a Lesbian, and the culture had to make room for me — nun and all! From there, I began to grow in my love for Rachel and in my identity as a Lesbian sister. Rachel and I became friends and are now lovers as well. We have moved into an apartment together. My order, respecting my choice to live out of a convent, approved my living with her as a roommate.

Today, I am a practicing Zen Catholic, Lesbian, feminist nun. I prefer no labels, but have chosen to identify with many. I have listened carefully to my innermost voices. I've had to develop my own philosophy based on the Gospel message of love and acceptance of all, while still being who I am. I am a Lesbian woman and I love being a Lesbian. I am a nun, and I love being a nun.

I can belong to my group because we have changed with the times. We don't wear habits. We are forward-thinking, politically-minded, hard-working, powerful women. When I read from our statements that we will collaborate with those striving to create a world in which we love, justice and peace prevail, and we will combat evil in all its forms: injustice, war, discrimination, oppression of peoples, and exploitation of the earth; when I see us working in our ministries to combat racism, sexism, and war; when I see our women risking their lives in the political upheavals of Central and South America; when I see us in the ghettoes and barrios of the United States; when I talk to my sisters who are political activists, and to those who have been arrested and jailed for participating in non-violent demonstrations for justice; when I listen to the women who work with battered women, homeless women, abused children, the mentally retarded, the aged and the dying; when I see all these things, I feel deeply bonded with my religious sisters.

My pain is that I can't share being a Lesbian with most of these women. Since my Lesbianism is a part of me, they don't really know me. Yet, if they knew I was a Lesbian, they might know me even less, because of whatever homophobia, stereotypes, or projections they might have. Another source of pain is my Church. I'm not sure what kind of a Catholic I am. I like the Catholic traditions and my personal history. However, I cannot reconcile myself to the Church's clericalism and sexism.

I am a feminist. I am becoming aware of women's spirituality and the Old Religion. I seek the universal truth, the Source of all, the Spirit within. One place I find universal truth is in the New Testament, in Jesus' words. Unfortunately, we sometimes throw out our whole Christian heritage because of the way male preachers have interpreted it for us. I am a Catholic. No man can deprive me of what I hold dear. I listen to my heart for direction, while being accountable for my actions. I keep the spirit of the law, rather than the letter.

It is in listening to my heart that I have chosen to remain a sister. I want to be a sister to all, especially to the sisters in my group and to my Lesbian sisters. My struggle arises from wanting to be accepted by both. My nun-sisters may not accept the Lesbian part of me, and my Lesbian sisters may not accept the nun part of me. And yet, I am not parts; I am whole.

I have been a sister for twenty years. Only in the past four years have I known that I am Lesbian. I feel no need to stop being a nun. I love the vows I have taken, and I believe in their spirit. The vows are meant to set us free, not to shackle us. My vows of poverty, chastity, and obedience set me free from undue attachments to material goods, people, and power. I vowed freely to give, freely to love, and freely to listen.

The vow of chastity or celibacy is a stumbling block for many people. I remember hearing, years ago, an old priest say that celibacy begins in the mind. We can be completely non-physical and yet so possessed and unfree that we are uncelibate. Or we can be physical while being free and still celibate. This has proven true for me. During the periods of my life when I was very emotionally involved with a woman, I gave up all freedom. I was completely attached, either wanting to be possessed or to possess. Because I was unfree to be myself or to love others, I would

call myself, during those times, uncelibate. During my life
now, when at times I express my love sexually, I feel free.
I neither possess nor feel possessed. I live my vow of
celibacy: my vow to love all. I am committed to my group
of sisters, as well as to my special friend-and-lover.

My relationship with Rachel is a gift. It has helped me
learn about the spirituality of sexuality. In Rachel's love
I feel close to God and to my friends. She makes no demands
on me to make a choice between my group or her. We both
live with the mentality that we can be all we want to be.
It's not either/or, but both/and. I am very happy. I am
balancing my community life and my lover. Sometimes
it is a struggle, but a struggle well worth it.

I don't know where life will lead. I need only be true
to myself and all else will follow. I've listened to my heart,
to the Spirit within, and I live my life on the edge.

*Born in 1945 into an Italian-American working-class
family, I presently live with my lover and teach in San
Diego. I have been a nun for twenty years.*

THE AWAKENING

Sister Maria Nuscera
(1976-present)

In my large Italian family touching, hugging, holding, kissing between people of the same sex and opposite sex were commonly enjoyed and encouraged, and attitudes toward sexuality were open and honest. My grandparents freely expressed off-color humor in front of us children. Since our bedrooms (for ten in one house) were close together, we children concluded from what we could hear that our parents and grandparents had active sex lives. Because of this, we learned that sex and sexual feelings are good. Although sexual intercourse outside of marriage was frowned upon, we knew that our mistakes would be forgiven. I have always felt an unconditional love from my family.

In junior high and high school, I felt an attraction toward

some girlfriends: I wanted to be with them, walk them home, carry their books, go on dates with them, dance with them, call them on the telephone, give them gifts. They were thinking about boyfriends the way I was thinking about them. Although I dated men in college, my real interest continued to be women.

Not until my first year of teaching music after college did I act out my attraction for women physically and emotionally. I became friends with a sister that I met at the Church I attended. We began to share moments together and look for each other. We touched and kissed (finally) and conjured up plans to meet and be alone together. Although we did not "make love," we were close and tender and spent evenings and nights together. Finally the community gave her an ultimatum: the religious community or her friendship with me. She chose the community and broke off our relationship abruptly. For months I was depressed.

At twenty-four I entered a religious community. Since twelve I had had a romantic attraction to sisters and convent life. Walking by the convent three blocks from my parents' house, I used to wonder, "Where are the nuns? Are they praying? How do they look without their habits?" Later I viewed religious life less romantically and saw religious women committed to Christ as a visible official woman-power force for the Church. Entering a religious community was making a choice to discover myself and my relationship to God.

I chose the Sisters of St. Joseph of Carondolet because I was attracted to their sense of freedom and respect for diversity. My community is a group of rugged individuals striving for unity with each other and God. I derive personal satisfaction from bonding with these women who have a deep passion for ministry in the Church today. I sense our heritage from women who gathered in France back in 1650.

Over the years many of the sisters have become my good friends.

If you asked me when I was twenty-four if I were a Lesbian, I would have said, "No." Now at thirty I say, "Yes, definitely." In the past couple of years I have become more aware of my emotional and sexual needs. I need to be touched, hugged, kissed, and held. I need tenderness and a few friends who will love me unconditionally.

Four years ago I had a sexual affair with a married woman about eight years older than I. After months of close friendship, one weekend when her husband was out of town, we shared her bed. She taught me how to kiss — tenderly, slowly, passionately. Her lips, tongue, fingers, explored my body. As she gently removed my bedclothes, she taught me how to make love with a woman. Later we talked about it.

Elizabeth initiated our friendship and sexual contact, and she ended it a year later. After she filed for divorce and began working at a local department store and dating a young black man, she called me less, neglected to return my calls, and avoided physical contact when she saw me. Repeatedly I asked her to talk to me about what was going on inside her. Did she want to break up? Finally she told me she wanted no further contact. When the relationship ended, I still didn't recognize myself as a Lesbian.

I talked about the relationship to my best friend, Judy, also a Sister of St. Joseph. She knew I was hurting, going through a sort of withdrawal. She was supportive, comforting, and tender with me. I could call her anytime of the day or night, crying or just needing to talk to an understanding person. My spiritual director was also exceptionally understanding.

Months later an "out" Lesbian friend unexpectedly visited me. We talked about sexuality and Lesbianism, and she gave me many books, which I read eagerly with a sense of discovering myself. One late October weekend we made love. After that I knew: I am a Lesbian.

The following weekend I attended the Conference for Catholic Lesbians in Kirkwood, Pennsylvania. It was exciting and confirming. Meeting such positive, deeply spiritual women I felt proud and fortunate to be a Lesbian among such great women.

When I call my spirituality incarnational I mean that I seek to find God in all things, especially people. Past religious beliefs affect my values regarding sexuality. I have no trouble reconciling my religious vows and my Lesbian identity as long as I am celibate. When I am not celibate, I cannot reconcile my actions with my vow. Although I have deep questions about lifetime celibacy, I have just taken my final vows because I feel that God has called me to be a sister and that this lifestyle is the best one for me.

My sexual/emotional relationships have brought me close to God and have helped my growth. Even at times of great anguish, the Spirit teaches me valuable lessons. I experience love of the Spirit through intimate love of people. My spirituality has revealed deeper possibilities for friendship than I would have known otherwise. Some of my most satisfying moments have been in the intimacy of silence with someone I love.

I have been a pastoral associate at a large suburban parish for the past five years, and prior to that was a liturgist and teacher. I am also a musician and active in many women's groups and Lesbian organizations. While ministering, I pursue graduate theological studies, hoping to continue them to the doctoral level in feminist theology. Besides reading, I enjoy yoga, Italian cooking, and travelling.

LOVE THAT LESBIAN MUSIC

Sister Sara
(1958-present)

(Sister Sara, forty-two and sexually active, has been a nun for twenty-four years. She is currently on leave-of-absence from her community. This interview with Nancy Manahan took place in Sister Sara's San Francisco apartment on October 31, 1982.)

Nancy: How do you reconcile your vow of chastity with sexual activity?

Sister Sara: I don't bother trying to reconcile them. Since I was twenty-two, I've never been able to fathom why sex causes such a fuss. Being sexual is so normally human. I never bought the chastity ideal. There's a place for celibacy, but I don't define celibacy as abstinence from sex for one's entire life.

Nancy: How do you define celibacy?

Sara: As being single. Not being married or in an exclusive relationship. The good of celibacy is that it frees people to concentrate on what they want to do with their lives. Being married and raising a family take a lot of time and responsibility.

Nancy: Doesn't an intimate sexual relationship take a lot of time?

Sara: Sometimes. But not as much as marriage or a family. I have been in intimate sexual relationships for three, four, or five years when my lover and I lived in separate towns and saw each other twice a month or less. Now that doesn't take a whole lot of time.

Nancy: How did you first experience sexuality in the convent?

Sara: When I was twenty-two and living in a community with twenty-five sisters on my first teaching assignment, the sister superior, who was forty-eight, liked me, and I felt attracted to her. One day I was feeling bad. She said, "What's the matter, Honey?" and took me into her office where I poured out my soul. When I got up to leave, she gave me a wonderful, consoling hug. Well, I just melted into her arms and cried. The next thing I knew her hand was on my breast! I moved her hand away and started to pull apart. She drew me closer to her, and I let myself feel how good it was. When she put her hand on my breast again, I thought, "What the hell!" We stayed in that embrace for awhile. Absolutely wonderful!

Nancy: How did you feel about her making a sexual advance when you were vulnerable and in need of mothering?

Sara: It bothered me. I wouldn't consider it appropriate behavior. But I don't feel it harmed me *at the time.* I don't know what implications this experience had on my subsequent relationships, however.

From then on, most of our exchange was on an

emotional level. Periodically we would have physical intimacy too. I took to it like a fish to water. She would run scared sometimes. When we started kissing, she'd get nervous and say, "Honey, not so long," or "Not with your tongue, Honey." But gradually she got more comfortable. We lived two and a half years together, but our schedules didn't allow many opportunities for physical intimacy. The whole physical affair was completely above the waist.

Nancy: Did you ever sleep together?

Sara: Not in that house. It was too risky. Once in a while we went to each other's rooms to chat and hug. But if anyone had knocked on the door, we would have died just to be caught in the bedroom together. When I got an assignment 150 miles away, we didn't see each other for months on end. When we did visit, we slept together. Fewer than ten times in our lives did we sleep together.

Nancy: Do you mean sleep literally or did you make love?

Sara: We always made love during those times, sure.

Nancy: Do you mean you had genital contact?

Sara: No. I mean we made love from the waist up. There are lots of ways of making love, and we definitely made love. We all have our lines of what's okay and what's not. Pelvic movement was okay, not direct genital touching.

Nancy: Did you feel guilty?

Sara: I knew what we were doing was fine. Given our natural ability to determine what's okay and what's not, I don't know why people have so much trouble about sex. I only worried about what would happen if it became known. Someone could hurt me with that information.

In my next relationship with a woman I felt more fear and guilt. It was in 1973, several years after my relationship with the sister superior had evolved into a close but non-sexual relationship. I lived with a sister and we grew very close. We'd sit up at night drinking wine and talking for hours. After two years I finished my graduate studies and had to move on. One night Lucy and I were holding each other and crying about our coming separation. Then we stopped crying and started kissing. That was the first time I ever went "all the way." I was scared to death. Scared to death. I'm not even sure what I was scared of, but the next day I told Lucy I did not want that to happen again. I did not want to be lovers with her.

Nancy: What was her response?

Sara: She's a woman of few words. She said, "OK." Later Lucy revealed that she was afraid too. She had had several sexual experiences with women in our community, and she had never been able to maintain what she called "a positive relationship" because sex always wrecked it. She tells me now, ten years later, that I'm the only person she's been sexual with that she's still close friends with. During those first two years of separation, we did a lot of commuting. We lived fifty miles apart. We'd visit each other on weekends and almost always sleep together — when we could get away with it.

Nancy: What happened to your earlier decision not to be sexual with her?

Sara: Well, our feelings were stronger than our fears, but that didn't seem to hurt anything. And I was still being a sister. You see, that worried me. I was afraid that we would have to stop being sisters because of how we felt about each other. In fact, it was all working out fine. I was having my cake and eating it too. But just as in my first relationship, Lucy and I didn't reflect together on what was happening. We couldn't afford to. Gradually we moved out of a sexual relationship. A few months later, I had a sexual/emotional/social relationship with a woman on my softball team. Dot was divorced and the mother of two kids. We never had much in common except sports. We met at a time of mutual need for closeness and comforting.

Five years ago I met a woman who had been an Immaculate Heart of Mary sister for nine years. Ann and I became lovers. For the first time we could both utter reflections on our experiences together. My other lovers had all been too scared to talk. Ann was no longer a nun and she wasn't the "straight" mother of two kids. She didn't have to lie to herself or hide.

Finally I was able to say, "By golly, I must be a Lesbian!" Don't ask me what I was thinking up to then. I wasn't thinking; I was just being. My relationship with Ann brought me into contact with other women who freely identified themselves as Lesbians. It became something I could think and talk about. Ann and I had been lovers for several months when I decided to move out of my community and live in an apartment. Ann had sold her condominium and had bought a house. But she had two weeks before she could take possession. I invited her to stay with me during that time. Well, two weeks turned into ten months.

Sisters in my community couldn't speak directly to me about my living with Ann. If they disapproved because they considered it sinful, they had to leave it for a confessor. One of my friends, a province administrator, asked me to consider an assignment in Hawaii. I told her that I wouldn't choose to live 1000 miles away from Ann, so I couldn't accept the assignment. She said she understood. I never said that Ann and I were lovers, but my friend respected our relationship.

Nancy: Why are you on a leave-of-absence?

Sara: Leave-of-absence gives me time to live another lifestyle. It's been the most difficult decision of my life:

whether to be a Sister or not. In the old days, when sisters walked away from the convent to start a new life, there was a clear distinction between being "in" and being "out." Today more and more Sisters live by themselves or with people outside the community. To be a Sister in my community means living and working around certain shared goals, such as working against racism and discrimination against women or working for peace and disarmament. Who could ask for more? I'm proud of my community, and it's exciting to be a part of this group of women. But I don't want to be accountable to them for my life. I have a need for autonomy and independence. I've been afraid that part of my motivation for having been a sister all these years has been my own lack of security. Now I want to be a secure person without having the community to fall back on. However, I'm not ready to say, "Yup, I don't want to be a Sister any more." I'm not ready to take my name off the roster until I feel comfortable about going through the process.

Nancy: When you take that step, how will your life change?

Sara: My external life won't change at all. I'll continue to live alone in this apartment. I'll continue to work where I'm working. Financially nothing will change. Since I've been on leave-of-absence, I've kept all my wages. Ordinarily each sister makes out a budget for herself. Any wages over and above that are donated to the province treasury for the retirement fund, travel fund, education fund, and other communal needs.

But I'll be able to be more open about my sexual activity. When I have a lover, I don't want to have to be secretive. I don't want to deal with the community's disapproval. I figure I can do it without that disapproval if I'm not on the community's roster.

Nancy: How do you think people will react to this book?

Sara: Lesbian nuns I know are going to dance! In convents this book will go around like hotcakes, just the way
The Hite Report did in my community. We were waiting
in line for that book. Everybody read it. Lesbian nuns will
be more self-conscious about this book. I can see them
dying to get hold of it, but trying not to show too much
interest. They're also going to be listening to the response
from other members of the community and praying to God
it's okay.

The book will also be an occasion for confronting a lot
of pain. Lesbian sisters who are not out in their communities (and I don't know anybody who is out) will have to
listen to homophobic reactions. But it will be a catalyst.
All hell's going to break loose. Religious communities are
going to have to discuss the book. They're going to have
to respond to the reality, and they've never had to do that.

Religious communities have progressed beyond the days
when we were warned about particular friendships. Now
they say it's okay to have good, healthy, intimate relationships. But homophobia is rampant, and Lesbian relationships
are still not okay.

Recently I prepared the liturgy for our order's assembly
meeting. The opening and closing song was Cris Williamson's
"Sisters." After the liturgy one of our international administrators beckoned me over and whispered very dramatically,
"Sister," (we never call each other "Sister" anymore) "Sister,
how *could* you play that Lesbian music during the liturgy?"
I replied, "Sister, I happen to *love* that Lesbian music." We
both had big smiles on our faces.

Section V

SURPRISES AND CONTRADICTIONS

Imagine our surprise! A Lesbian ex-nun daughter writes about her Lesbian ex-nun mother. Sisters sitting-in at the chancery for a teachers' union fall in love, leave the convent, get married in the Church, and have a baby. Many more surprises confound attempts to circumscribe our lives and realities.

Sr. Peter Marie, 1964

Mary Alice Scully, 1981

SECOND GENERATION

Mary Alice Scully
(1961-1979)

In the spring of 1965, I'd been a Sister of Charity for four years when I was invited to the fiftieth anniversary celebration of a nun in a semi-cloistered order. I'd never met Mother Katherine, but I'd certainly heard about her all my life. She was one of my mother's closest friends for longer than I could remember. Since my mother had died the year before, I decided to represent her at this Golden Jubilee. It has taken me almost twenty years to realize that my going represented the last episode in what was probably the main love relationship spanning almost fifty years of my mother's life.

Mom became friends with Mother Katherine back in the twenties on a retreat. Her family, I was told, always resented the "influence" the young nun had on her, especially when Mom decided to enter herself. I suspect that she had a hard time as cloistered nun. I he woman I knew as my mother was something of a free spirit given to odd outbursts of the unexpected. I'm sure she was censured for being singular, as I was many years later, and for pranks, such as sliding down the bannister. The photographs I have show a smiling novice, arms secure within her wide sleeves. I suspect her leaving religious life was with real sorrow, although she never talked much about it. Something vague about being sick. Recently an aunt hinted at a nervous breakdown.

Starting over at thirty-two, she got a job as a secretary in Catholic Charities at next to no pay back in 1931. She worked in a Catholic Action group of semi-professional actors, and shared her home with out-of-state unwed young women disgraced by pregnancy. During those years, I suspect she was active, outgoing, and gay. She had many friends. Her love for Mother Katherine continued through frequent contact.

Approaching forty and knowing she wasn't getting married for reasons I can only speculate about (and I do), she took a year-old boy to raise as her foster son. At forty-four, she took a new-born girl.

Being raised as a foster child of a Catholic Lesbian ex-nun had its peculiar aspects. That she was an unusual and adventurous woman was clear to me, even as a child. Unmarried, she'd blithely introduce her children and chuckle at others' chagrin. Poor, she worked two, sometimes three, jobs while continuing to be an active member of the acting group. The clown-life of many a party, she regaled friends with poems and stories. Among her many women friends, the memory of one deep-voiced, striding, laughing friend, Mary, who babysat while Mom worked hard and played intensely, stands out. I only vaguely suspect that Mary stayed overnight sometimes. My mother loved and, more than once, hurt hard. Fun times I took for granted; it's the tears I remember more. Off and on I heard of Mother Katherine and her alcoholic brother who inhabited the Bowery. There was the time we stood on a cold, windy corner waiting to give him Mom's last five dollars. "He has less than we do," she said.

How does a closet Lesbian who is a practicing Catholic raise two children with no money? In a Catholic boarding school. For me it was a prison where the French nuns believed child-beating stood for discipline. Real bad on the soul of a child. I was already coming up tough.

During my teens, I was busy growing up, active in school and playing hard in the streets. Only dimly was I aware of the other person inside my mother. At home she was tired and serious. There was little clowning around. She saw her women friends less frequently and never at home. I thought most of them were weird, very prim or very lonely "old ladies." What had she wanted, hoped, dreamed for her children? What were we to her? I was too young, busy, self-absorbed to ask. She was too weary, lonely, closeted to tell. Her spirituality was deep but private. She went to church alone, rarely received communion. Her Lesbianism may have brought her gaiety, but it was also, I suspect, a burden increasingly weighing her down.

At nineteen I entered the convent myself, and Mom died two years later. It took me years to realize that I hardly knew the woman who was my mother. They tell me that blanks and gaps are frequently encountered when one tries to piece together the life of a long-ago Lesbian, closeted in her truth. From my own and others' memories, I see the hilarious companion and the deeply private, sometimes puzzling person.

Yeah, I became a nun of the sixties — active not only in the changing Church but in anti-war and prison reform movements. Liberation theology and recognizing myself as a Lesbian liberated me, even while I continued to be a nun. Religious life was a freeing experience for me in a lot of ways. I stayed for eighteen years.

I suppose that subliminally I knew all my life that I was a Lesbian, and so did Mom. But it took the challenge of a friendly stranger to call me out of my unsuspected closet.

Because I was a nun, I was free to roam the corridors of the women's house of detention at Riker's Island in New York as part of the clergy volunteer program. My religious habit was the anti-war uniform of the seventies: jeans and workshirt.

"Hey, Bo-dagger!" shouted an inmate.

"Who me?" I glanced around to be sure she was talking to me.

"Yeah, you . . . You social worker or somethin'?"

"Uh, no . . . I'm a nun."

"You ain't no nun in them clothes."

I explained that I really was a nun, despite my clothes, and that she apparently had notions as stereotyped about what nuns are like as people outside have about women in prison. But at that moment the process of accepting myself as a Lesbian began.

When I knew it was time for me to experience the risks, demands, insecurity, and failures that most grown people face daily — the life of the jungle instead of a warm secure zoo — I left religious life. My mother and I continue to be an interlocking story.

Now that I've left home for the second time, I've had the experiences to flesh out the labels bo-dagger, butch, and Lesbian.

Yeah, I'm forty now; but no, I'm not planning to raise any foster kids. After all, enough's enough.

I live and work, love and search in New York City.

UNION ACTIVISTS, LOVERS, AND PARENTS

Christine and Sheila
(1971-1972 and 1960-1981)

Sheila: I was the oldest daughter of four children in a closely knit family. I grew up comfortable with myself and my religion. My mother's calm balanced my father's fervor as a convert. My parents' love and sensitivity also influenced me and my decision to enter religious life. Attraction for several caring nuns in high school made me think seriously about religious life.

Chris: Four wonderful years at a midwestern Catholic women's college prompted my conversion and my desire to enter the convent. The mystery, drama, and romanticism of listening to the novitiate choir in the eighteenth century Italian Renaissance Church gave me the shivers. I needed the structure and security of convent life. From 1968 to 1972 when I was in college and convent, the order was

163

going through "the great change." In the 1971–72 school year, I was the order's only postulant, immature and a bit rebellious but committed to religious life. When my superiors asked me to leave the convent at the end of my first year, I almost lost my sanity. I hadn't been the best possible postulant, but the convent was my life. I took an emotional nosedive.

After leaving I found a job teaching seventh and eighth grade at a middle school in downtown Los Angeles. I loved the teachers and administrators there. I could make mistakes, pick myself up, and start over. I really learned how to teach.

Sheila: In high school I had felt so close to my girl friends. Without realizing it, I seemed to be having typical adolescent feelings toward girls that most girls have toward boys. I knew nothing about Lesbianism.

Chris: While I was teaching in the middle school I began dating two of the male teachers. One was an ex-seminarian. I now know that the other was and is gay. Although both men were good friends, I felt uncomfortable dating and couldn't handle sexuality at all. I was miserable because I couldn't figure out what was wrong with me. I took it as a sign that I truly belonged in the convent, and so I re-applied. Even though I had matured and become a good teacher, I was turned down. I was crushed. Why didn't they want me? What was wrong with me? Maybe if I had joined a feminist organization, I would have found out sooner than I did that I was really OK.

Sheila: When I was in the novitiate, I became "involved" a couple of times, but this was nipped in the bud by those in charge. "Particular friends" were frowned upon but never really explained. Now I realize that even after final profession I searched out nuns I could feel close to, but no one reciprocated until I met Chris.

Chris: By my third year at the middle school, a Catholic Teachers' Union was forming. Working in this trade union changed my life. I grew along with the union. I became vice president. After moving out of the middle school into high school teaching, I was fighting for teachers' rights and students' rights to quality education. I had found my community. I was hard core union. Working seven days a week consumed my entire life. In 1976 we went on strike. We "sat in" all night at the chancery as a last-ditch effort to show the diocese that our strike was serious and to gain publicity. It was frightening. None of us felt revolutionary. After the strike organizers meeting on the first floor of the chancery, I crept upstairs to join those sleeping on the marble floor. Sleeping-bagged bodies were all over, and I hadn't brought a thing to sleep on. Sleeping on the hard cold marble was unthinkable.

While I was standing there, one of the strikers, a nun named Sister Sheila, offered me part of her sleeping bag. Not wanting to wake everyone with my protestations, I lay down next to her and felt the most warm and marvelous feelings I had ever felt in my life. I didn't sleep a wink all night and felt great the next day. The next night we spread one bag on the floor and the other on top of the blanket. We held hands through the night. I remember thinking, "What is going on?" I could only answer, "I don't know, but it feels fantastic!"

After the strike ended, we saw each other constantly, even though seeing Sheila was interfering with my union work. All of a sudden walks, beaches, mountains, and sipping wine with my new friend were more important than stuffing envelopes and designing membership drive programs. Neither one of us really understood what was happening; we only knew we wanted to be together.

And so I got a job at Sheila's school the following year. I decided that the best way to be near Sheila was to enter her religious order. Just when we thought that everything was perfect, I was informed that I was not to be accepted.

No reason. They had conferred with my previous superior. Again I asked what was wrong with me. I was furious, and I was plagued with self-doubt. I don't believe that I was refused entrance to Sheila's order for being Lesbian. I'd never even heard the word, and I'd never had a Lesbian experience. The union was sheltered and innocent. We were all so naive.

Sheila: When Chris and I met, and my feelings were reciprocated, I was frightened. My stable existence was disrupted, and the vows I had grown to value were all topsy turvy. Poverty and Obedience posed no difficulty. I still lived a simple lifestyle, and people were more important than possessions. But my relationship with Chris directly challenged my vow of chastity, which demanded celibacy. Even though I wanted her, I found it difficult to give up what I had had for nearly twenty years. When I finally admitted who I was to a good friend, she wisely observed, "Things don't usually just happen. People keep putting themselves in the same position until they are forced to make a decision."

Chris: Because of school and union work, Sheila and I were together constantly. We even took trips to see her family together. But we had covered up our lives so well that when we finally "came out" to our friends and family, they were astounded. We had been hiding and denying the facts to everyone including ourselves.

After I was refused entrance to Sheila's community, I began to try to sort out my feelings and discovered that there was nothing wrong with me. I simply loved Sheila, and I wanted to live and share my life with her. Although we began spending our weekends together, we still had not had a sexual experience. The tension was beginning to cause anxiety and crying attacks. Because Sheila was still a nun with vows important to her, she was constantly battling herself. I understood but I couldn't deny my desires. I wanted physical love; I had waited too long. I knew I was Lesbian, but I wasn't willing to admit it yet. I began to attend Lesbian group therapy sessions. I resigned my office at the union and changed schools. I was too scared to search out women's bars, but my new-found Lesbian friends took me. What a revelation! I didn't like the bar atmosphere, but I felt I could be myself at last. It was a heady feeling! I moved closer to Sheila's convent, and we saw each other all the time. Finally that summer we slept together. It was wonderful for me, but Sheila had an upset stomach the next day. By now I knew what I wanted. But I didn't want Sheila to leave the convent because of me and later blame me for ruining her religious life. It had to be her decision.

Sheila: I tried to live both lives for almost four years until I faced the fact that I was being dishonest with my community and myself and unfair to Chris. I explained the situation to my religious representative; she and my other superiors supported me and my decision. For twenty years I had always been proud of being a member of my community, so it was difficult to make the decision to leave. But I finally realized that the truth for me was my love for Chris.

Chris: The night Sheila signed her dispensation papers and received her dowry back, I held her close to me. My heart ached for both our losses. Since then our lives have grown and changed. We've gone through some bad times — one very serious one. I began seeing someone else until I realized how much I cared for Sheila. It was a growing experience for both of us because we might not have trusted how much we love each other without this test.

Sheila: Since leaving the community, I had not been actively involved in the Church until Chris and I decided to commit our lives to each other. When we talked to Father Paul, we both realized how important the Church was for us and have become more involved again.

Chris: On May 14, 1982, Father Paul performed our original "commitment ceremony." Our closest friends came. Using passages from the Old Testament and contemporary poetry, we used the Book of Ruth as our theme: "Whither thou goest, I will go." For at least two years Sheila and I had wanted to have a child. In April 1982 I became pregnant by artificial insemination. On February 11, 1983, Patrick was born. On March 26 he was baptized by Father Paul, who named the two of us the parents.

It hasn't been easy for us. Some of our previous friends are no longer friends. We have experienced discrimination. When I became pregnant, the principal at the Catholic high school where I taught called me a sinner. I walked out of her office and the school that day. A lot has happened to me since I became a postulant in 1971. I believe that changes regarding homosexuality are needed in the Church. The Church hasn't always been there when we needed help. But Sheila and I live our lives as we feel we should.

Sheila: We are very happy together. We have had our crisis and feel stronger for it. We have done a great deal of growing in the past few years and intend to do much more.

Now thirty-five — Christine — and forty-three — Sheila, we live happily in Los Angeles.

COZIER THAT WAY

Terry
(1969–1971)

What red blooded Lesbian wouldn't have enjoyed my high school? Hundreds of teenage girls and dozens of nuns nestled cozily together, in L.A.'s suburbs. When I was a freshman, I told myself that when I was a senior I would tell Sister Charlene that I wanted to be just like her. I imagined her and me in a quiet empty classroom. All the other students home. But she left the high school when I was a sophomore, and now I think she was carrying on with a senior student.

I promptly found a fresh young nun to dream about. Sister Terese was barely six years older than I. From my sophomore to senior year I played volleyball and basketball, and she never missed a game. She was my greatest fan and my sponsor for the convent. She gave me my first real woman's kiss when I was a postulant.

Sister Terese and some other nuns had come to the novitiate to make a retreat, but we postulants weren't supposed to talk to the "holy sisters." I remember walking down the stairs from study hall. As I came around the corner I saw a habit, but being a conscientious beginner, I didn't lift my eyes from their guarded position — checking out the floor. The habit stopped parallel to me. I felt a gentle tug at my arm.

"Oh, I didn't know —" I started to whisper. She put her finger across her lips: "Shhhh." Leaning against my side she cradled my chin in her hands, not saying a word, but with a look in her eye that nailed me to the wall. She kissed my lips so softly. I specifically remember the "so softly" part.

Dumb me. I thought, "What do I do now? What is this all about?"

She whispered, "Goodnight, Terry," and crossed my forehead with her thumb. I didn't sleep too well that night, even after an extra rosary.

When I told my folks in 1969 that I wanted to go to the Sacred Heart Convent, they went for it at first. I was their oldest child, and they wanted me to go to college, be a teacher. I spoke in religious jargon: "vocation, calling, God's will." What I didn't know was that I wanted to follow the women I loved, and the women I loved were nuns.

The summer of '69 I ran around trying to do everything I could for the last time. I smashed up my '56 Chevy, and with no regrets entered the convent in September with three other girls from my high school. Three years later I discovered that one of them was having an affair with a classmate when she started the novitiate, and the other two had developed a "particular friendship." I was the ignorant, naive one.

By June of '70 I could see through a lot of hypocrisy. In November I left Sacred Heart. It was more like being shuffled out the back door so that no one could see me go. "One bad apple spoils the whole basket." So what if I couldn't say goodbye to a few friends. They left a few months later anyway. And I started my search for the perfect religious community.

During the next year I went to twenty-five retreats, think-throughs, and discovery weekends sponsored by different communities. A friend who had been in Sacred Heart with me tried to get in the Daughters of Charity. After they gave her a psych test, they told her they didn't want her because she showed homosexual tendencies. This friend was having an affair with a Daughter of Charity, and it suddenly terminated with the good sister's transfer to another city. So my friend gets a "no thank you" letter from the D.C.'s.

OK, we're young. They're not the right community anyway. We're still very religious — not gay yet — but wondering how they could say those things! If they say we're gay, let's check it out, cruise a few bars. You go in first. No, you go. Let's both go see what it's like. My college roommate gives me a few Lesbian lessons — physicalness, no love emotions. I go through a period of deep regret and repentance: God, I'm sorry. I shouldn't have done it. I'll never do it again.

Then in the summer of '73 I'm working at a summer camp in the National Forest with a few Sisters of St. Joseph helping out. Beautiful! Well, I'm minding my own business being a good camp counselor when Sister Beth comes on to me like a diesel dyke in a honkytonk bar. For the next two and a half years I hitchhike from Southern California to her convent in the Midwest to visit her whenever I can. My first serious lover. My head is changing. I'm ready to say I'm a Lesbian. But she's a nun and getting ready to take her final vows. She wants me to be in the ceremony — give the homily. Wait a minute. What kind of a lie is this? She's preparing to make a promise of celibacy in front of everybody, and she still wants me whenever she can get me? Come on now.

It's time for me to admit a few things to myself: 1) There is no such thing as the perfect religious community. 2) Church isn't all it's cracked up to be. 3) I'm gay. For a while I tried to salvage religion by joining Dignity, Metropolitan Church, Jesuit Volunteer Corps, Pentecostals, Newman Centers, Christian Ministry. Finally I decided it was all a bunch of baloney.

I'm happy now. I rode my motorcycle in the gay parade last year, and I'm making a decent living as a police officer. Three years ago in the police academy I met a female cadet who had been in the Sacred Hearts about three years after I'd been there, and she's now dating one of my ex-lovers. It's a small world. That's OK. It's cozier that way.

I must be getting older. The rookies at work look like babies, and recently at a women's bar, I ran into one of my former campers. I regret disguising names and places in my story. Let's call it professional discretion. It would be fun to see Sisters Charlene and Terese today, fifteen years later. I wonder if they would make me all goose-bumpy.

Sr. John Ellen, S.S.N.D., 1954

Charlotte Doclar, 1984

TWO CLOSET DOORS

Charlotte A. Doclar
(1952–1981)

Religious women who happen to be Lesbians live behind two closet doors. The one called religious life keeps us protected from the world, that sinful entity that we are taught we should be in but not of. The other door hides our sexual orientation. We learn by bitter experience to keep that door tightly closed lest "we all become suspect."

I lived and loved behind those two doors for twenty-nine years. I was not conscious of the second door until twenty-two years had slipped away. Finally, I knew that the only way to be true to the person God called me to be was to open both doors and walk away free.

I write my story not because it is special but because I now know that it is *not* special. I share my story because in unity there is strength. As long as society can keep us isolated and invisible, it succeeds in keeping us powerless.

As I grew up I was not aware that I was different. I was a tomboy, and I avoided boys whenever I could. Now that I have acquired 20/20 hindsight, I wonder what my family and friends thought about me, but at the time, I thought my loves were normal. I had heart-wrenching crushes on several older girls, my PE teacher, and my band director. My loves seemed normal to me. I never associated these feelings with anything sexual. I was not aware of sexual needs before I entered the convent in 1952. At eighteen, sexually naive and terribly attached to my mother, I entered a world of women, and at eighteen I had my first affair — with an older nun. Although I was not to put a name on it for many years, it was at this time that I began my life of short-term Lesbian relationships.

In the beginning, the relationships were basically what was known as particular friendships. With each relationship, the sexual aspect became more defined. That's a polite way of saying I learned by doing. I cannot remember having to fight the authorities over one particular lover; no romantic "us against the world." I had many affairs in the convent. I'm not sure if that makes me promiscuous or if it was due to the many transfers.

Religious life can be a stomach-wrenching experience for one who falls in love easily and is an incurable romantic. I would become emotionally attached and then be forced to live through the trauma of one of us being transferred to another convent. My world ended every time I had to say good-bye. Looking back I cannot imagine how I survived. I can only conclude that I must have been having an awfully good time between good-byes.

Triangle love affairs were very common in the 1950s and 60s. Convent couples did not fluorish until we began living outside of convents and had more input into where and with whom we wanted to live. In pre-Vatican II days frequent and indiscriminate transfers created a familiar scenario: Sister Charlotte and Sister Anne love each other dearly. One day Sister Joan joins their community; Sister Anne falls in love with Sister Joan, and Sister Charlotte begins to cry at night!

And where was my spiritual life during all these years? At first, when I was young and dedicated, my conscience would get the better of me, and I would go to the chapel, fall on my knees, cry, and promise that I would never stray again. It was all very dramatic. But my resolutions did not last long. Eventually I stopped going to the chapel. Nothing happened. I did not come down with some incurable disease. Lightning did not strike. I began to feel as if god really did love me. I was faithful about keeping the rule. (Well, most rules.) I was a good community member, a good listener, and an awfully faithful friend. I was intense in my desire to remain forever as a good religious. I was not exemplary in any sense, but I felt safe and I had a purpose in life.

As the years went by, my personal affairs became more physical and therefore more demanding. I found myself wanting more and more. Finally I wanted someone to love me, and only me, forever. My vow of celibacy made my desire for a personal love illicit and illegal. I knew that some choices would have to be made.

In 1978 I named myself Lesbian, and the struggle with hypocrisy began. When I first entered the convent, I felt called apart to be someone special, a religious. Then I felt a call just as strong to claim my identity as a Lesbian. (Straight people may have a difficult time understanding this desire to say our name because they have never been forced into deception.) I felt as long as I remained in one world, I could not be true to the other. My Lesbian sisters "in the world" were struggling with identity and closet doors while I lived behind the facade of convent walls, quite protected. It came down to personal integrity and the old cliche of waking up each morning and liking the person in the mirror.

I did not just leave the convent. I struggled with my decision for several years. I went for counseling, made a thirty-day retreat, spent four months in a renewal program, and interned for a year in Washington, D.C., with New Ways Ministry. I tried to work it out within the convent structure, but I could not. On the surface it seemed so simple. But beneath it, I wondered how it could happen to me. What had I done? What had I neglected to do? Was it my fault? Who was to blame?

I am not saying that it is impossible to be a gay religious: I am saying that for me it was not possible. I could not keep the two worlds apart. I wanted to be part of the Lesbian community, and I also wanted the awe and respect that "Sister" evokes in the Catholic community. Not being true to either world was causing havoc within me. For me the bottom line was celibacy. Although I am more celibate now than I was in the convent, I am free to choose it, and that makes all the difference.

I have been "in the world" for three years now. My freedom has not been all fun and games. I am very lonely at times. I have discovered, however, that loneliness is a widespread malaise in today's world. I am teaching again. I thought I was through with teaching when I left the convent but it happens to be the only profession that I do well enough to earn money to survive. After twenty-nine years in religious life, I have a difficult time adjusting to the fact that I am not formally ministering anymore. (I suppose the Messiah complex dies slowly.) I feel a need to minister in a special way to the gay community, but now that I am out on my own, I do not have the time or the resources to do so.

I consider myself quite fortunate because I received

cooperation and support from my Congregation from the beginning of my struggle. I have spoken to many who have been put through hell because of their honesty and forth-rightness, and so I know that my experience was an exception to the rule.

My spiritual life is in a state of shock. I have been drawing away from the patriarchal heterosexist Church of my youth. I cannot worship god as male, and the male-dominated Church is not my Church. I do not miss the legalistic ritual. What I miss and what I am searching for is a supportive community. But if I have learned anything from my life, it is that we never really arrive. It is the striving that gets me out of bed in the morning.

At fifty I am standing on another threshold. I remind myself that not everyone has the opportunity to begin again at my age. I consider it a challenge and a blessing. I have been blessed in many ways. My only wish is that all those whom I have touched over the years are a little better for having known me. If heaven is anything, it is the journey we make together, holding hands as we go.

I was born in New Orleans in 1934. I was in the School Sisters of Notre Dame from 1952 to 1981. I now live in Houston, where, at fifty, I am slowly but surely beginning again.

Sr. Mary Benjamin, I.H.M., 1963

Coriander, 1983

REVOLVING DOORS

Coriander
(1962-1968)

Some people think I'm tall till they get up close. I'm only 5'1", but I stand straight and hold my head high. I'm compact and muscular. I walk with purpose. My eyes are clear and deep and reflect what's going on around me.

I was born in Leo during World War II, the granddaughter of Polish and Irish immigrants. They left me a legacy of dreams and the will to work for them. From my father I learned to work with my hands. My mother taught me how to laugh.

·As a child I loved the sunshine, got angry a lot, and always colored with red. I followed my brother into the world, and nine more kids followed me. We grew up in Hollywood. When I was seven, I wanted to be a movie star or a nun. I was an obedient child. Terrified by visions of hell and damnation, I was both a sunny adventurous child of the day and a lonely brooding child of the dark. I feared God and my father. But wishing I had been born a pagan with the freedom to live by my own instincts, I harbored a secret desire to rid myself of my baptism and my parentage.

I was most often seen in my jeans and T-shirt with a tool in hand. Whether it was scissors, hammer, or paintbrush, I enjoyed using my hands, never imagining that the skills I was learning could earn me a living as a woman. In our large family where everyone had work to do, I took for granted my role as mother's helper. But when I considered assuming my mother's job for real, the future looked like nothing but hard work with no vacation. That was so intolerable that at twelve I decided that I wasn't going to grow up.

At fifteen it was inescapable. My body was changing. I was full of yearnings and excess energy. And my poor little heart was going crazy over a couple of nuns and some girls on the varsity team. In sixth grade I'd had a boyfriend, but only because he was my ticket to the movies. My loyalty and affection were reserved for my girlfriends. In high school the pressure was on to start "blooming" into womanhood with bras, girdles, and makeup. My father, who had bragged about my biceps a few years back, now looked at more than my arms in a way that made me uneasy. My girlfriends were seeing less of me. When my dearest friend Katie wrote that we must stop seeing so much of each other and start spending time with boys, I felt betrayed.

During my senior year I went through the motions of preparing for college and the adult world, but I was panic-stricken. Confronted with graduation, I fled to the holy and more familiar ground of religious life. The women I had loved as my teachers took me in as one of their own.

Of course, it was a life of sacrifice. But I hadn't learned to want what I was giving up.

On a sunny day in September 1962, my family drove me to the novitiate of the Sisters of the Immaculate Heart of Mary. We piled out of the station wagon like a baseball team. The priest greeting families looked us over and asked, "Which one is entering?" I stepped forward and began my life as a nun.

The first few weeks were like a honeymoon. We were feasted with food, song, and celebration by the group ahead of us. They taught us the ropes of community living and welcomed us as new members of the family. It was like going to my girlfriend's house to stay overnight and never having to go home. I could hardly believe my good fortune that this family of women could be mine for the rest of my life.

I loved the early morning hours, the walk to chapel through the citrus grove in the fading starlight. We gathered in silence and gently began chanting psalms. As a child I had been intensely religious. Now I was anxious to learn the secrets of the mystic life.

Of course there were more than seeds of mysticism germinating. We were young and passionate. Romantic crushes were sprouting like weeds. I was growing several myself. What I remember from our first trip to the beach was not our singing around the campfire but the light in Betty's eyes as we held hands and gazed at the stars. But the fathers of the Church were one step ahead. Our rule book was clear: No Particular Friendships. Love everyone, but no one in particular. Our superiors did their best to keep us alone or in groups and warned us not to walk in two's.

In my second year of training I was appointed choir director of novices and postulants. My group was noted for its inability to carry a tune. Choir practices were awful until we got to sounding like a regular group of voices. A couple of times we were visited by one of the professed nuns from the college, a real musician and conductor. She didn't stand demurely with a hymn book in one hand while the other marked rhythm in rigid patterns. She waved both arms through the air. I liked her style, so I started memorizing the hymns. One day at mass I got up there with nothing but my bare hands and waved those rhythms like I was directing the Salvation Army in Central Park. I must have looked like a swallow returning to Capistrano with my long sleeves swinging and the tails of my white veil flapping in the wind of my exuberance. We sang a mean Magnificat that spring. The next year I heard that directing with two hands had been axed at the Novitiate.

On the surface I was adapting well to convent life. Letters to my family sounded like theology books, and I was constantly reassuring them I was happy. But I was a lonely child with no one to tell me what to do with my need for touching and loving. My journal was filled with treatises to myself about overcoming cowardice and sensitivity. I saw my passions only as signs of immaturity and childishness.

Shortly after Christmas 1964, I was assigned to teach fourth grade in the San Fernando Valley. I was frightened because I'd completed only a year of college and three classes in education. Besides, I kept getting sick. I'd feel it first at the base of my spine, a creeping affliction that crawled up my insides until my head was pounding and I was vomiting. At its peak I was helpless. It was bad enough that I had so little preparation in teaching without this painful illness. When I pleaded with my superior to postpone the assignment, she refused to listen. The sickness was my fault. I was acting like a child. The responsibility of teaching would snap me out of my immaturity. I couldn't believe what I was hearing. But I had no choice. I had taken a vow of obedience.

I'll never forget my first day teaching. I stood in front of a large classroom wishing I could shrink into the woodwork while fifty nine-year-olds filed past and stood expectantly at their desks waiting for this stranger in black to stimulate their wandering minds. After lunch another fifty appeared before me. Responsibility came only in large numbers.

My sickness came in weekly cycles, the pain increasing daily until I'd be vomiting bile and feeling my head would explode if I moved. After my body exhausted itself, I fell into a deep sleep. But after a day of respite, the cycle began again. At her wit's end, my superior wanted to let me stay home on my worst days, but she couldn't. There was no one to take over my class. So I went to school and tried to function. I could usually manage to wait until my students filed out for recess before I ran to the restroom to heave. Once I threw up in the desk drawer. During this painful time I often imagined that I could escape from my body. I wanted to walk away and leave myself behind. I'd buried my feelings so deep I was numb to all but my pain and isolation.

After three months of teaching with no success at willing my sickness away, I was sent to a hospital for tests. I was relieved that my superiors considered my illness real. But nothing came up positive, and so the doctor sent me to the motherhouse with a prescription for tranquilizers and sleeping pills. I turned down the option to attend classes at the college. I simply lived at the motherhouse and performed small tasks.

With the time and space to heal myself, the spiraling darkness that had been my life lost its hold, and I found myself on solid ground again. But the crisis had pushed me to a turning point. All my life I had acted out of guilt and fear, fitting myself into a mold fashioned by my parents, teachers, superiors. I had feared authority and never questioned its demands. Now I found that those who dictated my life had power neither to destroy nor heal: they were weak and impotent in the face of my suffering. Only I had the power to heal myself and the wisdom to live my own life. A peace I had never known came into my soul. I knew that guilt and fear would never possess me again.

My recovery was rapid. The sickness returned a few more times at longer intervals, but it was waning. I started doing volunteer tutoring at a housing project in Watts and was pleased with the way people responded to me. My feelings were coming out of hiding, and though I was still confused, I felt nourished by a new inner strength and self-love.

In summer 1966, I was introduced to sensitivity training, my order's first venture into the human potential movement. There I met Eva, a heavy, dark-skinned woman with deep brown eyes and black hair. There was a softness about her, a quiet strength, and an ease with which she expressed what was in her heart. Tears came easily to her as she talked about her family conflicts and painful events at her convent and school. I felt a warmth for her and a closeness that surprised me. At the end of the third day, everyone had spoken but me. Hesitantly I recounted some of the events of the past few years and spoke of my loneliness. There were no tears. I spoke as if it were all over and done with. But as I looked around the room, I saw my pain reflected in the eyes of others — particularly Eva's.

A week later in the college parking lot, a nun rushed over and threw her arms around me in a warm embrace. It was Eva. Her eyes were full of tenderness as she greeted me like an old friend. Since we were both taking classes at the college, we saw each other often. I talked. She cried. We laughed. I told her I was worried that I had a terrible crush on her. She said, "Great! Enjoy it!" Enjoy it?! After all these years, someone was telling me to enjoy my feelings.

In August we all received our assignments for the fall. Eva and I were missioned to teach at the same school in San Diego. I couldn't contain myself! I walked around with a grin so wide my face was in danger of cracking. I was ready to make any sacrifice (except Eva, of course) in thanks for this favor.

We drove down together and were the first to arrive at the convent. That evening we sat in the light of a kerosene lamp that cast colored patches of light around the room. As my ritual to begin the new year, I taught Eva my favorite folk dances. Her eyes sparkled like the lamp as we danced.

I taught sixth grade that year; Eva taught first. She had a wonderful rapport with her students. I was lucky if there weren't dogfights in the aisles. Life was tough, but not at all like it used to be. I was loved, and I knew it. Each evening I crossed through the bathroom into Eva's room, and she read to me. We sat very close on the bed, her arm around me, while I listened to stories like *The Little Prince* or *The Wind in the Willows*. Sometimes we lay down for awhile before I went to my bed. Before long my initial feelings of affection became desire. The night Eva asked if she could put her hand on my breast, I was only too ready to comply. From there we went in the direction of least resistance, and finally I had to admit that what we were doing was sexual.

Never in my life had I felt so alive. My spirits were high. I was healthy and strong and enjoying pleasures I'd never dreamed of. But along with an appreciation for the pleasures of our intimacy came gnawing feelings of guilt. Surely we had gone far beyond the imagination of those who said "No particular friendships." Was I still celibate? If not, what was I doing in the convent? No one had ever said that celibacy meant not loving women. Was I doing something terrible? I talked to a priest who refused to pass judgment on my actions. He said it was up to me to decide if they were right or wrong. He opened a door, and I walked through, realizing I was on my own.

I continued my relationship with Eva and finished my year of teaching. But the guilt lingered until I could no longer ignore the contradictions embodied in my relationship. All my life my parents and teachers had used guilt and fear to get me to do things their way until I became so sick I couldn't do anything. Only at the end of my illness could I see my life as my own. In loving Eva I was growing in a direction at odds with convent goals of obedience and service to the Church. I began to make decisions, not out of guilt, but according to the voice of my intuition and the wisdom of my body. I began to see the Church more objectively. It was run by men, not God. My allegiance to the Church was no longer fate but choice.

I left the convent in 1968 because its walls had become a prison. The fear that drew me there for protection had lost its power. The convent could do nothing now but hold me back. My spirit was starving for the life I had surrendered as a child. It was time to catch up. I felt like a long-distance runner about to run the first mile of her marathon.

It's painful to remember my blunders as I tumbled back into the world. I had no idea how to dress. My attempts at dating led me into bizarre situations. More than once it was a priest who offered to purge me of my virginity. After six years as a nun, I needed to pass as "normal."

I thought a woman was supposed to want a man and babies, or at least pursue a "womanly" career. But I was swimming upstream with bright purple fins. I was at heart a dreamer, a lover, an artist. And I couldn't imagine a life without Eva. She was my lifeline as I balanced on the threshold between the convent and the secular world. Eva was still in the convent, and I'm sure I raised a few eyebrows with my frequent appearances at her back door, helmet in hand, on my Honda 90. Together we got involved in radical politics. Unknowingly, I allowed the left to become my new religion.

I became an angry militant. It was easy. I'd been angry for years. In the sixties, anger was a virtue. And I had so much stored up virtue, I was a veritable arsenal of rage. I yelled at my parents, the government, the Church. I baited cops and ran from tear gas and clubs. I threw rocks at windows, rolled flaming trash cans into the street, learned to shout, "Fuck you!" For a year I majored in the politics of rebellion and clung to the only love that meant anything to me. Just when I began to feel strong enough to let go a little, Eva turned on me in anger and walked out of my life.

In spring 1970, I flew to New York with a little money and a suitcase full of second-hand clothes. A psychic there saw my life as a spinning ball of light, pulsing with color, growing bright and then fading, but always spinning. That's how New York was for me. I studied bellydancing, ate pizza, braved the subway system, and watched a solar eclipse in Central Park. I became lovers with a guy named Larry who sucked his thumb in his sleep, and I walked out of a bookstore one day with seven paperbacks on sex. I picked up crabs and trichomonas and read my first book on health foods. I was fired from my job at a publishing house when I took time off to go to an anti-war march.

From New York I traveled to Wisconsin with a busload of hippies and a store of brown rice and granola. I lived as a squatter on Mifflin Street, the hippie village of Madison. I made friends with women at the University and learned about the women's movement. The high point of my year was playing a lead role in a feminist play. I loved performing. When I returned to L.A. that summer, I acted in guerilla

theater on women's issues and the Vietnam War. Hovering
on the fringes of the Lesbian community, I still thought I
needed a man.

When Will came along, I was attracted to his kind, gentle
ways. He was a bear of a man, six foot four and hairy, but
oh, so vulnerable. Our love was born of a mutual need for
healing deep wounds of the past. Our intimacy was sweet,
and life began to feel different. After years of soaring on
the clouds of mysticism, consumed with intense love or
outraged by injustice, I was learning, with Will, to enjoy
the ordinary.

Will was opinionated about everything, from the chair
he sat in to the handle of his coffee cup. He surrounded
himself with colors and shapes that pleased him. He was
an expert at puttering; life was too precious to spend it
working. Money, when he had it, slipped through his fingers
like spaghetti. But he enjoyed it. When Will worked we had
steak and wine for dinner. When I worked, we paid the
bills. We fought over money as we tried to come to a balance
between work and play. When we weren't fighting, we made
a good team. We developed a style as a couple, expressive
of our love for play and disdain for the status quo. Always
we were teaching each other. Will taught me about herbs
and architecture and French toast. I taught him to crochet
and juggle, and together we studied gardening and health
foods. He learned to dance. I learned photography. I quit
driving a school bus and began to make a living at woodworking, a skill that had lived in my hands from the beginning.

After three years it was becoming clear to me that we
were best friends and soul buddies, but not lovers. Will had
given me a sense of belonging, a safe place in which to
explore my creativity and skills. Despite the growing sexual
tension and money problems, I knew I had a special place
in his heart. Because I wanted the best for both of us, I

urged Will to find a lover and began to separate myself from the image of "couple" we had developed. I felt a great restlessness. I longed for the country places I had dreamed of, and I wanted to settle once and for all the question of my sexual identity. There were tears in Will's eyes as I climbed into my VW bus bound for Colorado. It was 1978: ten years since I had left the convent. This time I knew what I wanted: to live in the country, to seek my spirituality, and to love a woman. Changes have never been easy for me. But they're easier in a new place. Like a chameleon, I can change colors, and no one's the wiser.

It took me over a month to find the Lesbian community in Boulder. When I did, I let them assume I'd been out for years. I was readily accepted and trusted. The little bit of doubt I kept to myself was dispelled when I fell in love with a woman from Oregon who called herself Gnome. The night we first kissed was a full moon in September. There was no holding back the night we made love. My body responded with natural ease, and in my heart I knew I had finally come home to myself. Women's music was never the same after that. All of a sudden the words were really about me. I had joined the club, declared myself a dyke. Gnome had to restrain me in public. I was sixteen again and in love.

Gnome and I moved east to New England. We spent several months in Maine, struggling through the cold and isolation of winter, and then moved to Vermont where we rented a farmhouse and bought a couple of milk goats. In one year I had realized two of my three goals. My search for spirituality was a more difficult and mysterious quest. The first year I spent with Gnome was not conducive to peace or solitude. We were plunged into one crisis after another over money, jobs, illness, and the extreme cold of the northeastern climate.

By the end of two winters, our initiation was over.

We had passed the test, survived the changes. I began to anticipate the seasons, to prepare for them, to celebrate them. I became aware of their effect upon my whole being. Here was a new holiness, a conscious union with the elements, and rituals that grew up out of a natural harmony with the earth.

Two years after I met Gnome, we decided to move apart. It was a sensible decision, but painful. I was alone again. Since it was summertime, I decided to buy a tent and live in a small wooded pasture. With nothing solid to keep out the night, I snuggled deep into my sleeping bag and tried to ignore the unfamiliar sounds of the woods. That first night, I was visited in my dreams by a little elfin creature who assured me I would be safe. After that I began to relax and feel the peacefulness there. The woods and meadows became a healing place, sometimes the only place where I felt whole. I met a woman named Tree who introduced me to Native American ritual and goddess worship. She introduced me to the healing power of the sweat lodge. We worked together on ritual celebrations attended by local woman.

I left Vermont in the fall of 1981, grateful for the gifts I had received: an understanding of the land and its gifts, skills of self-reliance, and a deeper sense of self. I loved the land and knew I would return, but it didn't feel like a permanent home. I needed to explore, to experience other places and to find more of the scattered members of the family of women I belong to.

The day I left Vermont, I got as far as Pennsylvania where I headed for a campground to spend the night. As I drove down a dirt road, a large doe leaped across the road in front of me. For an instant, she was fully illuminated by my headlights. Then she was gone. In that split second, we almost touched. I remembered my own leaps out of darkness, and I know I carry her spirit with me.

When people ask me what I do or who I am, I think how all my life I have been a clown wearing my various costumes and philosophies — nun, militant, hippie, goatherd, gypsy. I see all my identities as play — and as real. I want to play all the parts I can. And I can do it more freely now because I don't have to become any one role — (as I did the nun). I have myself behind my masks, and my self comes out into the masks, and my playing is real. As long as I can go on playing, I have courage to go on living.

My wanderings have brought me to Austin, Texas, where I work as a vocational trainer for mentally retarded adults. Here I hope to earn the funds needed to realize my dream of a house and woodworking shop in the country.

Section VI

CLOISTERED SENSUALITY

Sometimes it started with a sisterly backrub between novices, a charitable visit to a bed-ridden sister, or a theology discussion late into the night. Decades after leaving our religious communities, we remember our clandestine rendezvous, our confusion and excitement, our terror and avoidance, our frequent return to the arms of particular friends who became lovers. Yes, Sisters, some of us "did it" even in the convent.

FINDING MY WAY

Mary Brady
(1956–1970)

It was a moment of blinding revelation, like the ones the saints claimed on their conversion to the love of God; but for me the message was different. It happened in a convent in South America in 1969. I was in my young superior's room, on her bed, lying full-length atop her warm and sensuous body. At that moment I knew what it was I had been missing, needing, wanting, through thirteen painful years of religious life. I knew I needed love, sex, a woman — and I knew, without any doubt, in spite of thirty-one years of Catholic training, that, for me, it was good.

I graduated from high school in 1956: a basketball player, honor student, class officer. I had been taught that the best thing I could do with my life was to be a nun, so that fall I entered the novitiate of the Grey Nuns of the Sacred Heart. I really intended to be perfect, which was what all nuns were striving for in those days. (Nowadays I think their ambitions are less elitist.) But on entrance day I fell desperately in love with a senior novice who was kind to me. She obsessed my thoughts and energies, in spite of my best efforts, for the next three years.

After the novitiate, I fell for the nun who helped me with my first teaching assignment. We were inseparable. Once she told me she had heard that sex is the most intense pleasure a human being can experience. That aroused my curiosity, and I wondered what it could be like. When the superior eventually told her to stay away from me since people were beginning to talk, I felt embarrassed and guilty, even though I didn't know what I had done wrong.

Transferred to another convent the next year, I did it again. This time I got involved with an older nun who persuaded me to spend the night in her room, not once, but many times. (Yes, in her bed, though nothing ever happened beyond a few kisses and lots of delicious body contact.)

Those were the days of waiting for everyone to retire, and then creeping up the stairs and down the hall to her room. Even worse was trying to wake up hours before dawn to get back to my room before anyone was up. Always there was the terror that someone would go out to the bathroom and wonder what I was doing on the wrong floor in the middle of the night.

One morning the crude-mannered superior accosted me in the kitchen before morning prayer just as I finished putting the milk in the refrigerator.

"Did you spend the night in Sister Martin's room last night?" she blustered, shaking a finger at me.

My heart stopped. What could I say? I knew that visiting another sister's room was forbidden.

"Yes, Sister Superior," I answered, looking her in the eye

and feigning a calmness I did not feel. Again I felt embarrassed and dirty without understanding why. I waited for
the anger and punishment I knew would come, but the
superior turned on her heel and left. She never mentioned
it again. Perhaps she was more embarrassed than I.

I discovered how to scratch my genital itch, literally,
as I lay in bed one night after about ten years in the convent. Late in life to discover one has a clitoris; but the
attitude in Catholic schools and homes in the forties and
fifties kept little girls ignorant of our bodies. The taboo
was so strong that I never looked, or touched, for almost
thirty years.

Then, the combination of continual sexual frustration,
an irritating menstrual pad, and a maddening itch made
it impossible to ignore those forbidden parts. They were
keeping me awake. I rubbed, and the itch turned into
pleasure. I remembered that tantalizing statement about
sex I had heard years before. My mind kept telling me I
should stop — it was a mortal sin to enjoy a sexual feeling
for even a second. I tried to maintain an attitude of un-
willingness while my fingers went about their delicious
business on their own. The feeling got better and better
until I forgot about my soul and went on to have my first
orgasm. So this was what my friend had meant!

Not surprisingly, once was not enough. There was no
way I could not continue to masturbate once I had discovered how; and I, who had never done anything more
serious than whisper during Sacred Silence, engaged in a
constant struggle with the specter of mortal sin.

Oh, the humiliation of going to the sacristy before
Mass and confessing that I had "willingly touched myself
and took pleasure in it." Some mornings I couldn't face
it and just skipped communion with the sisters, leaving
them all to wonder what terrible thing I had done. That way
I could get several nights' mortal sins into one confession.

In the mid-sixties, homosexuality began to be mentioned in magazines and news reports. I devoured *Newsweek,* ostensibly to keep in touch with world affairs for my teaching, but in reality to maintain contact with what seemed like a saner world than the one I found myself in. (Now, I'm not sure.) The word "homosexual" began to appear in the book and theatre reviews. Every time I saw it, a thrill of recognition went through me. I started skimming for the word, and read every reference, no matter how obscure. I remember telling myself I shouldn't be reading such things, and resolving to read only the news articles in the front. But still I would skip right to the back and look for that fascinating word.

Then I was asked to go to South America. I accepted eagerly, hoping the challenge of the missions would end this unhealthy preoccupation. But it was there I met Beth. It was Christmas morning 1968, after Midnight Mass, when she first came to my room. Beth was my superior but only two years older than my thirty years, and we knew each other from the novitiate.

"I wanted to see if you were all right," she said, looking a little flustered. She sat beside me on the bed and put her arm around my shoulder. I can still see the dimly lit room, the tan bedspread, the Sacred Heart Statue on the nightstand. She began stroking my back, then held me against her breast for what seemed like a long time. I was afraid to breathe. She was warm and soft, and before I went off to sleep I was in love again.

A week later she retired early, not feeling well, and I took a tray to her for supper. We talked, and when she finished eating, she asked me to lie beside her on the bed. Ignorant and shy, I never initiated such moves, but was only too glad to accept an invitation. I lay down and she held me, stroking my back, her hand running thrillingly under my pajama tops and eventually even under the bottoms. I grew excited and confused, but it felt so good I didn't want to ruin it by asking questions.

After that I contrived to visit her room almost every night. The caresses grew more intimate, and she taught me to touch her in ways she liked. At last I had found what I'd been needing all those years. I was bursting to talk about how she felt about our loving, how she thought it fit into a life of vowed chastity. I wanted to explore the powerful emotions I was feeling, and ask her why she never touched me as she wanted me to touch her. But whenever I approached her during the day, she acted as though nothing had happened. At night, she wouldn't talk about it. It was unreal. I did the only sensible thing to do in such a situation. I went crazy.

I returned to the States and slowly put myself together with the help of a few good friends. Yet I could never be the same. My vow of chastity haunted me. I searched the theological literature, both current and traditional, for some justification of a celibate lifestyle that made sense to me. I didn't find one. What I found was disturbing evidence that the Christian faith was not the One True Revealed Religion, but just one among many religious myths invented in the long history of the human race. For both of these reasons, I asked for a dispensation from my vows in 1970 and, painfully abandoning my entire adult life and my only adult identity, left religious life.

I moved into an apartment with a friend who had left the community at the same time. We grew very close and soon became lovers. I found that loving a woman could be an ecstatic experience without the guilt and restrictions of convent life.

I still didn't consider myself a Lesbian, just a woman who happened to love another woman. It wasn't until I met another Lesbian in a NOW consciousness-raising group that I began to think I might really be one. I resisted the idea since I still had hopes of fitting into the mainstream. But finally I looked myself in the eye and said, "Yes, you are a Lesbian."

That was the hard part. From there it was easy. I began going to ALFA (the Atlanta Lesbian Feminist Alliance), and coming out to my friends and co-workers. I developed real pride in loving women.

My spirituality was in limbo, however. I went to Church intermittently when I first left the convent. In spite of my doubts, I was unable to let go of another shred of my identity right then. The rising feminist tide came to my rescue and, in the course of my reading and thinking about the oppression of women, I saw the Church for the oppressive institution it is and rejected it altogether. This left me in a vacuum. The Eastern religions helped for a while, but I finally had to admit that no one had any more clues to the meaning of life than I did. The emptiness of living without a faith was scary, but it was the only honest position for me at the time.

Then one afternoon in late 1975 as I was working on the newsletter at the ALFA house, the phone rang. A few minutes later a woman rushed into the room and exclaimed, "The witch is here!"

Witch? I thought, seeing visions of broomsticks and Halloween masks. This must be a joke. But no, the woman said that a witch from California had come to talk to Lesbians about her religion. Intrigued, I came back that evening to hear what the witch (ha ha) had to say. She changed my life.

Z. Budapest's talk was the first I had ever heard of women's religion, the thousands of years when the Goddess was worshipped, the overthrow of the ancient matriarchies. It was a revelation almost as great as that first contact with a woman's body. Here was a sensible spirituality of harmony with ourselves and our universe. There was no dogma, no guilt, no avoidance of pleasure, no judgment, heaven or hell. The universe as Female was suddenly more friendly, and I, a more integral part of Her eternal cycling.

And so I have managed to find a life that is right and good for me. I live joyfully with my lover of seven years; working, writing, gardening, loving the Earth and Her creatures. I try to live a healthy life and quietly honor the cycling of the moon and the seasons. All the while I am grateful that, after so many false starts, I have finally found my way.

Born in Buffalo in 1938, I finally moved south to get warm. The world amuses and horrifies me, and I write science fiction to explore the implications of what I see. The girl who entered the convent so long ago seems like a stranger. I give credit to my lover, Diana, for the present richness of my life, and look forward to being a truly eccentric old crone, if the boys will permit the earth to live that long.

Susan Weaver, 1983

RECOGNIZING MYSELF AS LESBIAN

Susan Weaver
(1948-1954)

I grew up in a white, middle-class family in the suburbs of New York City and went to Barnard College. My three sisters and I were brought up Catholics. Because both my parents had strong, liberal attitudes, we did not have a narrow, rigid education. But even in this unconfined household, it was not until my sister and I were adults that we realized our uncle, who was a professor at Columbia University, was gay. Complete silence surrounded the subject of homosexuality.

I entered the cloistered Carmelites two years after finishing college. This was the first of three endeavors to find a contemplative religious vocation. I was briefly in the Carmelites, then the Trappistines, and later with a French community, The Little Sisters of Jesus, who had just arrived

in the United States. My attempts at contemplative community life were sincere, and I left each of these communities
with good feelings and friendship toward my superiors and
sisters.

At the time, I did not recognize that one reason for my
feeling comfortable in the religious life was the strong attraction to be with women — a Lesbian sentiment. Although
I was attracted to others in the community in Carmel and in
the Trappistines, I did absolutely nothing to answer these
attractions. In my twenties, I could not call myself Lesbian.
I hardly knew the word!

My initiation to sexual experience occurred in the Little
Sisters of Jesus. The community was located in a Montreal
ghetto. I had tripped and fallen down a flight of old wooden
stairs. That night one of the Little Sisters, Sister Huguette,
came to my bed and gave me a kiss on the forehead. This
simple act was so moving and caused my first recognition
of sexual love for another woman.

Sister Huguette and I walked to work together, and I
waited for her after work. Huguette had a job in a candy
factory, and I did housework. At the time, Huguette and
I only held hands and rarely kissed, but I felt a deep sexual
love for her.

That same year Huguette and I were sent to Vancouver,
to a new community of the Little Sisters. We traveled three
nights in the railroad coach. We were together all the time
and kissed during the night. When we arrived, I sensed
that the Vancouver community had been told to watch us.
I had known all the members of this community; but now
Huguette and I were treated with suspect caution. Although
no one spoke directly of it to us, we knew we must change
our relationship.

Huguette and I voluntarily left the Little Sisters. As I

look back, I do not know to what exent the love between us was responsible for our departure from the community. As a fact in itself, I knew I would be happier outside of religious community life. And, amazingly, at the time, I was still not aware enough to call myself Lesbian.

Huguette returned to France, and I soon joined her in a funny, tiny attic apartment in Nice. Neither of us felt altogether at ease about our sexual love. I would go to confession, and then, with a sense of confusion and guilt, return to our emotional, sensual love. Within a year, we decided to have no more love-making or sexual intimacy. Guilt made this so.

We returned to the United States and began working at a secular institute in Mississippi, where we caused suspicion simply because we were together. I remember one afternoon, vividly, when we were in my bedroom laughing about some everyday event. Suddenly, the head of the institute pushed open the door to check on our laughter. I realized that, all along, we were being watched. After about a year at the secular institute, Huguette returned to France because her father was sick. I returned home. Although I saw Huguette again, our love was never revived.

Years ago I could not believe it possible that I would feel a sense of freedom and peace away from the institution of the Church. I do owe much to my friends and religious sisters and to my religious reading. My favorite author continues to be Mother Janet E. Stuart, who, I would guess, unrecognized to herself, was Lesbian.

Recently I have had some marvelous religious experiences with two psychics. The fact that these women know I am Lesbian has in no way hampered our friendship. Clear and sure psychic communication with people in the spirit state has given me a new approach to prayer.

I am alone now; but I hope this will not always be the case. If anyone would like to write to me about her own religious thoughts, I would be glad to correspond.

Peace, Joy, and Thanks.

I am fifty-nine. I live in northern rural Vermont, where I write and illustrate children's books.

SOUTH AMERICAN LAWYER IN A CLOISTER

Maria Cristina
(1963-1975)

When I entered the convent I had already had one relationship with another woman. Ena was a teacher at my law school. Although we were intimate only three months, our year-long lover relationship was very fulfilling physically. During the rest of the time there was an equally intense emotional attachment.

Ena was killed in an airplane crash, and one reason I entered the convent was that I did not see any other future in my life. I knew I was a Lesbian; I had never had any attraction to a man. To get married just because I was supposed to would be tragic, not only for myself but for the man. I had wanted to be a nun before I met Ena; when she died I felt guilty, as if I was being punished for something that was not proper.

The only way I could forget what happened was to dedicate myself totally to study. In South America a law degree takes five years in my specialty. I did it in four. Those years did not help me to forget her, but they did help me to realize I could find the answer in the convent.

When my family moved to the United States, I visited a Benedictine cloister in Connecticut. I liked the nuns, I liked the place, and I was accepted. I knew I was going to live very close to women, but I never thought I would want to have a relationship with one of them. Perhaps in my fantasies I thought I could have friendship and closeness with a woman without touching her, but later on I wanted something else.

The convent community was small. There were thirty-three enclosed nuns and six external nuns. I was enclosed. We dedicated ourselves to contemplation, to recitation of the Divine Office in Latin, and to performing manual work to help the convent's economy. I worked mostly in the office typing correspondence dictated by the Mother Superior. I also did the convent's bookkeeping. My specific task was dealing with the revision of the Canon Law sent to us from dioceses in different areas of the country. It was meticulous work, but it was easy for me because I had a background in law.

It was very hard to become accustomed to waking at 2 a.m. for Matins. The habit was heavy and black and sometimes uncomfortable. On hot days we roasted. Part of the veil was long enough to cover our faces entirely; we could see, but not in detail. When we received visitors we were separated from them by a grille and a heavy curtain as well as by the veil.

Each afternoon we had one hour of conversation, but always within the limits of the Rule. Never was it possible to talk about some problem you had outside, even if you had recently arrived. We were supposed to deal only with matters prescribed by the Rule and dedicated to the thought of God and of cloistered Benedictine work. The recreation hour was the hardest time of day for me, especially during the first year. I could not exchange ideas openly and say, "This was my experience," like I used to do outside the convent. And close relationships were not permitted. We were supposed to confess whenever we got attached to someone.

When I was a novice, I was attracted to a woman very much, and I believed she was attracted to me. Her name was Sister Dolores, and she was beautiful. We sat close to each other at table. Then we had to confess this feeling. We were separated and forbidden to talk to each other during recreation.

I knew what was happening because I knew I was a Lesbian. But since I was a nun who had freely taken the vow of chastity, I could not consider breaking that vow. It was a very serious, deep commitment. It was painful to be attracted to her, and it was painful to break that relationship.

I could never tell if Sister Dolores knew what was happening because we never had open communication about it. Since we were supposed to be physically detached from everything and everybody, there was never a close touch. The only time we could touch was during recreation when we had a chance to talk and touch hands. According to the Rule the sisters were supposed to touch both palms to the other nun's open palms. But it was a very neat, short, physical contact. There was no possibility to say, "I have this feeling for you."

The kiss we received on some occasions — when we took the veil, when we did our final vows — was from the whole community. But again, it was a very short, very special embrace which conveyed the feeling of community but nothing else. In an enclosed community, we sisters had the feeling that we were protected and belonged there, but it was hard to say, "I have a closeness to one of the nuns." It's a life against nature, and I just accepted that I couldn't be close to another woman.

The best part of the day was the two hours in the afternoon when we were supposed to kneel in the front of the chapel with the sacrament exposed. That was the time when I was most in contact with God. I was dedicating my life to Him in a lovely, enclosed place. When I was with Him in that intimate contact, it was very beautiful, close, and rewarding.

We had to kneel in a very special way: erect with no help from the furniture, and without even the skirts to protect our knees, with our arms extended forming a cross. Pain helped us to be in the Presence of God and to attend to the communication we were supposed to have when we were praying. Some days praying was very easy, and I had a rewarding experience. Sometimes I just could not reach any sort of communication, and my mind wandered. I would remember things that happened during the day, or years ago, or sometimes even when I was outside the convent.

The Rule did not permit those thoughts. In the Chapter of Faults, we had to admit that in prayer we thought about this and that. We had to explain those thoughts in detail to the whole community. We had to confess our peccadillos against the Rule, the things we were guilty of during the day, like breaking silence or swinging our arms when walking. We were also supposed to accuse the other sisters of any of these things we had seen them do. In the beginning, this rule was frightening and difficult for me to understand. The first time somebody accused me of doing something wrong I was hurt and furious that my fellow novice would spy on me! I learned to believe this detail of the Rule was good. To do my very best to communicate with God, I had to disrobe everything that was external and communicate only with my spirit.

Another difficult practice was flagellating ourselves alone in our cells every Monday, Wednesday, and Friday. The two flagellation devices were called the minor and major disciplines. The small one was supposed to hurt but not show anything on the skin. The other one was heavier and sometimes drew blood. The disciplines were to be used on the buttocks and legs.

When I was a postulant I heard about the discipline. When I was a novice I actually had to use it. The first time was a bit frightening; I did not understand any purpose but to have pain. Later I learned it was a very good way to try to achieve perfection.

The purpose of flagellation was to dominate our sexuality. But sometimes when I hit myself I awakened my carnal desires. When our carnal or sensuous side was aroused we had to explain what had occurred to the Mother Superior. It was difficult for me to share with her because I felt guilty and ashamed. I knew that as a woman there were moments when my sexuality was there. This flagellant device did arouse my feelings, and it was hard for me to control them. By obedience to the Rule, I had to use that device on myself every Monday, Wednesday, and Friday. There was no escape.

Many times masturbation, which was forbidden by the Rule, happened. I had to confess, in front of the community, "Last night I had impure thoughts and impure manipulations." I felt guilty and remorseful, and I requested heavy penance, which was granted. Heavy penance was self-inflicted flagellation, which sometimes aroused me again. It was a cycle, especially right before or during or after my period. We also had belts with small crosses to wear around the arms, thighs and waist. Those small crosses caused a lot of hurt. Some days, doing this penance was quite helpful and rewarding for me in trying to achieve perfection.

Our beds were very hard. We had a white flannel nightgown to sleep in and since we didn't have hair we used a bed cap to cover our heads. The Rule prescribed the shaving of heads. There was a coarse mattress. We didn't have pillows or sheets, and the blankets were changed only once a year. We were supposed to change our nightgowns every six months.

According to the Rule, we were supposed to lie flat on our backs and sleep without moving. Our arms were supposed to be crossed in front of our breasts, our legs were to be straight, and we had to cover ourselves to the chin. It was hard to learn to sleep the whole night without moving. In the beginning I did move, and I had to confess this to the community the next day. I felt very guilty being unable to sleep without moving.

There were not any physical Lesbian relationships in my convent because we had complete separation of bodies. Each one of us had a cell, and each cell was locked from the outside before retirement by the Mother Superior. Not locked exactly, but latched outside the door.

I decided to leave the cloister because of the radical changes made by the ecumenical movement and Pope John XXIII. The rules, the habit, everything I had known and grown to love through all those years was changing. These changes were not made at our request or with our knowledge. My vow of obedience said I had to accept without question everything that happened, but I could not accept all those changes. And once there was conflict, everything became heavy and impossible to accept.

My Lesbianism was coming to an uncontrollable point. I wanted to have a physical relationship with a woman, and I could not do it because of my respect for my vows.

I confessed my conflicts, and the Mother Superior begged me to reconsider, to pray, to analyze my thoughts, and to do penance. For a year I did pray and do heavy penance, but these conflicts became too difficult for me to deal with. I told the Mother Superior I wanted to leave. It took a year to process the papers.

My last remembrance is of the night before I left. I was excluded from the community already. That day I remained in my cell and walked in the garden. The Rule forbade saying goodbye to anyone. Only the Mother Superior came to talk to me, and it was very painful for both of us.

I was unable to cry when I left. And my ring . . . my ring . . . the most painful thing I had to do was return my ring to the Mother Superior. (I still have my crucifix. The ring I wear now is similar to the one I had then.)

The first two months it was terrible for me to deal with the world: noise, money, confusion. I was in limbo; I did not belong to anything. I was frightened; I did not know if I could cope.

I remembered how to drive when I left the convent but I could not do it. The first time my sister took me from New York to Washington, D.C., was a nightmare. The noise of the traffic, the speed at which she drove — I was frantic. I had not been in a car for thirteen years. I also had not seen T.V. or read a newspaper or magazine in all that time.

I had forgotten how to use money. I had used United States currency only a short time before I entered the convent. I could not tell the difference between the ten and one dollar bills. When I received change, I could not count it; I did not know if they gave me the right change or not.

When I first left, not having a veil on my head felt strange and naked. I started using a scarf, and I said, "Well it becomes me, it is nice. It is a little bit of a gypsy touch."

Sometimes, I remember little things. I can see my cell

right now. I can see the chapel. Somehow I cannot see the garden; it is lost. I walked there many times but I cannot see it now. Some faces I remember: some faces and names are gone.

After I left, my spirituality was blank, empty. At first I did not go to Mass. Then I went, but it felt empty, like going to a theater. I even tried going to some other Churches, not Catholic, but they did not have any meaning for me. Then I heard about Dignity. The first two or three times I went to these meetings I also felt nothing. But then I met two beautiful women there, and slowly gained the feeling that I belonged. Now, the services hold a very deep feeling for me. I really feel God in the community.

I have friends in Dignity, and though it's nice to meet people outside, the feeling in Church is very special. If something happened to me, they would be concerned. Many times I go from work to that Church, and I am able to talk with God; I always come out fulfilled. I call God "My Beloved," in Spanish, "Mi Amor." I have this renewal every Sunday which gives me the energy to go on the next week.

Right now I feel I am able to cope with the world. I have been out of the convent for nine years. I have a relationship with a woman which is beautiful and rewarding. I am not promiscuous. We share an apartment and we hope to have a house in the future.

I am active in Lesbian and feminist organizations. I have memberships in Dignity and Catholics for Human Dignity, an organization derived from Dignity. It is political and uses democratic processes to demand change. I am also a member of Women Over Forty, which is composed largely of Lesbians.

I work as a legal secretary; I cannot say where nor can I use my last name in this book. I hoped I could come out totally and say, "I am a Lesbian," but I already lost one job this way. So, I know the risks. In San Francisco, even though we have acceptance in many ways, we still have problems of losing almost everything just because we are Lesbians.

I grew up and went to college in South America. After getting a law degree, I moved to the United States and entered a Benedictine Monastery in Connecticut. Thirteen years later, I left religious life. Now I work as a legal secretary, since my South American law degree is not recognized here. I am active in Dignity and live with my lover in San Francisco.

This story is based on an interview with Nancy Manahan in January 1982.

Sr. Mary Gregory, S.M., 1949

H. M. Fairfield-Hickey, 1982

CONVENT REMINISCENCES

H. M. Fairfield-Hickey
(1947-1953)

In my thirty years since I last wore the habit of a nun, I have subjected myself to some pretty hefty self-analysis about my motives for entering the convent. Besides wanting to live a life as religiously fulfilling as possible, I wanted to escape a home life dominated by a mother who was suffocating me. I wanted to do it in such a way that she would approve and not begin yet another domestic war which would sadden my dear father. My mother, through no fault of hers, was born into the Baptist religion. Therefore, she was scandalized by my decision, fearing I would be ravished by priests and have my babies murdered. But she came around when she saw the favorable reaction from friends, relatives, and neighbors.

Most importantly, I desired to be with women, even

though at my sexually undeveloped eighteen years I did not know that I was a Lesbian. Wrapped in my ignorance, I wanted to live in a female-dominated environment because I was more comfortable there.

I remember my first morning in the convent. The mother superior called me into her office for her standard pep-talk to new postulants who had lain sleepless and crying, wracked with homesickness and timidity the night before. I suprised her by bouncing in, smiling all over myself, well-rested and full of energy. My mistress of novices encouraged my natural ebullience and nurtured my artistic talent. She was exceptionally perceptive about how to help the blithe spirit she had in her charge along the road to moral and spiritual maturity. We remained friends to the day of her death in 1980. I pray we are still friends.

It was not until I was a white-veiled novice that I had my first romantic attachment. We had a torrid affair that never got beyond the grope and fumble stage. The relationship was terminated rather abruptly when, in order to make points with the new mistress of novices (my mentor had been elected mother superior), my friend told all and did not hesitate to name names. Since I was a senior sister, I bore the brunt of the blame.

After I exchanged the white veil for a black veil and took my temporary three year vows, I awakened sexually. Along came Sister Claire. Grope and fumble just would not do. We both knew how and what to do and definitely needed to. Our affair was moderate but certainly helped the days to pass in an interesting fashion until, after a few months, her sensitive conscience called a halt. She was my first genuine lover.

A few months before I was to ask permission to take my final vows, I admitted to myself that I was being a hypocrite. My feelings about women were so strong that I felt I could not do justice to the vow of chastity, so I departed. I still did not think of myself as homosexual. I dated men a great deal, but could never bring myself to let these encounters become intimate.

Six years after leaving the convent, I looked myself in the eye and said the word "homosexual" out loud. I was not involved with anyone at the time, nor did I have any prospects. I just had a sudden explosion of insight. From that point on, I felt an enormous sense of relief. I have been comfortable with my Lesbian self ever since.

Shortly after that, I met the woman I lived happily with for sixteen years. She is the first mature love I had. But as so often happens, she met someone else, and my life took another turn. During those sixteen years, I came to realize that organized religion had inhibited my spiritual growth. Once I gave it up and became what I call a pietist, I felt closer to and more comfortable with God. I have been able to home in on the essentials of spirituality without the clutter of minutiae that organized religion must insist on to retain its structure.

During these last thirty years out of the convent I have lived a full Lesbian life with all that implies. Not all love and prayers, many years have been hell with a little insanity thrown into the brew. If it had not been for the training of those convent years, I could never have survived to the present with my sanity and my life intact. It is as absolute as that to me.

Convent experience provided guides for my personal standards. Without them I most likely would have changed direction with every opinion breeze that came my way. I have a tendency to see reason in everything everyone says or does. Since the convent, I can see why people act the way they do, but I am not moved from my own purposes by them. With my artistic temperament, I do not need chaos, too! The time I spent in the convent was essential to my development as a person and as a Christian. This was the most enriching experience of my life. I have never escaped the influences and hope I never will. My vocation is for all my life.

I have lived in Massachusetts since my birth in 1928. I have been a nun, bookseller, tutor, day nursery operator, retail salesperson, artist, craftsperson, teacher, portraitist, designer of stuffed toys and soft sculpture, consultant for an avian medicine clinic, and director of a wild bird hospital. I am bright, talented, dogmatic, reclusive, inclined toward mysticism, non-social, and happiest in the woods listening to opera. I am still trying to decide what to do when I grow up.

CLOISTERED SENSUALITY

Monique DuBois
(1964-1976)

(Monique DuBois grew up on an island in the West Indies in her black, middle-class Catholic family. Presently she lives quietly with her lover of several years in south Florida. Rosemary Curb interviewed her in December 1982.)

Rosemary: When did you decide to become a nun?

Monique: When I was three years old, I saw a nun for the first time. Right then I decided I wanted to be like that when I grew up. As I grew older, my attraction developed more toward wanting a life of prayer and solitude, not the life of the active sisters I knew.

Rosemary: You mean teachers and nursing sisters?

Monique: Yes, but since I didn't know that cloistered nuns existed, I thought what I wanted was unique. So, naturally I thought that God wanted me to start such an order. Then I found out from my sister that such orders already existed. I was relieved that I didn't have to go through the whole process of starting one myself.

Rosemary: What attracted you to that life?

Monique: Two things, I think. First, a desire to be alone with God. Now I can see that my desire came from my disillusionment with the relationships I saw around me and the lack of love I saw in them. I was very shy and withdrawn then, and I didn't want to relate to people. I didn't want to be hurt. I felt secure in a life with God alone. My other motivating desire was to serve the world in as large a way as possible. I felt that as an active sister I would be limited to just the specific people I would be dealing with, whereas a life of prayer was more universal because I could touch the entire world.

Rosemary: Do you think that your attraction to monastic life was in part a desire to live in a community of women only?

Monique: Not at all. I didn't think in terms of sexuality. I always knew I was attracted to women, but I didn't choose sexuality to be a part of my life at all. When I was twelve, I got permission from the bishop to take a vow of virginity. I was in love with God. That was enough for me. I knew I would be with women in the monastery, but I didn't conceive that I would have any kind of personal relationship with them. I thought we would pass each other in the night or in the day in total silence.

Rosemary: Did the Poor Clares fulfill your expectations?

Monique: Ironically, during my time with the Poor Clares, I developed a real positive people feeling of being loved and being affirmed as a person. I was feeling close to people for the first time. But spirituality, no! They put me down for being too "holy" and made me feel it was just a first fervor phase I was going through. I wanted prayer, solitude, and fasting. But they said I was too young to fast.

I felt patronized! I entered in the sixties when all the Vatican II changes were going on. Old rules were being dispensed with.

Rosemary: You thought it was lax?

Monique: Yes! I wanted some kind of support for real spirituality, not the kind that's found in mere observance of the Holy Rule.

Rosemary: Did you think of spirituality as communal, or was your goal to become a solitary mystic?

Monique: When I entered the cloister, my goal was to become a saint by twenty-one and then die and go to heaven! But as I was nearing twenty-one and saw that it wasn't all going to happen as I planned, then I started becoming more realistic.

Rosemary: What did becoming a saint mean to you?

Monique: Being perfect. Never getting angry or having any negative feelings, always being accepting and totally forgiving. I would have a perpetual smile on my face. I'd be filled with love, have elevations and be able to pray with my arms raised for hours at night like St. Francis of Assisi. I'd live solely on the love of God.

Rosemary: Living outside your body?

Monique: Oh, no, I didn't go that far. I just wanted to be a saint — perfect.

Rosemary: I wanted to be a saint too, but I thought of it in terms of mysticism, of being transported out of my body like St. Teresa of Avila. I wanted to be raised up beyond physical needs. I liked the idea of penetential practices, such as fasting or kneeling motionless for hours; but I wanted some visible sign of my growth in aesceticism, such as the stigmata.

Monique: I had my first mystical experience about two and a half years after I entered. I was walking out in the courtyard, and all of a sudden I just knew that everything was One, and that God is the unity that binds us all together.

Everything was transformed. A leaf wasn't just a leaf anymore. It was a living part of an infinite One. For about six
months I was out of the world. I was up here. I transcended
everything. I didn't need to eat.

Rosemary: Up here in your mind or in your spirit?

Monique: In my spirit. I saw everything differently.
Everything that happened, the rain or the sun shining, was
God. Then I lost it. I succumbed to the pressure to be like
the others: "What do you think — you're holy?" I spent
the next god knows how long trying to recover that feeling.
I was depressed for years, and I was angry at them.

Rosemary: Angry at your community of sisters?

Monique: Yes. I hated the pressure to give up that side
of me to become more acceptable to them and not to stand
out anymore.

Rosemary: Weren't you worried about spiritual pride?

Monique: No, why?

Rosemary: If you were lifted above the community . . . ?

Monique: I wasn't lifted up above them. I was lifted in my
spirit. In that space you don't look down on anyone, because
everybody is One.

Rosemary: How did your sensuality germinate and develop while you were in the cloister?

Monique: As I felt loved and became more outgoing I
started to express myself in physical affections, which were
returned; and then I began to develop a more conscious
awareness of my sensuality.

Rosemary: Were any of your friendships sexual?

Monique: I had a relationship with one nun that was
more sensual than sexual, and that lasted for about six
months. It provided me with the experiencing of feelings I
had never stopped to consider before. Then I started falling
in love quite easily with other Sisters. Now I was feeling
jealousy, passion, and all other kinds of feelings.

Rosemary: How did your feelings about your body and sensual pleasure change?

Monique: Well, I became more aware of my body and how I looked. The new feelings I was having were quite pleasurable, and I explored them mentally with lots of sexual fantasies and physically by masturbating. But eventually I felt all this was not in accord with my vows, and I remade my choice for celibacy.

Rosemary: Do you think that their racism made your white sisters perceive you as more sensual than they?

Monique: That never occurred to me. It may have, but I was certainly never aware of it. I never experienced racism of any kind.

Rosemary: When did you first become aware of homosexuality and of the gay liberation movement?

Monique: In the monastery through documentary films on TV and articles in magazines like *Time* and *Newsweek*. Then I finally put the name "Lesbian" to my feelings and myself.

Rosemary: How did that affect your life?

Monique: I became increasingly uncomfortable and amused at the disparaging remarks the nuns made about homosexuals. At times like that, I always wanted to "come out" to them and let them know that one could be a Lesbian and a nun as well. I became aware that there were others out there like me and that it was possible to live a life of love with a woman. That really blew my mind, and for a while I didn't know how to deal with it. But again, my primary love for God prevailed and my choice of celibacy was again reaffirmed.

Rosemary: Did awareness of your sexuality lead to your departure from religious life?

Monique: No. Complete disillusionment and rejection of the Catholic Church and a need to preserve my psychological and emotional sanity did!

Rosemary: How long ago did you leave the Poor Clares?

Monique: Seven years ago.

Rosemary: After you left, did you seek relationships with Lesbians?

Monique: Yes. After I left, I felt that loving and being loved was important and that I could only know how real my love for God was in the context of how real my love was for others. So I sought out Lesbians right away through gay centers and the *Wishing Well* magazine. Quite unsuccessfully, though! Eventually I gave up, and then much to my surprise I found I was meeting women in my jobs and at women's groups.

Rosemary: How long have you and your present lover been together?

Monique: Six years now.

Rosemary: Describe your present spirituality.

Monique: The essence of my spirituality now lies in my striving to be constantly aware of God's presence, in knowing that there is that of God in everyone and everything, and sincerely following the consequences of that belief as I see it in every moment. To me this has nothing to do with formal observances, rituals, worshipping on Sundays or saying my morning and evening prayers. But it is something that must dominate my entire life and influence my every action, so I can walk constantly with God, live in his love and know every day and every act to be a sacrament.

Sr. Jean Marie O'Leary, 1968

Jean O'Leary, 1984

Steve Stewart

GOD WAS AN INNOCENT BYSTANDER

Jean O'Leary (with Jan Holden)
(1966–1971)

There was no anti-war movement, no women's movement, no gay movement in Ohio in 1966. I wanted to do something special, to have an impact on my world. I was a senior in high school when I decided to enter the convent. Once I had made up my mind, there was no wavering or looking back.

My parents were good Catholics. We all went to Mass and to confession and recited the rosary together. When I was in second grade, my father promised to send all of us to Catholic school if my mother recovered from a serious illness. I went to Catholic school from third grade through high school. But when I told my family I was going to be a nun, it didn't seem like the Jean they knew. I had always been independent and rebellious. I'd been suspended from

231

high school two or three times for organizing bands marching through the cafeteria or putting goldfish in the holy water font. Everyone liked me, and it was important to me to be popular.

I was a drummer in a teen band. We played school dances and teen canteens. Bobby, the lead singer and sort of my boyfriend, wanted to marry me, but I knew I didn't want to get married, and I didn't want to go on the road with the band. A professional women's band from Chicago asked me to play with them. Even though I loved playing the drums, I didn't want to end up with their booze and drugs.

Nuns particularly influenced me. I had a crush on Sister Mary Thomas, who inspired my interest in religion. I read the philosophy and theology books she gave me in one or two nights and went back for more. I became serious about religion. In my senior assembly speech I announced my decision to become a nun. My friends were shocked. But I really thought it was my vocation to be a nun. Now I realize that I was also running away. I thought that if I dedicated my life to God I could get rid of my feelings for women.

When I was in third grade in an all girls school, I knew I loved women. I had fantasies of living on an island with women. I was a tomboy, and my girlfriends loved my boyishness. In high school I dated boys because everyone did, but my real emotional ties were with my girlfriends. I took a secretarial course just to be near Betty James. I should thank her for my learning to type.

The order I joined had only six or seven hundred nuns, mostly nurses and teachers. A modern, liberal order, with the motherhouse in the United States rather than Europe. When I joined the convent the sisters still wore habits, but uniforms were modernized during my first year. The motherhouse in Pennsylvania was on a huge estate called

the Villa with woods and a lake. It was beautiful and wonderfully serene.

I arrived there in the evening with my drums because I
couldn't bear to leave them at home. Sister Carrie was excited to see them because she played the piano. We set up
my drums in the recreation room. I pulled up my shift,
sat there in my pantaloons, and played for the whole class
of novices. When I started my drum solo, the room went
crazy. Sister Carrie loved it. She played the piano and we
were jamming, having a great time, when the postulant
mistress and the novice mistress walked in. They just looked
at us. The chimes rang nine o'clock, the hour of Grand
Silence. They made the sign of the cross, and we said a
prayer. Nobody even whispered. I was sitting there with
my drumsticks in my hand.

Relationships in the convent were more intense than
almost any I've known on the outside. We were together
constantly: talking endlessly and intensely in sensitivity
and encounter groups about love and hope and philosophy.
We studied great thinkers and modern psychology. Up to
a point it was all intensely emotional: the order emphasized
personal growth. Inevitably natural sexual feelings came out,
but we never said the words *Lesbian, gay,* or *homosexual.*

Sister Jackie and I were postulants together. We took
the same courses, worked together in the Villa, and lived
on the same floor in the dorms. Talking, always talking,
we explored our innermost feelings. The energy between
us was amazing. She was my opposite — quiet and introspective. She was my first love.

After months of building, our affair finally began with
a backrub. We were in a classroom when the convent bells
chimed Vespers. The building around us was silent and
empty. Everyone was in the chapel in prayer. We should
have hurried there ourselves. Jackie and I looked at each
other as we listened to the bells. Neither of us moved. She

spoke softly, answering the question I'd asked before the bells. Her voice seemed to fill the room. The end of her sentence finished our conversation. I watched her face, so strong and intelligent, her eyes mysterious, passionate, their distance muted. She stood finally and touched my shoulder. I looked straight ahead as she massaged my neck. We were drawn so tightly together, invisibly held by the emotion between us. When she paused, I turned and gently pulled her to the seat beside me. I could hear her soft breath and feel her pulse as I touched her neck. Magnified in the silence of Vespers, the tension between us exploded in our first kiss.

We never acknowledged our relationship. Jackie wrote poetry to me. We slept together in the minimal privacy of the sheets hung between our dormitory beds. We made love very quietly while others slept. It was scary and risky and exciting and wonderful. We never said we were lovers. Jackie's poetry was romantic, idealistic, and tragic. We had long conversations about community and love. We never said the word Lesbian.

The environment was closed, isolated. We denied the sexual element. We were warned against Particular Friendships. Jacke felt a great deal of guilt over our relationship. I wanted to redefine celibacy to mean a shared love, an expansive love for people, eliminating possessiveness and jealousy. But there was no support for that. When I decided to leave the convent, I told my juniorate mistress I was a Lesbian. Her response was "Don't you think we all have feelings like that?" She kissed me on the mouth and said, "What you have to do is stay and try to be celibate." It was an inherent conflict — the recognition of sexual desire but the denial of its expression. I refused to deny my feelings even though it was years before I could openly acknowledge my Lesbianism.

Jackie and I found places to be alone after they took

the sheet partitions down in the dorm. They thought they were being liberal, removing the sheets and letting everyone dress together. I was devastated. We went to the rec room or to a great spot we found behind the stage in the cafeteria or out to the woods on the pretext of having a smoke.

Smoking wasn't permitted, but it was very common. I'd quit six months before I entered the convent, but started again the first week I was there. Smoking provided a good excuse to go out in the woods alone. To get more cigarettes, I'd change clothes in the cafeteria, take the bicycle we kept backstage and pedal to the gas station down the road. Since we couldn't smoke openly, a carton lasted a month.

Once I began the affair with Jackie, I was more aware of being attracted to other women. I was idealistic: I believed love energy was boundless, that I could love many people. I didn't want to stop the relationship with Jackie, but I realized I was also drawn to Sister Carrie in the class ahead of us, Jackie's best friend before she went into the convent. Carrie was like me, outgoing and lighthearted. She was the one who had played the piano that first night. When I recognized the attraction, I pursued it. I sent her messages on holy cards; I made sure I saw her whenever possible. I pursued her for months.

One afternoon, Sister Carrie and I went out to the meadows. It was a beautiful day, every leaf shimmering in the sunshine. We *had* to be outside on a day like that. We pushed each other on the swing; higher and higher. We played chase and wrestled on the grass. Carrie ran into the woods, dodging behind a tree, not really trying to escape. Laughing and out of breath, I caught her, and we collapsed on the grass. I could feel her warmth and vitality. I put my hand on her shoulder, bringing her closer. I kissed her lightly. It was an electric jolt. Carrie did not respond; she froze. She looked at me wide-eyed. Then she ran.

I caught up with her at the swings. "It's all right. It'll
be OK. Please, listen to me," I said. I wanted her to understand. I loved her. I didn't want her to be afraid. I didn't
want to lose her. We talked a long time about love, about
friendship, about sharing. Carrie was honest with herself
and with me. She recognized the intensity of our feelings. She
wasn't afraid to explore their meaning verbally or intel-
lectually. She was innocent of prejudice against love. That
day we only talked, searching for clarity. It was inevitable
that we love each other; it was inevitable that we would
make love.

Jackie was overwhelmed with jealousy. I'm sure she
loved us both. Jackie wrote letters and poetry telling me
how awful she felt. Sometimes she cried all night. I didn't
want to cause her that pain. I tried to reassure her, but I
couldn't deny my love for Carrie. It was a celebration, an
affirmation of love for the whole community.

One evening after theology class, I asked to share with
everyone a paper I'd written analyzing Hope. It was an
independent study, and I was excited about it. I was explaining a point about emotions that Jackie insisted I didn't
understand. But I was explaining it very clearly. Jackie
bolted out of the classroom into the woods. There was a
terrible storm. We all went out to look for her. Nobody
could find her. She came in later, soaking wet. The priest,
a psychologist brought in for encounter and sensitivity
groups, asked to talk to Jackie and me. He counseled us
and helped us through what was essentially a break-up,
although it was never openly acknowledged.

Carrie also began seeing the priest for counseling. She
discussed in total innocence everything we were doing. It
took me six months to build enough courage to talk to
him myself. I blurted out that I thought I was homosexual.
I couldn't bring myself to use the word *Lesbian!* That was

the first time I had said it, after years of knowing and denying. We talked about my attraction to women. But when he started asking me questions, I gave him the "correct" answers, not the truth. Finally, he assured me that I shouldn't worry — I wasn't homosexual. I left thinking, "Oh my God, this guy hasn't heard anything I've said," but I guess I wasn't telling him anything. There was a huge empty silo at the Villa, two or three stories tall. I went inside and sat down. Staring up into the emptiness, I felt utterly alone. That was the first time in my life I'd ever told anyone else how I felt and he'd denied it because he didn't want to hear it.

Everyone denied it. Carrie and I were seen once walking by the lake, holding hands and kissing under the light by the bridge. The novice mistress called us to her office. She said we shouldn't walk by the lake because we were breaking the rules. Nothing else. We knew she knew, but she said nothing.

One night the postulant mistress, Sister Martha, caught us. Everyone was in the rec room. Sister Martha was working on a mosaic. She asked me to get more tiles from the laundry. I asked to take Carrie with me. At first, Sister Martha said no. But when I said I'd like company because it was dark there, she consented. Whenever Carrie and I were alone we became very passionate. We always schemed for those moments of privacy. Getting the tiles shouldn't have taken long, but once we were in the laundry, it was dark and quiet and we were alone, lost in a world of each other. Suddenly the room was thrown into glaring light. Sister Martha stood in the doorway. She just stared at us. Our headdresses were off, and there was no question about what we were doing.

I was in agony that night. I knew I was going to be kicked out. I knew tomorrow would be my last day. All

three of us walked around the Villa saying nothing. We
went to bed without talking. I didn't want to leave the
convent; I wasn't ready for the world.

Sister Martha called me into her office the next morning. I could barely look at her. I wanted to be anywhere
but in that office, knowing she was going to dismiss me.
She said, "The least you could have done was talk to me."
I was stunned. She wasn't angry. She wasn't going to throw
me out. She was jealous! I left the office floating.

The next day Sister Martha asked me to take her to
the store. When we returned, I drove the station wagon
into the garage, turned off the ignition, put my arm around
Sister Martha, and kissed her. It was that simple.

Sister Martha had been in the convent for twenty years.
She followed the rules meticulously, and she set the rules
for everyone: lights out at ten, no radios, no smoking,
walking correctly, no cutting up, maintaining an attitude
of dignity. She didn't encourage familiarity.

After we began having an affair, Martha changed dramatically. She began to express her wonderful sense of humor.
A spontaneous, warm, creative person emerged. And, of
course, the convent changed, too. We became a family, a
community of intimacy and love. Not that we were open
or direct about our love, but the atmosphere became completely supportive and nurturing.

Eventually all of my friends were transferred to other
places. I, too, left the Villa to go to college in the midwest.
I became more aware of events in the world. I wanted to
march on Washington, D.C., against the Viet Nam war,
but was denied permission.

Most of the women I knew and loved except Jackie
and Claire left the convent. Claire, my last relationship,
was like Jackie, intense and guilt-ridden. Claire was the
first woman to close off communication with me. She

was seeing another nun, and I never knew what their relationship was. With everyone else gone, it was very lonely.

I was ready to leave. Consciously I wanted to participate in the world; subconsciously I was ready to acknowledge my Lesbianism. The convent had given me a sheltered, protected environment in which to explore my feelings for women. Even its denial and restrictions couldn't suppress my instinct. Martha says I changed the environment to fit my own needs, but all the women I loved there made a profound impression on me. We shaped each other's lives. It was five or six years before I stopped thinking of them daily. Even now they are often in my thoughts. And the only guilt I ever felt was not for loving women, but for cooperating in the hypocrisy of denial.

In spite of my experience, I wouldn't say the convent is a hotbed of Lesbianism. I think that many women have joined convents to escape sexuality, whether Lesbian or heterosexual. A desire for obedience and dedication to God are often secondary to a need for celibacy and denial. The convent appears to be a haven, a world apart from the pressures and risks of this world. But such shelter exacts a price in self-denial that I was unwilling to pay. I wanted to affect this world, not remove myself from it.

I have been working for gay rights for fourteen years. I am Executive Director of the National Gay Rights Advocates, a gay public interest law firm which handles precedent-setting cases involving discrimination against gay people, and former Co-Executive Director of the National Gay Task Force. I am past President of the National Association of Business Councils, a gay business organization. Presently I serve on the executive committee of the Washington-based National Gay Rights Lobby. I was the first openly gay person to serve on a presidential commission. I organized with Midge Costanza the first meeting of gay people in the White House in 1976. For the past four years I have been an investment realtor in the Los Angeles community.

Section VII

HEALING IN THE DARK

Growing into independence and strength has been difficult for many Lesbian nuns and ex-nuns. During and after religious life some of us suffered physical or emotional illness. Some of us numbed the pain and confusion with alcohol, tranquilizers, or marijuana. Gradually we have recovered through meditation, psychic work, therapy, and most importantly, breaking the internal and external silences to name ourselves: Lesbian.

GOD'S LOVE IS PRICELESS

Ann Campbell
(1955-1971)

Traveling alone through Scotland, fulfilling a childhood promise to myself, actually opened the door to the room in which I now find myself. I see my life as a passage through a series of rooms, each of which has its own special door and key. In Scotland, in a remarkable moment of clarity, I released a long-held and tiresome burden of guilt. I saw that my life and conflicts were unique, but not so singular — as my ego had convinced me for years — that I could not fit comfortably into God's harmonious plan.

From my childhood through adolescence I had interpreted my parents' and teachers' instructions about God to mean that I was in great debt to Him. I had been born into the one true Church. My family was fairly well situated financially and emotionally. I was a gifted student. Surely

God would demand His price from someone who had been given so much. From first grade Catechism through college theology, I wanted to know all the truths and all the nuances about God and religion, as if by knowing I could somehow avoid my debt. I became expert in the fine distinctions between venial and mortal, perfect and imperfect, dulia and hyperdulia, proximate and remote, Petrine and Pauline, and even between the Immaculate Conception and the Virgin Birth. I flirted with venial transgressions, but never came close to a mortal sin. I never tampered with sex in thought, desire or deed because I knew there are no venial sins where the sixth and ninth commandments are concerned. I excelled scholastically and religiously. I even crowned the statue of Our Lady twice: in my eighth grade May procession and at a Sodality Ball in my senior year. My heroes in high school were saints, nuns, and contemporary religious figures like Thomas Merton, Dorothy Day, and the French worker-priests. In pursuit of a spiritual, intellectual and (in retrospect) a woman-filled life, I packed a trunk, left a world I hardly knew, and went off to the convent in 1955. At seventeen I believed that I had found the price that would compensate God for all the good things. I would be safe and saved for all eternity.

In the novitiate my reasoned, theological, carefully defined religion was less valued than domestic skills, good conduct, and unflinching adherence to tradition and rule. From the outset, I was not good at convent life. I developed a mildly abrasive, cynical and disruptive approach which persisted throughout the sixteen years I tried to live it. I became even more intellectual in my approach to God and remarkably arrogant for someone so young and naive. Spiritually I never learned even the ground rules for prayer and meditation. I thought the readings we were given were childish, the maxims self-evident, and the rules and traditions archaic. Strangely I never seriously considered leaving.

I just looked for ways to survive and to keep my superiors reasonably ignorant about my distaste for the whole thing.

Since I was bored, it was natural that I would seek and find distractions. One of my earliest was a first year novice, a girl a year ahead of me. She was attractive, graceful, and an expert in sewing, cooking and cleaning. I had none of these talents so desirable in the novitiate. Naturally she caught my eye. I must have caught hers also since we spent a lot of time exchanging covert glances across the dining hall. On those rare occasions when postulants and novices did get together we talked. Once at a piano recital when the lights dimmed, she reached over and held my hand. That innocent gesture still stands out as a momentous experience of joining. My subsequent guilt was the logical consequence of my inability to escape my obsession with the price I believed was due on all "non-spiritual" good things, even moments of happiness. Our low-key relationship ended abruptly when our respective mistresses became aware of it. I was warned about the danger of particular friendships. I made other friends, but I steered clear of any other sentimental entanglements in the novitiate. My distractions were more childish and overt: general mischief making, rule bending, and overeating.

I made my first vows in 1958, just in time for the movement toward more modern scholastic and spiritual preparation for nuns. I got to finish college instead of going out to teach as most of my group did. Although I was told to major in Latin, I wheedled my way into science and math, and this major field put me into contact with a brilliant, witty nun-professor. I virtually idolized her for the next ten years.

During my college years all of my emotional energies were focused on her, and I dogged her path both inside and outside the classroom and laboratory. I could think of no one else. Even now when I pass a chemistry lab with

its familiar acrid odors and sounds of clinking glassware,
I am aware of an intense nostalgia. Was my feeling sexual?
At some level, yes. I certainly touched her whenever I could
in the context of playing around and joking. I managed to
conceal this side life from almost everyone. I did well in
my studies, showed up for chapel, continued to be mildly
eccentric, and provoked very little negative attention. Ultimately I graduated and went off to teach, believing that
I would get over my infatuation. I didn't, but she, wisely
enough, became increasingly aloof. I got the point, visited
the college less often, and quietly decided that the pain
was one more price.

My years of teaching — three in elementary school and
eight in high school — went by quickly. In the midst of
them I made a thirty day retreat and final vows. I spent
a year or so mildly involved with a nun with whom I lived.
But for the most part, I was engrossed with teaching,
moderating activities and spending my time with my students. I was determined not to get seriously entangled
with anyone. I considered my tendency a weakness, and
it frightened me.

After Vatican II I became a mild radical. I loved the
debates, the arguments, and the challenge of being in the
minority. I felt involved in religious life for the first time.
Then came the civil rights, social reform and peace movements. I was in love with being the rebel — not with religious
renewal.

During the summers at the end of the sixties, I went off
on National Science Foundation grants to finish my degree.
I met men and women from all over the country with whom
I shared meals, liturgies, and fabulous summer evening
conversations. I buried my old ideas about God's exacting
price and bought into the new theology of the secular city.

In the midst of this personal transformation, I suddenly

became seriously involved with a nun I had known as a friend
for years. Living in the same convent we discovered new
emotions for one another. In 1969, at age thirty, I had
my first sexual experience. I continued to teach, to be
an activist, to go off in the summers and flirt harmlessly
with the men in my classes. I never admitted to myself or
to anyone else that I could be a Lesbian even while engaging
in sex with a woman on a regular basis.

Gradually I backed away from Mass and the sacraments.
By then there was so much flexibility in scheduling that
no one noticed. I would sometimes go to confession and
allude to my transgressions; at times I went guiltily to Communion and asked God to forgive me. This went on for
two and a half incredible years.

Finally I left the convent in 1971. I claimed that my
convictions on social justice, racial equality, peace and
intellectual freedom were the reasons. Although I still
believe they were part of my motive, I had finally acknowledged that my love for this woman was inconsistent with
my vows. And since I judged this love to be incompatible
with God's plan, I also prepared to pay the price in guilt
and inner misery until I could extricate myself. My theology
of freedom had deserted me.

My lover left the convent with me, and I lived with her
for a year. When I moved out and went back to school, I
immersed myself in study, family, teaching Catechism,
and work. And I drowned my anguish in alcohol.

That year my one good friend was a gay man. In a
moment of alcohol-induced intimacy, I confessed that I
thought I too was gay. He tried to convince me to give up
the Church and my family to resolve my guilt. That was
what he had done. In one sense that encounter was a breakthrough: I had finally verbalized my worst fear. His response,
however, simply confirmed my apprehensions that I was

heading into an unknown, sordid, Godless existence. Most frightening was the sensation that I had lost control over my own life's direction.

After that year, I moved back in with my lover. I worked hard, went to Church, made very few friends, drank more and more, and pulled my companion into my self-inflicted isolation. We traveled, went to the theater, and led a very self-contained life. Eventually the churchgoing stopped. I could no longer even cope with the questions, let alone seek the answers, about where my life was going. Drinking to blot out feelings became a nightly ritual.

I started back to school — always the safe haven — to finish my doctorate. While I was running to stay ahead of my life, my lover became seriously ill. Terrified, I saw her illness as the price of our relationship. A reawakened sense of guilt and my old schizophrenic approach to religion and prayer impelled me back to Church. That she lived was a miracle to me, and I was filled with gratitude to the God whom I simultaneously believed had cursed our union.

During her slow and anxiety-filled recovery, my moments of lucidity were few and far between. I managed to work, get through my classes, and take care of her. But my times alone were spent mostly in an alcoholic daze. After a series of bizarre drinking episodes, I decided I had to do something about the alcohol. I sensed that drinking was closely related to my sexual and religious conflicts. Finally in the summer of 1979 I called a gay and Lesbian center and asked if they had alcoholic counseling. I was referred to a gay women's Alcoholics Anonymous group. There I could talk about God and being gay in the same sentence. God was still a possibility for me after all.

Within a year of joining A.A., I could pray a little, I knew many happy Lesbians, and I was liberated from alcohol — one day at a time. I couldn't deal with being gay in all areas of my life, but I had definitely turned a corner. To celebrate the completion of my doctorate I went to Scotland for three weeks. Since my childhood, when I had listened to stories about my mother's homeland, I had hoped for this trip.

My visit there with an aging cousin began my real spiritual awakening. We talked about the Church, the family, the convent, and our lives. She told me that she had lived with a woman, now dead, for sixty years. She had seen her through her last illness seven years earlier. She had always enjoyed the company of women more than that of men, and she guessed I felt the same. Even though I assume this devout Catholic woman did not share my sexual experience, I felt validated by this ninety-year old gracious lady. She was right about my enjoying the company of women.

Later, high on a hill overlooking the castled countryside and the isle-filled sea, I became transfixed with the sensation of the presence and power of God. His limitlessness and timelessness that I had tried so hard to define and measure poured over me, and I knew what it was to enjoy the divine embrace. I remained there for a time, and when I left it was with a sense of freedom and release.

Three years since that trip I wish I could say that all my negative attitudes have been swept away. They haven't. Because I'm still a bit paranoid about my gay identity, I'm using a pseudonym for this story, and I don't feel comfortable with the Church. I'm over-committed to work and other activities, but I no longer suffer as much from guilt. I know there is no terrible price to pay for happiness. Best of all, I experience God daily in my life in a way that is still new and wondrous and joyful.

What lies ahead for me? I wish I knew. My long relationship which began in the convent has ended. My new more elusive love demands more from me in the way of maturity and positive thinking, but she promises nothing.

She loves God openly and freely. I pray that I'll be given the key to the room I can share with her.

Since completing my Ph.D. in 1980, I have been working as a budget and personnel administrator in a large university library system. Although much of my time is spent on professional activities and writing, I enjoy reading, theater, and films.

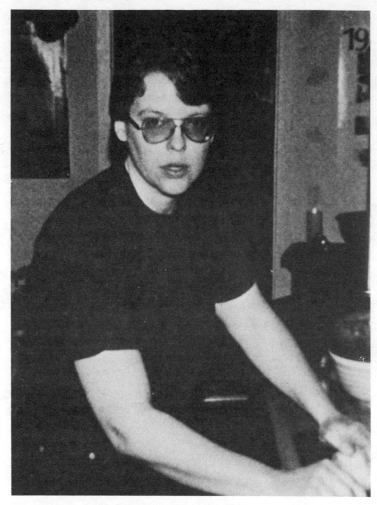

Teresa O'Herlihy, 1982

AGORAPHOBIA

Teresa O'Herlihy
(1972–1978)

Dear Nancy Manahan,

This is a very difficult letter to write. I believe that nobody has a right to ask me for my excuse for living as I do. Upon reading your and Rosemary's reasonable list of Lesbian nun question, I bellowed, "Confession! They want me to confess!" Had I not been shut up in my room to cool, I would have discarded your letter in a rent up wad.

Let me see what I can tell you. Presently I am a musician specializing in pre-Baroque keyboard works. Since eight, I have been musical. I found it easy to say, "Yes, Mother," to everything and then go off to practice for hours. My practicing was always something to hide behind, you see, and an excellent and approved excuse for not confronting emotional issues or making decisions for being involved in most of human life. During my teen years, I did a lot of crying for no clear reason, avoided making friends, picked at my face, and learned a lot about Palestrina. Providing a musical background to other people's lives can take extraordinary time and energy. It tends to make a child a loner and fosters dependency upon providers: parents who pay teachers and teachers who dispense musical instruction and praise. It made a fat timid sissy out of me.

Around the age of ten I knew I would be a nun because my music teacher, a nun, said I should be. "Yes, Sister," I said and kept on practicing.

The only choices I could see after high school were getting married, getting a job in the dime store, or becoming a nun. What I really wanted most was just to be left alone. I assumed that convent life was sure to provide solitude after some trial period during which I would be expected to answer difficult questions about what I was thinking. Although neither verbally nor socially skilled, I was prepared to give a good accounting of myself. In exchange for being let alone inside a good music library, I was prepared to play the organ eight hours or more a day for the rest of my life.

It almost worked out that way. My novice mistress thought I was the closest thing to a musical genius she'd ever known, and said, in effect, "Just go on reading your musicology books, dear, and we'll make you into a good little nun." I was the pasty novice in the corner who never lifted her eyes from the prayer book and did just what she was told, the one everybody thought stupid but who had to confess prideful satisfaction over her secret and unrecognized genius, a rare baby mumbler with delusions of grandeur.

I stayed for six years with no perceptible increase in self-awareness — only boredom and anger toward the end.

I was a good nun. I did everything I was supposed to do and had time left over to research the life of Orlando di Lasso. I was probably the most repressed, completely passive individual you could find.

I believe that musicians develop like toadstools in the dark. We don't always know how we do it or what we're doing or why, but sooner or later in our preoccupied minds, at first dimly, a change registers. I believe that I finally left religious life because it was too perfect, as deadly boring as a piece of good music played too often. I doubt whether my explanations were coherent or satisfactory, but sheer insistence rather than adequate reasoning carried me. In the face of all the coldly logical emotionalism opposing me, reasons adequate for leaving would not have been recognized. Everybody felt brutalized in my quiet and miserable departure.

Rather than returning to the home of my Irish working-class parents in Ohio, I went to California to stay with my sister, her husband, and three children. I didn't have much money, had never held a job, and had a habit of mumbling when spoken to.

When I found a job as a file clerk, I moved to a motel in West Los Angeles, dressed out of Good Will, and ate canned soup and yogurt. Not having a piano was terrible because I had to think a lot. Unable to sleep, I also cried a lot. I lost fifty pounds from sheer terror. Frightened once too often by the flasher next door, I took my suitcase full of Good Will clothes and my carefully hoarded money on the bus to San Francisco, where I answered an ad for a woman-only to share an apartment. There I met my first real Lesbians.

I was twenty-five and had never had sex with anyone. When they asked if I was a dyke, I said, "Sure!" because I wanted that apartment with a piano in plain sight. Then, feeling suddenly bereft of my baby fat and not knowing

where to look, I said, "No, I'm a nun." They laughed at
me, and I cried. They figured me out almost at once, and
wouldn't let me near the piano until I'd told them what
they wanted to know. We sat up that night smoking marijuana and eating spaghetti and meatballs. I got the apartment and a job, and I taught myself how to type out of a
book. I decided that if I was a Lesbian — even though I
didn't have a lover — I could no longer be a Catholic. Everybody else seemed to be in couples; I bought a second-hand
car and acquired a cat.

Then I fell into a long and debilitating depression with
bouts of private hysterics. I felt suicidal for six months. I
couldn't describe the problem, but the feelings were
miserable and overwhelming. That spring I moved to Santa
Rosa, hoping a change would snap me out of it. I believed
that by keeping busy I could ward off my sense of isolation.
I rented a two-room apartment and a piano, bought some
new clothes, got a part-time job, studied bookkeeping at
night and gave piano lessons. But I was still depressed. I
went to a doctor complaining of the weeps, irrational fears,
insomnia. Naturally he gave me Valium, and naturally I took
it right up to the maximum dosage. I just floated along so
fuzzy-wuzzy — oh happy coping Teresa — until one weekend
my prescription ran out and couldn't be renewed until
Monday. When I played organ for a Protestant Church that
Sunday, Bach never sounded so much like the jitters. I
knew I was addicted.

I joined a women's meditation group, where I met the
woman who became my lover. She is a rather bad musician
but a person of excellent sense. When she found out about
my Valium addiction, she moved in with me to help me
taper off in case of medical emergency or a shortage of
will-power. This worked out very well, and she hasn't moved
out yet.

When I had the Valium licked, I knew I still had problems.

I didn't like answering the phone or going outside the apartment. I shopped for clothes by mail order, found a grocery store that delivered, stopped taking outdoor exercise or driving my car. I got panicky in the elevator at work. I found myself standing in open doorways hesitating for up to twenty minutes before I could go outside. I was afraid to look at high ceilings in public buildings such as banks and the Church where I played. I quit my outside jobs, took on more piano students, and practiced, practiced, practiced, so I'd have solid excuses for never going out.

Finally I went to an outreach clinic where a bright young man diagnosed me as agoraphobic and recommended San Francisco specialists whose fees were beyond my financial capability. Instead, my lover and I decided to move to a smaller, nearly rural area. A woman who has lived a reclusive life, hiding behind a keyboard since eight and being cloistered for six years, might well be expected to have trouble coping with an urban environment.

I am no longer afraid to go outside or shopping. I enjoy walks, even overnight camping, and do not fear attacks of hyperventilation in natural surroundings. Commuting to work is difficult, but I know other people have to fight some reluctance to go to an office job. I avoid elevators, crowds, and large enclosed spaces when I can. Because of this I miss concerts I would like to hear, but I have developed a number of musical connections and much more confidence in my dealing with people.

I miss my religion, but missing it has caused me to improve my education by reading about past and present world religions. I cannot permit myself the emotionally overwhelming submissiveness I once believed was religious. The first time I was in a Catholic Church I had to go outside and vomit. I don't know whether my agoraphobia or a soul-felt rejection of the Church brought on the nausea. One day I hope to be able to combine the emotional, intellectual, visionary and expedient principles of religion into a coherent whole.

My lover, an artist who makes icons, describes herself as a matriarchal pagan. She declares she is satisfied with her faith, but to me paganism seems anachronistic and exotic. She says that I am oppressed. I have certainly been repressed. It has been frustrating, annoying, and an offense against personal pride to have to learn at my age about my own body and emotions as well as my lover's.

I hope I have in my rambling fashion answered some of your questions. I was planning to write all this out someday. Your letter just prompted me to do it sooner.

Sincerely,
Teresa O'Herlihy

I am twenty-eight and live in northern California. From eighteen to twenty-four, I was a Benedictine nun. I work part-time, practice the piano, camp in isolated areas, and read. Right now, I'm reading all thirteen volumes of The Golden Bough.

Sr. Helen Horigan, 1967

Helen Horigan, 1983

I ALWAYS KNEW YOU WOULD

Helen Horigan
(1963-1968)

Periodically throughout grammar school, a visiting priest or nun is introduced to my class. All fifty of us rise: "Good morning, Sister Mary Lucille. Good morning, Father Burns," we say in one sing-song voice. Our teacher Sister Mary Eustacia begins pointing out children who have relatives in religious life. "Monica, stand please. She's Father Rafferty's niece. Thank you, Monica. John Flynn. He's Sister Catherine's cousin. Now some of you children will have a vocation. And you will know. God will let you know somehow."

I have a fear, a twist in my gut. "It's me. I know it's me." And I don't like it. But what are my choices? "Be a teacher, Helen. Good pay for a girl. Summers off." Or a nurse, or a secretary.

In high school I take college prep courses. I don't believe I'll marry and have kids, but I don't want to be a
lonely old maid either. I can't let anybody know I'm thinking about being a nun or I'll get isolated: "Holy Mary. No
fun. Can't swear around her."

And yet nuns fascinate me. I try to look inside those
stiff, tight habits for a hint of a breast or a whisper of hair.
My brother Eddie shocks me by saying they go to the bathroom when they leave the room during class. Many nuns
seem strict and cold. They're not allowed to make decisions
for themselves or own a car, as priests do. Yet the nun rules
are so clear, the boundaries definite and safe. Nuns are
intelligent women, educated. They know their purpose in
life. A big purpose.

My sister and brothers have all chosen safe institutions
with concrete purposes. My sister is in nursing school, two
brothers are in the military and one is in the priesthood. I
make the only choice I can.

It's my senior year at St. Clare High. My brother Dick,
who has just been ordained a priest, goes with me to the
Provincial House of the Grey Nuns in Lexington. The sparky,
dynamic novice mistress talks about valuing the individuality
and wholeness of each sister. Though much of her talk
about community involvement in social and political issues
is directed toward the handsome, newly ordained priest,
I watch and listen and feel drawn.

But how am I going to tell Ma? I'm standing in the hall
when she comes out of her room. I "come out" to her for
the first time. "Ma, you know, I'm going in the convent."

She comes toward me crying and a little angry. "I always
knew you would. From the time we named you Helen."

We sit at the top of the narrow stairs. "What are you
talking about?" I ask surprised.

"All the people in our family named Helen are nuns."

"Who are they?" I'd never heard of these hordes. One,

it turns out, is a cousin of hers I'd recently met, and another a distant relation I've never heard of before or since. I wonder why she never told me.

The last day at home and the hour's drive to the novitiate are painful. I've given away all my prized possessions, thrown out scrapbooks. A clean break. We all cry on the drive out: my sister-in-law, my youngest brother, Ma, even Dad. But I feel relief and excitement when I see the big brick building calmly overlooking the willow pond. I am here. No more sadness. No more trying to be understood by my family or to meet their unspoken demands, no more struggling to fit in with friends.

Safe inside the novitiate, I've just turned eighteen. We study the new "opening the windows of the Church" encyclical from Vatican II. We're in the Ecumenical movement, sharing religious services with local Protestant groups. We join clergy and parishioners in civil rights marches and freedom rides. We watch news on television and are expected to vote if of age.

For the first time in my life sexuality is acknowledged by adults. My religious superiors say, "Yes, you are a sexual person, Helen. You may have certain feelings. Choose not to encourage them. Be careful not to wear a sanitary pad too tight because it can arouse feelings. You can and should have friendships, and every one is 'particular.'" The novice mistress tells us that the community warned against particular friendships in the past for fear they would turn into homosexual relationships. "It is possible, my dear little sisters. There have been cases. But it doesn't have to, and you should be able to have friends. Just watch out for it." We even have seminarians visit to allow us to develop non-sexual relationships with men.

We're expected to sign up periodically for structured emotional counselling called "going on guidance." I cry at guidance almost all the time. What about? Perhaps loneliness, peer relationships. "The real Helen Horigan is just coming out," the mistress says. "Who is this real Helen Horigan," I wonder.

We can also speak to the confessor who comes once a week. I tell him about strong attractions I'm feeling for two nuns I've met at the college and to one of my own sister novices. I want to acknowledge these feelings, explore them. "These are normal sophomore feelings — not knowing where you belong or what you're about. It will pass. Don't worry about it." Then he gives me a big hug. I'm concerned that someone will look through the window and see us and think we are being sexual.

After two and a half years, I make temporary vows for a year. I'm in college full time now. The safe womb of the novitiate with no more than twelve postulants and novices has burst. I'm living in the main part of the provincial house with at least fifty sisters. I see more clearly that our innovative novice mistress, our brilliant mystic theology teacher, and the few other professed sisters we'd been exposed to are exceptions. Most of the others are dedicated, hard workers, willing to accept whatever is handed down to them. They are not active in making change happen.

No longer do I have close nurturing supervision. And I don't trust that my new superiors have the skill and intuition I need. I'm relying more and more on myself and my peers. Yet I still don't have the freedom to make important decisions. I'm supposed to rely on authorities and obey the rules. All around me in the Church and the outside world, I see radical change. Famous theologians are questioning Church authority, leaving the priesthood and religious life, and even leaving the Church itself.

After renewing my vows for a second year in 1967, I'm assigned to a summer project in Boston's inner city with women from different religious communities. Nuns, priests, and local residents work together in social agencies, settlement houses, and parishes. We celebrate our life as a community in a weekly ritual that includes mutual evaluation and nurturance. Our Mass is a meal. We break real bread and share wine and sing folk songs with guitars. Music, visual art, and poetry are interwoven with the social/political/ religious work. Local anti-poverty and anti-war religious leaders sing and chat with us. I feel a growing force, a powerful link to the world.

Back within my own community, our constitution (the Holy Rule) is being discussed, evaluated, rewritten. Superiors are now elected rather than appointed from above. Hierarchic titles are abolished. We now use "sister" instead of "mother." But there are too few members of my community who are radical enough for what I envision. I see few women I can vote for as leaders. I'm stuck! I am looking for a leader informed about radical theology and politics and inspired from her heart to throw off outdated rules. Most are still looking to the Motherhouse in Montreal for direction, clinging to the "old ways." The structure itself feels too outdated to be able to change enough. I long for community living, but not the kind where sisters sit around the community room mending socks and T-shirts. I begin to think of leaving.

In the middle of my junior year of college, my provincial superior and her assistant call me in: "With your personality, Sister Horigan, we think you need more community life. We're taking you out of school and sending you on mission to Worcester." Flashes of that ancient orphanage, of women chatting about recalcitrant children and about "The Sound of Music" flood my mind. "No," I scream silently, "You can't. I know you'll never send me back to school. I'll be stuck like all those frustrated, little-educated women who never had a chance. You're not going to isolate me there. Let me out!"

A few days later Ma and I have tea in the parlor of St.

Elizabeth's. As we stare at a bowl of plastic fruit on the low Danish modern coffee table, Ma says, "Helen, you know you make choices when you're young, and sometimes it's hard. You have to think about whether you're happy here. If not, you can come home and live with me. I'll support whatever you do."

Instead of going off to Worcester or out on my own to find community life, I go home and become Ma's roommate. "Helen, I'm so glad you're out of that prison."

"Oh, Mother, why do you tell me these things now — after the fact?"

Soon I feel stuck again. I'm twenty-two and doing social work at the Welfare Department. Among my co-workers is the man who eventually becomes my husband. Michael and I share a disdain for the System and compassion for clients — products of economic injustice. We join the Vietnam Moratorium and march on Washington. We laugh. Our friendship deepens into sexual expression.

One night after I've known Michael for a year, I have a heated discussion with my mother and my priest brother Dick just back from missionary work in Peru. "Marriage is unnecessary," I insist. "Why must the State and the Church have a say in such a personal commitment between two people?"

"That's the way it is," says Dick. "You can't just live with someone. It's immoral."

"Indecent," says Ma. And a part of me knows the only way out of my mother's house is getting married.

During our six year marriage, I become aware that in dance and other creative expressions I feel most myself. I leave social work, but still struggle with the idea that a practical career is necessary. I go to graduate school to study special education, thinking I'll integrate the arts in the classroom. But I find myself teaching in suburban public schools with little support for my ideas.

As my feminist consciousness grows, I feel more sexual. I'm repeatedly attracted to other people. I know something is wrong with marriage, and I want to open mine up. Michael doesn't. Again I keep my feelings inside.

After five years of living in Brighton, we move to the country. The confines of a close relationship and the institutional strictures of marriage become clearer than ever. I feel trapped inside the stone walls surrounding this beautiful country home. Again I cry, "Out!"

Alone in Cambridge, I'm scared to death, but I'm drawn to independent creative women who spurn convention, traditional work roles, and lifestyles. These women have wild, untamed spirits. They love music and storytelling. "Sing, Helen. Tell us the story about the kids at school. Tell us a joke. Dance." We are both audience and performers for each other. We nurture each other through faltering relationships, repressive jobs, lost homes.

As a community, we study sexuality and our bodies. We make holiday cookies. We take field trips to Crane Beach or the Blue Hills. Always laughing, singing, telling stories. On Friday nights at Fran's apartment, Camp Cuckoo we call it, we drink and get high smoking pot. We vent the week's frustrations and dream our fantasies. Eventually, I become involved with my first woman lover. We are drawn to each other within the group as women friends. I know Lesbians exist, but I have no idea of the extent of the women's network or the size of the Lesbian community.

Tee and I struggle with the relationship for over two years. Moments of tenderness alternate with angry outbursts, and much of our relating is clouded with alcohol.

"What do you want from me?" Tee asks. "Why do you stay with me?"

"I want a travelling companion, someone to make the way easier."

"You mean like springs in a buggy for the bumpy road?" she asks.

"Yes."

"But I can't give you the affection and nurturing you want. You never have enough. You always want more. Besides," she snaps, "I'm not even sure I'm a Lesbian. I just don't want to bother with birth control."

"Bullshit!" I retort.

Seeking out the women's community and making new connections on my own, I realize I can break off this addictive relationship. I see that my alcohol abuse is letting me avoid taking more direct control of my life. As I find more of my own inner power, I no longer want to be absorbed in old patterns, in alcohol and drugs.

I get sober. I call myself a Lesbian. This identity becomes a growing source of strength and comfort. As my involvement with women and the Lesbian community grows, so does my understanding of non-hierarchical politics and spirituality. Now I am searching for expressions of my own creative sources and sexual empowerment.

At thirty-seven I still seek a tribe, a community of women creating new ways of being in the world with rituals and celebrations rooted in daily life and rising from a collective spirit.

"Helen, when was the best time of your life?" a friend asks. Perhaps the first few years in the convent. Life seemed simple and clear then. I can see now that it was the beginning of a long journey.

One of the few natives living in Cambridge, I work at Modern Times Cafe, which has a strong feminist history.* *I am currently studying astrology, swimming as much as I can, and actively waiting for the next step to be made clear. I am on the editorial committee of* Women of Power: A Magazine of Feminism, Spirituality and Politics.

*[Editor's note: This restaurant, formerly called "Bread and Roses," was started by Lesbian ex-nun Patricia Hynes.]

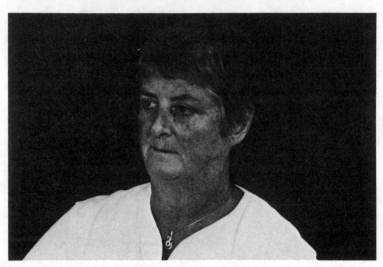

Elizabeth Malloy, 1983

MYTH FOR A WINTER'S EVE

Elizabeth Malloy
(1952-1967)

I was born a child of the moon. A woman mothered me to life, then lost her taste for earth and left me orphaned from the field of her twelve years later. Her death blew a great hole inward drawing me into a vaulted space inside myself. After seven years of deep ache, I brought the hole hollowed out in me to the vaulted place of vow and eased into the journey of my soul.

This journey gave me space for that mooning need which welled up inside. I moved into solo flights of fancy to the universe of upper air where only the soul breathes. I knelt in the night light of the moon and waxed full of her white reflecting light. For eleven years, the mooning light of my spirit led me on a journey through black habits and solitary keeps, through places where bodies darkened each other's doors but never touched. To keep moving, to keep floating in that moon-filled time, I bound myself to their rule: NO HARBOR OF HER.

Harboring of Her was greatly feared in the rite of that journey navigated by him in the Exodus from Her Garden of Eden. She was doomed with her snake, the Eve of his Adam. From the dawn of his day, he feared the strength rising from Her Harboring Her. In his new world, we were wed to him, we chanted. We were his brides, veiled from the world of our bodies by flowing cloaks of black, uniformed for the journey beyond the physical plane. We were soul sisters, set in silent pairs on this night journey.

Before my trip through this night, I had stayed at Harbors of Her, lingering lovingly locked in the strong embrace of that life-giving force. Forgoing this for the celibate cell was a high price, but I was willing to pay the fare to set my hollowed space in a hallowed place. This riteful course eased the pain that pooled around the death of her.

Under cover of vaulted vow, a lovely, lanky, friendly tree grew next to my wall. Her leafy boughs shaded me from the heat of the sun. After many years, a harrowing wind uprooted the tree, and cracked the mortar of my celibate cell. The loss of this friend welled up in me the knowing which loss had placed there years before. With her uprooting, I lay bare to the rays of the blistering sun. It burned my skin, so long veiled from sight. A vortex of pain welled up in me and, as I opened my parched lips to cry, a storm spewed out, pitching my vessel from the comfort of that cool, vaulted sky.

There welled up a wave of tears which crested high, arched, and drove me into a Harbor of Her. A force coiled within had had enough of the segregated slight of the body. It slithered from the inside out, deflating my spiritual sails and driving me into a Harbor. I took refuge there until that storm eased; then I journeyed on, away from that Harbor, but the familiar coil hung now in the forefront of my mooning time. I felt bound by the support of that Harbor place. I could not re-sign to the solitary keep of the celibate cell.

I lived now in two spaces. The vowed words which moved me stood separate from the Harbors of Her who moved me too. A wall of silence parted those two channels of wind which blew me on my course. The face of that wall looks flimsy in the light of today, but in that other life of mine, that wall stood sentinel to the transition from soul to whole. It saved me from shredding apart. The wall formed a friendly cave which allowed life to grow on either side. The vaulted chapel stood walled away from the Harbors of Her. Each grew side by side until one pressed painfully against the other. Six years of separate lives wore me down.

Then one fall day my vaulted chapel and Harbors of Her collapsed in a heap and buried me deep in the wreckage. The walls of both sides folded over, folding me in, and I lay in fear of death beneath the rubble. I had no life but that vowed veil. As it rent and fell from me, a howling rage seared my life.

I could find no bottom to my fear as I was carried out into the open ocean far from the vowed place and my Harbor of Her. Constricting fright gripped me as I was pulled under again and again by the maelstrom from within. Then I floated solitary in no-world, holding in fear to the backbone of work. Important work filled my unimportant world. I gripped at a structure, knowing in my well-worn knowing place that no structure could save me.

Once I emerged from that rim of despair, I lashed myself to rafts floating by. Safe, hollow work and a Harbor of Her held my life together for seven years until that night began to dawn which held secrets to unite the two parts of me. After drifting in the world of him, there dawned on me the rite of passage to my own being. I was able to name myself: Lesbian. Hovering in fear, I heard what it meant: a woman who defies his patterned world, a woman who defies his rule that there be no Harboring of Her, a woman who journeys in both the night of the spirit and the light of the body. Deep within myself I knew I had been born such a woman. This knowing swelled up a new tide, and the split began to merge into one ground of being without a wall binding them apart. A new strength surged. My vows were now made within myself at the strength of my own direction. I was a woe/man transubstantiating into a womb/on/ground. A whole new life now flows in and out from the motherlines of womb/on who re/create this world, this hallowed place, this Harbor of Her.

I left the Sisters of Charity in the late sixties after seventeen years. I am an associate professor of history, principally interested in women's history. Right now I'm writing a book of myth and saga on the stone age epoch of women culled from research begun in Ireland which took seed in me and is in the process of being birthed.

Sr. Angela of St. Margaret Mary, 1963

Helga Dietzel, 1982

FROM GERMAN LUTHERAN
TO EX-NUN MYSTIC

Helga Dietzel
(1959-1966)

For me to enter the convent was as natural as breathing because in some of my previous lives I was a monk and a mystic. Whatever I wanted to accomplish in that way of life has finally been completed, but not without tremendous spiritual and psychological anguish. Today there are no regrets. I am a far richer and deeper person because of my experiences as a nun.

My parents were from Germany and moved to California in the 1920s. When they returned to their homeland for a visit in 1938, the war broke out. Thus I was born in Germany and lived there the first ten years of my life. In 1948 my family moved back to Los Angeles. Although my parents were non-practicing Lutherans, they sent me

to a Catholic school. Within a week, I knew I had to become a Catholic and a nun. Within a few months, I understood more about Catholicism than most of my peers who
had been raised in Catholic schools. I slipped easily into
the spiritual life, feeling as if I were coming home. Secretly,
and against my parents' wishes, I was baptized as a Catholic
at age sixteen.

Sex and feelings about boys were very confusing for
me during those teen years. I masturbated, but with
tremendous guilt, ending up in the confessional two or three
times a week. My emotional ties were always with girls and
the nuns who taught me. I was uncomfortable with boys
because they wanted me to behave and dress differently
than I felt. Feigning helplessness and dressing in binding
clothes didn't fit my love for the outdoors and sports.

I was always in love with one or another of the nuns
who taught me, but my first deep involvement was with
a fellow student. Cecilia and I spent every spare moment
together, wrote each other long letters, and talked for hours
on the phone. My body felt charged with electricity whenever I was near her. We hugged, held hands, and once kissed.
Since sexual feelings were supposed to be in connection
with boys only, I defined what Cecilia and I were doing as
expressions of a deep platonic friendship. Others noticed
our closeness, and eventually one of our love letters fell
into the hands of a nun, who handed it over to my confessor. Convinced that Cecilia and I had been sexually involved, they separated us for our remaining two years in
school. I felt as if we'd done something very shameful.

After I graduated in 1957, my parents shipped me
off to a Lutheran college in Germany, hoping to bring me
to my senses and convert me back to Lutheranism, or at
least to get the notion of becoming a nun out of my head.
That was a wonderful and happy time for me. During vacation breaks, I traveled alone through Europe with only a

knapsack on my back. My Catholic faith grew even stronger, and I became increasingly impatient to enter the religious life.

In 1959, at twenty-one, I entered the Little Sisters of the Poor, an austere, mendicant, and monastically structured community whose primary work was caring for the aging poor while maintaining a life of prayer and monastic austerity. However, some sisters, like myself, were teachers for high school girls aspiring to enter the Little Sisters.

Sisters were not allowed to write or receive visitors, except their parents. Since mine had disowned me, I was completely cut off from anyone I had known. Despite this, I was never lonely because I became totally immersed in my new life. Aceticism fit perfectly into my spiritual/mystical belief system: the less of me and earthly satisfactions, the more of God within me. I often suffered intense mental and emotional pain. Yet I enjoyed a closeness with God which gave me deep inner joy, peace, and ecstasy. Sometimes I would be so enthralled by the beauty and oneness of the universe, that I'd forget about my body or what I was supposed to be doing.

On the psychological level I punished myself severely. I had one aim in life then: to be perfectly in tune with God. To do this, I deprived myself of all emotional ties, welcoming humiliations and constantly striving to cleanse my conscience of anything that might offend God. A passionate and deeply emotional person by nature, I was denying myself the most necessary nourishments for my emotional well-being: intimacy, deep friendship, and self-esteem.

Several times I fell in love with sisters stationed in the same convent. With each woman, I kept communications on a strictly intellectual and spiritual level. I avoided seeing or being with her and never touched her. Those brief moments I did allow myself to be with her alone, my body and mind were on fire, so intense were my feelings. When she transferred to another convent, as always happened, I knew I would never see her again; but I did not allow myself to feel the pain deep inside me, ready to explode. I wanted to develop only universal love.

Under such self-torture, something had to give. During my fourth year in the order, my spiritual life went dry. Suddenly the one area into which I had put my entire being was empty. Since I had been depriving myself of the emotional and psychological joys of life, I felt excruciating loneliness: a black hole, a void.

For the next two years I went through the motions of Mass, Communion, meditation, the Office, penances, and the many daily rules that make up the monastic life. None of these made sense without God. Since my vows meant a commitment for life, I never considered leaving the Little Sisters. Furthermore, the Church taught that those who left the religious life had failed: they had been given the "highest" vocation, but somewhere along the road to perfection had fallen by the wayside. Finally, in my sixth year as a nun, plagued with tremendous guilt, I decided to leave. My superiors transferred me to another state. They decided I was emotionally disturbed: who in her right mind would want to leave the religious life, and horror of horrors, doubt the existence of God?

After my superiors realized I would not change my mind, I was transferred to another convent to await the dispensation from my vows. At this convent I was treated like an outcast by the superior who knew of my plans to leave, and by the sisters who were told to keep away from me since I was "mentally disturbed." I felt totally alone, honestly believing that neither God nor people wanted me. I bought into my superior's beliefs that I was emotionally disturbed. I even rejected myself, thinking I was ugly inside and of no value. After three months of this isolation, my dispensation arrived and I was finally permitted to leave in January of 1966.

For several weeks after leaving, I was in deep cultural and emotional shock. Gradually I conditioned myself to block out any memory of my convent life. I re-entered college and worked part-time as a teacher. During those college years, I was so deeply depressed that I eventually questioned my reason for living. I had put 200 percent into the religious life, and now it was gone. I was alone in my struggles through almost five years of depression, anger, frustration, and confusion about life's meaning. Spiritually, I was dead.

In 1968, at age thirty, I had my first sexual experience. It was heterosexual, and for the next two years I led a very active heterosexual lifestyle. Sex was easy for me, great fun, and very natural, but none of my involvements with men had any emotional depth. In 1971, it finally dawned on me to relate physically to a woman I loved. When this happened, my entire life of emotional involvements with women made sense. I had no problem admitting I was a Lesbian; I felt free and whole.

My first committed Lesbian relationship commenced around 1972 when I still hadn't let go of my need to nurture. My lover wanted a mother and I needed to be needed. I remained in that relationship for almost eight years, even though it began falling apart during its third year. The patriarchal/heterosexual concept of marriage ("until death do us part") was my idea of commitment and the reason I remained in the relationship so long.

Around 1971, I became aware of the women's movement. I read everything I could find on that subject, and became involved with feminist groups. Initially, I felt rebellious towards men and society's oppression of women. I could now see my life as a Catholic and a nun as submerging myself in the patriarchal belief system, which is so contrary to being fully a woman. I realized that I had bought into what the male-dominated Catholic Church states a woman should be: non-sexual, less in every way than the male, not in control of her life or body, always nurturing and supportive, financially dependent, never assertive or in a leadership role. I believed the biblical emphasis on a woman's evil nature. Seeing my past in this light helped me to face my oppression and work through the anger and frustration I felt as a nun. It took ten years of painful struggle for me to come to feel good about myself and get in touch with all of me, including the spiritual. Maybe those many years of painful growth could have been avoided had I not bought into the Church's belief systems, but I wonder if I would be as free and whole a woman as I am today without the struggle.

After graduating from college in 1971, I earned my living as a teacher. In 1975, I came to realize that career-wise I had been doing everything our male-dominated society expects of a woman, never considering other alternatives. I became a life insurance agent for the next two years, dreaming of big business and piles of money. Although I was very successful, it didn't feel right for me. Since 1977 I have been happily hammering away in an all-male trade: cabinetmaking. Four years ago I became the first female journeyperson in this industry.

From 1979 until recently, I've dated women and had a few short-term affairs. Presently I am in a committed relationship. Socially, my friends are primarily women, the majority of whom are Lesbian. Politically, I consider myself a Lesbian/feminist and am very comfortable with that.

Spiritually I am alive and well again. I do not belong to any institutional Church and completely reject the patriarchal structure of society. My concepts of the creator and the universe have changed drastically. I believe that I create and am totally responsible for everything in my life. The word mystic probably best describes my inner life. I feel in touch with the universe, experiencing and seeing its immense beauty and unity. Today I am genuinely happy inside and out, take great pleasure in being alive, and am at peace.

Although currently employed as a cabinetmaker, I am concentrating my energy and skills in the area of metaphysics. Soon I will be devoting my full time to this field. I have run the gamut from an austere monastic life to a very worldly one, apparently devoid of spirituality. In the process of experiencing these extremes, I have integrated the best parts of both, thereby creating a balanced whole.

Sr. Mary Ethna, O.S.F., 1958

Mab Maher, 1984

HEALING IN THE DARK

Mab Maher
(1956–1974)

When I left the convent eight years ago, I tried to stammer out the truth about the split between my spirituality and my sexuality. My spirituality had forked off into light where my sexuality and creativity could not follow. I wanted someone to help me as my unconscious bubbled up in anxiety and rage.

A dream which I had soon after leaving the convent became a great friend on my journey: *I come to a large church with my three cats. We process down the aisle looking about but seeing no one in the heavy masculine pews. The church is empty. When we arrive at the front of the church a voice says, "Choose one of your cats to preach." I ask my grey cat Buber to go into the pulpit. He jumps up on the lectern and begins to twitch his whiskers. I feel afraid: what if no*

*one is there and he is making a fool of himself? I look around
to see the pews filled with brightly dressed people listening
intently. I feel proud.*

This dream meant to me that the repressed instinctual
side of my spirituality was taking a lead. Formerly
spirituality meant a system outside myself. I was addicted
to religious "fixes" outside myself, even though I taught
theology as a way to discover self. I was deep into burying
myself so as not to hear my own heart and body as the
source of revelation. Letting go of Catholicism happened
quickly. I simply stopped going to Church. Letting go of
the mind set that underpinned Catholicism was much harder.
I believed that revelation from outside myself would make
me full. So I continued to believe in things outside myself:
professional status, financial security, social prestige,
clothing, even a specific weight. They became identity-
givers holding me at the threshold of the door of the darkness I needed to journey into. I knew that I needed to
change; but only slowly did I learn how chaotic, painful
and liberating real change is. When I saw other friends leave
the convent and adjust quickly with seemingly little pain,
I wondered what was wrong with me. Then I began to see
that the structures by which religious communities hold
together are not much different than the structures of
government, IBM, and the university system. I began to
feel terror at these insights. I saw I would never fit into
the conventional mainstream again.

Somewhere in the swirling chaos of those first years
out of the convent, I began a switch in life and mind direction. I began transpersonal therapy. I slowly began to perceive myself as the center of revelation. That was an
enormous leap for me, far more radical than leaving the
convent.

With much indecision and pain, I began to see that the
sexual choices which corresponded to my deepest needs

involved women. All the hungry ghosts of my novitiate training came out to chew at the vulnerable areas of my soul. These ghosts were my training on the evil of particular friendship, my sense of shame at even thinking of loving another woman, and all the inner manipulation patterns I had taught myself in order to survive in the convent.

In the novitiate I loved to kneel next to one classmate. Usually we were assigned places in chapel, but not when we knelt through the night before the casket of a dead sister. The intent of this observance was like that of the Tibetan Buddhists: by seeing death clearly, we were to become aware of the passingness of all things. But I never felt so alive as during those nights when I could kneel next to my friend. I felt as if I would live forever.

In our large motherhouse there were a dozen or more walk-in lockers in which food was kept in cold storage. One day my friend and I were accidentally locked into the one which stored milk. As the door jammed, I felt my anxiety rise. Everyone would now see that we were particular friends. (Actually, I am not sure that my friend knew she was my particular friend.) I huddled up in the corner with the cream cans. Much more pragmatic, she pounded on the door. After several hours of physical cold and psychic heat, the sister who managed the kitchen found us. As she released the latch, I blurted, "We didn't do anything." Laughing, she shook the bag of apples she was carrying at us and said, "Too bad. Too bad."

As a professed sister, my Lesbian awareness grew slowly. The year of Vatican II, I went to Europe. A group of sisters in my community spent a night in Lourdes in the grotto where the Mother of Christ is said to have appeared to Bernadette. The more spiritually hardy knelt most of the night. I took hourly lunchbreaks of dark French chocolate and Lourdes water. As the sun rose over the grotto, I felt a miracle trying to get in. We were kneeling all night in veneration of a woman whose statue was enthroned above the earth. On the earth were ten women, flesh and blood women, and we were not touching or honoring each other at all. Much later, I was to see that although religious life looked like a matriarchy, it was but a carefully decoupaged patriarchy which used women as its veneer. That day I simply ate more French chocolate to keep down this insight.

At twenty-eight, in graduate school in Washington, D.C., I had my first experience of triangular love. A handsome young nun from Detroit and I grew very close as we studied in the library, ate together, and took long walks each day. I loved Ann. I had so much energy I could have sold it. Ann was also a close friend of a priest from Ireland whose years of scholarship had left him physically blind. When the three of us went on an outing, I usually drove. One day we went to the ocean in Delaware. After we finished our picnic, I hiked two miles back over the dunes to find the car and drive it back to them. When I returned, they were lying under several blankets. I could see him sucking her breasts through her opened habit. Overwhelmed with my own sexual yearnings and loss, I fell to the sand and sobbed. I never revealed that I had seen them. One day Ann said to me, "I know you are happy that Dennis and I have found each other, for you are my best friend, and I want to share that with you." I said thanks and tucked it into that place in my throat where I had stored a good many words.

Before I started my dissertation, I left graduate school and came home to the college my community ran. I taught there during those years of thinning out convent membership. Most of my friends left. I was often on committees of leadership trying to make sense of implementing the new policies of Vatican II. But that was not the most important thing I did. The dean of that women's college was homophobic and did dreadful things to students who showed interest in other women. Many students came to me to share their confusion and distress. Perhaps they knew I was a Lesbian. I surely did not let on. But I supported their right to their lifestyles. I knew deep within me that I was supporting them at the very root of their lives; in jeopardy was not simply what they did but who they were.

One year I lived in a small house on campus with three other nuns. I shared a room with one of the nuns; the other two were close friends. As time went on, I knew that our bedroom did not have the same activity as theirs. I felt left out, but I also supported their loving. Several years later one of the women in that other bedroom announced to the community that she was leaving the convent because she was a Lesbian.

One year before I left the convent I took a leave of absence to do consultation work in the East. It was both gratifying and frightening to be living away from my community and making it on my own. My credit card assumed proportions beyond its pragmatic value. I entered the social scene fully intending to make myself love men. I was tired of being different; I longed for the anonymity of being just like everyone else. Luckily my friend Sarah taught me to look carefully at society's expectations. She urged me to trust my own heart. During those first few months I learned how much inverted interest there is in the lives of nuns. Sarah taught me to treat questions as projections and to have fun with them.

A few weeks later a man with whom I worked asked me over lunch if there were underground tunnels between rectories and convents for easy access to sex. I said, "Sure."

"But isn't that awfully dangerous? You could be found out."

"Oh yes," I assured him, "that did happen."

Two weeks later he called to confide that he had been

having an affair with his neighbor's wife. There was a secret
path in the adjoining orchard. But he had been found out!

When a woman asked me if nuns masturbated, I said,
"Sure."

She was shocked but interested. "I suppose it did help
a tense situation."

"Oh, of course."

A few weeks later at the swimming pool I overheard
her say that she and her husband were again having sex.
She attributed this marvel to her newly discovered joy in
masturbating.

Perhaps all this was not exactly what Ghandi had in
mind when he spoke of experimenting with the truth, but I
was learning who I was not and how easy it is to be caught
in the web of projection.

I applied to Rome for final dispensation from my vows.
On a cold, winter morning, five months later, I left for
Minnesota to sign my departure papers. It was my birthday.
I couldn't sleep that final night at the Motherhouse, so I
got up and walked out into the cloistered outdoor court
where a statue of St. Francis of Assisi was banked into the
snow and I sobbed out all my memories.

When morning came, and I was warming myself with
a cup of coffee in the cafeteria, my oldest and dearest nun
friend came in. "I see you couldn't sleep last night either,"
she said. "I saw you from my window. You must be frozen.
So little sense." I loved her. Bent and aged at seventy-five,
she seemed to have the happiest face I had ever seen. She
had cared well for my mind and my professional life by
engineering a fine education for me.

As we drank our coffee, she counselled me with long
selections from Dante to let go of whatever does not lead
to life. I stopped shivering. She looked at me from top to
bottom and then pronounced, "Yes, you will be fine. Hard,

but fine. For you, I am glad you go; but for me, well, I am sad."

On the way to the taxi I met two young nuns who assured me that I would soon marry. I wanted to shout at them that marriage was not the only justification for leaving the convent. I yearned for some rich quote of Dante to hurl into their faces.

The following Christmas I flew to Ireland. I needed to see the roots of myself more clearly. I rented a car and began a trip to the farthest Western Point, Dingle Peninsula. I felt completely free and at one with myself as I drove along. The roads grew narrow and cut into rolling hills. Almost imperceptibly I became one with the round, soft hills that curved into each other from every direction. They were the shape of women loving each other. I have never felt such an overwhelming sense of being at home. In that moment all the Earth was saying *yes* to my Lesbian identity. I got out of the car and opened my arms to the Irish hills; I ran up and down them calling them my lovers and my sisters. As the sun began to set I reluctantly left them to find a hostel with a huge feather bed and to sleep until the middle of the following afternoon.

Sometimes I regret the lost time in the convent. I was split from my womanhood in my long years within Christianity. I was living with a logic foreign to my own inner rhythm. Now I am returning to my original face, that which was mine before I suffered the blindness of too much light. The Sumerian myth of Inanna has been the mirror of my journey. Like Inanna, the light goddess, I go to meet my dark sister, the goddess Ereshkigal, my woman strength.

The deepest closet I have come out of has been my own heart. "Lesbian" is a soul term as well as a behavioral way to go in the world. It is as much a mystery and a gift as why and how I breathe. It is my spiritual home. But professionally and socially it is easier if I just stay out of that "spiritual-sexual oneness."

Most people can accept me as a behavioral deviant. But if I say that being Lesbian is not a deviation from the normal pattern of life but my gift to the larger Pattern that unites us all, that is often offensive. I can be accepted if my sexual identity is Lesbian but not if it is also my spiritual identity. Like Inanna, transformed in her exchange with Ereshkigal, I have been transformed by my journey to the Underworld of my Self. I may never "fit in." But I know now, that in healing my split, in living my truths, I am moving toward the Whole. I belong in the Pattern, and I am at home living with my great lover, the Earth.

I am a Bay Area writer and therapist. I recently completed a Ph.D. dissertation on humor and transformation, and weekly I convene a feminist salon.

Section VIII

ON THE BOUNDARY

Lesbians who remain in religious life after decades of personal and institutional change live on the boundary between groups male culture regards as mutually exclusive. We are learning to define our own values; to re-claim our ethnic heritages; to make our own political, spiritual, and emotional commitments; and to create our own lives. We claim both identities: Lesbian and nun.

TO SHED THE VEIL OF ANONYMITY

Sister Esperanza Fuerte
(1967–present)

A meeting of Lesbian nuns and former nuns which I recently attended became a place of "coming out" for me, but coming out just so much. Retreating to the closet of anonymity, I must use a pseudonym: Esperanza Fuerte, which means "Strong Hope." One of my strong hopes is that someday I will be able to use my own name publicly as an Hispanic Lesbian nun. Another strong hope is that I may continue to be a sister, if I choose to, while being accepted as a Lesbian woman.

My story is one of a growing awareness of myself being double-closeted in a world where both racism and homophobia have shared unspoken space in the convent. When I first entered the convent nearly two decades ago, I was an unassuming, quiet, passive girl. My Hispanic background

had been negated both by the values society placed on it
and by my own need to be accepted by a white world.
Yet I moved in that world as a stranger does in a foreign
land — with apprehension and ignorance. I met people who
assured me of their acceptance with veiled racist statements: "... but you don't look Spanish" or "You don't
sound Hispanic" and "It's a good thing you don't get too
dark in the sun."

Praying, living, and working in a convent environment
that neither questioned nor challenged my ethnicity (the
first closet), kept me lethargic and unconcerned. In addition, after almost a decade as a nun, I remained unaware
of my Lesbianism (the second closet). There had been a
six-month period in the novitiate when another sister and
I got physical in a relationship she had initiated. It was
nothing serious; we were just two people overwhelmed
by the stresses of a lifestyle we couldn't understand. I
didn't think then about the poignancy of that relationship,
for I placed the experience into the recesses of my mind.
I wanted to be a good sister; I needed to be accepted.

Toward the end of my tenth year in the convent, I
felt as if I was losing touch with reality. I didn't realize
that my depression was really anger turned in on myself
for all the thoughts I'd never had, for all the actions I'd
never performed, for all the risks I'd never taken — in
essence, for a life I'd never lived. As I tried to deal with
my anger, it began to be directed outside of me toward
people I lived and worked with. My feelings of "going crazy"
were leading me to act in order to save myself. At first,
I started lashing out irrationally, when I dared. Later, the
anger took healthier forms as I spoke out at meetings, committees, prayer groups, workshops, and rallies. I pleaded
with God, "Don't let me feel crazy all of my life!" I began
to read voraciously: books of psychology, of racism, of
women's issues, of warfare, of the struggles of the human

spirit. While all of this was going on, I felt less and less of a connection with my community. I can look back now and know where the isolation came from. There was no one in my community of over five hundred sisters who shared my experience of being an Hispanic woman.

The person who emerged first was the Puerto Rican, followed by the woman, and then by the Lesbian. The Puerto Rican woman realized that she missed eating her native food, missed speaking "Spanglish" (Spanish and English mixed together), missed the beat of the congas with swirling Latin rhythm, missed the fun, the noise, and the celebration of a culture that was foreign to the cultures celebrated in the convent. I had changed in order to be accepted by their dominant society; I had become a cerebral person and had squelched the heart person. Now, the feeling person began to emerge.

As my Puerto Rican identity grew stronger, so did my woman-identified world. I became aware of the double-standard prison of my Hispanic culture and the structured roles that our women had to play. I realized that my own mother never fully emerged as a fulfilled and complete individual, and I knew that I would Identify more with the struggles of my oppressed Hispanic sisters. Their "lucha" became my struggle, and their "suenos" became my dreams. I began to look at the religious congregation I had joined to see how we were "enabling" the poor that we proclaimed to minister to. I began to feel the pain that comes with the awareness that what we professed and what we actually did were different.

Why didn't we reflect within our congregational ranks the numbers of black and brown people we served?

Why weren't we providing educational curricula that would magnify the self-worth of those we taught? Why were we still dealing with those we ministered to in the same way we did during the founding of our congregation?

I wanted answers! I then realized I no longer feared criticisms from my white community; I was now criticizing it! Once my eyes were opened to see the truth, I was able to focus on my identity as a Lesbian woman. The oppression of my Puerto Rican sisters and brothers is similar to the oppression of my Lesbian sisters.

The fear that I experience as a Lesbian woman who is a member of a religious community is sometimes paralyzing. I know that all of the pain, struggle, death, and rebirth I have experienced over the years could all be swept away in a moment if my community knew of my sexual identity. This is why I have told only two close friends in my community. They and a couple of former members of my congregation continue to provide me with love, understanding, and support. They encourage me to believe that there are other Lesbian members sharing my struggle. At times, I want to stand up and "tell it like it is" in front of my congregation, but my fear of losing my credibility and of being rejected silences me.

Several years ago, lasting less than a year, I had my first real woman love. She was a sister from another congregation. She helped me to get in touch with my feelings and to question who I really am. I am a stronger person because of that relationship.

Since then I haven't loved another woman. The relationship couldn't be an open one, and I'm not ready for that. I don't want to work on being a Lesbian while I'm involved with someone, and I'm not ready to work out the implications of having the vow of celibacy while being in an intimate relationship. However, I will not rule out the possibility that if I fell in love tomorrow, I might take the risk.

I must not be completely critical of my congregation. I know that the opportunities afforded me as a member of my community have taken me to where I am today.

Who I am today, a Puerto Rican woman who is also a nun and Lesbian, is both because of my community and in spite of my community.

I am Esperanza Fuerte. My hope is strong: hope for the future, hope to one day share with the world my identity as a Lesbian woman, hope that my congregation may someday know who I am and say "Good" or "We're glad" and "Let's celebrate the gift of you." I will continue as a member of my congregation with hope that, as long as I am filled with life and love, I will remain a Puerto Rican woman who is also a nun and also a Lesbian.

I was born on the mainland in a large city on the East Coast. I have been a member of the Dominican Sisters for almost twenty years. My involvement continues as an advocate for feminist, Lesbian, and anti-racist issues.

Sr. Rosita, O.P., 1965

Sister Pat O'Donnell, 1983

DREAM JOURNEY TO MYSELF

Sister Pat O'Donnell, O.P.
(1955–present)

I am a Lesbian nun. If I had a choice, I would be exactly who I am. It has taken me forty-five years to come to this acceptance of my Lesbianism.

During college, before entering the convent, I loved several women. One demonstrative relationship frightened me. I confessed to a priest that I had petted, but I did not mention that such was with a woman. Society's rejection of homosexuality, and thus my self-rejection, was already well-ingrained.

In the Dominican novitiate, I was attracted to another novice. My arousal had been triggered by feeling Sue's leg next to mine as we sat at table. This disturbed me so much that I went to the Mother General and tried to explain my distress. I had no vocabulary for what I was trying to communicate and no awareness yet that I was a Lesbian. I requested that I never be assigned to the same house as Sue. The Mother General laughed at my agitation.

Even though she said I was overreacting, novitiate training prohibited particular friendships. To me, that meant no close friends at all. Friendship was connected to an evil inclination in me. That evil must be kept locked up. If it escaped, if I let it surface, I'd be sent away.

After final profession, I did graduate work in pastoral theology. The rug was pulled from beneath me when I realized that one cannot love God if one cannot love another person. To my horror, my conclusion was that I did not love God! My strict guard fell, and I let my feelings for another sister surface. Soon Donna and I became lovers. But guilt paralyzed me, and within three months I was unable to get out of bed to enter the classroom to teach. I seemed encased in a doorless, windowless, one-by-one inch room. I requested help and was sent to a psychiatrist, who medicated me with eight Valium a day. After four years of his prescription, I began to dislike the zombie effect and dropped both the Valium and the psychiatrist. In the meantime, Donna had left the congregation.

I became a workaholic in order to suppress my feelings. My superiors appreciated all the work I produced; but I was a robot, an efficient machine with no warmth, no sensitivity to the needs of others, and no will to live. Then two years ago, I requested from my superiors an extended retreat time. I was able to verbalize that my need was a matter of life or death. Fortunately they believed me even though I could give no detail.

I went to a desert house of prayer. There with the help of a skilled facilitator, intense prayer, a woman I came to love, and a series of transformative dreams, I finally named and then claimed who I am. It was the hardest year of my entire life.

As a starting point, my retreat facilitator suggested I draw my recurring childhood nightmare: a huge open mouth about to gobble me up. Although I no longer had this nightmare, I was terrified of something, and that fear was eating me alive. Then I had a dream which initiated my inner transformation: a thief was at my door attempting entry! I awoke so frightened that I got out of bed to see if the door was locked. My heart was pounding, and I felt paralyzed. This was the first step in my journey to the locked parts of myself.

During the next eight months I had four dream journeys. My first set of dreams pushed me to confront the fear of some unknown, to face the parts of myself that were terrifying me. It ended with a dream of an elongated face that looked like me. I had been taping drawings of my dreams to the wall of my room; and, although I disliked this image, I put the face on my wall. After several days I could look at her more comfortably. She became known to me as The Voice. I often dialogued with The Voice, my deep inner core, for she knew the truth about my self.

In the dreams of my second dream journey, I felt excruciating fear and anger. In waking life I continued to contemplate suicide. As I was about to give up the struggle, I found my dream self on the trail with Rose, the woman with whom I was in love. As we reach the edge of a pond filled with debris, an immense whale emerges from the water, opens its cavernous mouth, and sucks up the debris. I am rooted to the spot, terrified that Rose and I will be devoured. But the mouth doesn't touch us. It's miraculous. I'm saved with the woman I love, who, of course, is a part of me I'm finally able to explore. Loving Rose is good. God will clear away the debris and keep me safe — I hope. My life might be worth living.

The third dream series terrified me by naming my Lesbian sexuality. I am at our Motherhouse, in bed with a high school classmate. I am astonished that she is naked with me like this. Her body is so warm and good, and it feels marvelous that she cares for me. Awake, I fight the naming. No, no, I'm not a..., a.... Eventually, I say the word, but only in a tiny whisper.

The series ends with a terrifying eight-day dream sequence. I am climbing down the sides of a great black spiral hole. When it gets too steep to continue, I sit down. Two motorcyclists offer me a ride out, but I say no, I must go on down. They leave. But I can climb no further. Then I hear myself say, "I am ready," and I leap into the hole. For several days I fall, banging the sides, being bounced back and forth. Even awake, I feel as if I am falling. I am paralyzed. I can't breathe. I have let go of everything.

On the eighth night, I fall through the bottom of the spiral hole out onto the palm of an enormous hand. I am held so lovingly and caringly that I know I am safe. Once safely there, I realize that what I was so terrified of was claiming my Lesbian identity. For the first time in my life, I can say out loud: "I am a Lesbian." I write to New Ways Ministry for information on homosexuality and the Church. I read books from the library. I begin coming out to selected members of my community. In both my dream life and my waking life, I am taking risks I never could have dreamed of before. I am daring to be myself!

In the fourth dream journey, I am rolling in a giant sail ship like one from the fleet of Christopher Columbus. I hang on by my fingernails while a fierce storm tosses the ship back and forth. I want to live! I come to shore safely and find myself walking with Rose in the desert. We are completely surrounded by radiant gold light. I give praise and thanks to God. In this sequence the fearful mouth and the threatening thief reappear, but as friends.

The culminating dream in this long journey is one of

ecstasy and immense peace. I am a large jug, floating in the ocean. I am one with the ocean, one with the universe. I am overflowing with joy. I have faced my worst fears, descended into the depths of my nightmares, and emerged with my Self, alive and whole.

My waking life and my dream life have let me know that I can no longer separate my spirituality from my sexuality. I cannot trust God while being terrified of my Self. God has called me to be who I am: a Lesbian sister. To deny the Lesbian in me is to live in fear of the mouth, the thief, my own face and inner voice, the spiraling hole of my unconscious, and the ocean of my being.

I came to the desert to face the truth — or die. There I found another woman, the Self I had locked away for so long. Now two years later, I am at home with that self and alive in my love for others. I still have fears, of course. I am afraid of sharing my story in this book. But more important than my fear is owning who I am. No thief can ever again rob me of that power.

I was born in Texas in 1936. I have spent twenty-five years in religious education and pastoral ministry. My theological background and my own inner journey have led me to my present work: facilitating private retreats and offering spiritual guidance at a desert retreat center near Tucson, Arizona.

ALTERNATIVE COMMUNITY

Sister Anne
(1956–present)

(Sister Anne has always been considered a radical in her community. The focus of her her work has been social justice and spirituality, and most recently, feminist spirituality. Nancy Manahan interviewed her in September of 1982.)

Nancy: Are you living with your religious community now?

Sister Anne: No. I've moved into a house with my lover, Marie.

Nancy: How long have you been together?

Sister Anne: Six years. Sometimes when I think of what we've managed to do — but I don't often think about it. Some of my community members are aware of our relationship. I think they hope it's just a stage I'm going through. They really care for me and don't want me to leave.

Nancy: Are you *out* in your community?

Sister Anne: Well, I don't call it *out*. People know.

Nancy: People know. What's the difference?

Sister Anne: Some people know, and other people don't. Marie and I have some of the sisters over to our house all the time. It must be apparent.

Nancy: Is Marie a sister too?

Sister Anne: No, she's not, but she is involved in ministry.

Nancy: Is she your first lover?

Sister Anne: Not exactly. Over the years I've had relationships with several women and men.

Nancy: Were you attracted to women before you entered the convent?

Sister Anne: No, actually I was engaged to a man when I decided to enter. I didn't become aware of the possibility of loving women until my mid-twenties. I was working in New York and met a young woman from the parish teen group. She made appointments to see me and attended retreats I led. She said she loved me, but I was too busy to love anybody.

Nancy: I think it's part of the program: keep us so busy we don't have time to feel much.

Sister Anne: Yes, and when we'd be transferred, a whole block of people were finished — Christmas card, that's it. But Virginia kept in touch with me over the years.

Nancy: Did she become a nun?

Sister Anne: She entered our order.

Nancy: Of course. Following you.

Sister Anne: I didn't know. She keeps telling me she entered to be with me.

Nancy: It's one of the most effective recruiting practices of religious communities. Women fall in love with nuns and enter; then younger women fall in love with them and enter, and the chain goes on.

Sister Anne: Well, I didn't know until years later that that's why Virginia entered. She eventually left the order and started living with other women. But she kept checking in with me, almost an annual visit. Then I experienced a couple of relationships in the community.

Nancy: Lover relationships?

Sister Anne: Yes. By that time, I could see that people who had same-sex relationships weren't sick.

Nancy: What about your vows?

Sister Anne: I had studied theology in the 1960s. We questioned the hierarchical structure of the Church and found that the structure does not assure God's Will. Then we began redefining all three vows. I worked through my sexuality and felt I had a theological basis for entering into relationships. At that time, I was having some problems with an ulcer and sought help from a Roman Catholic doctor. After a couple of sessions I realized I was essentially going for counseling. He had me write down all the dried up, frustrated women in my community; he said that if I continued neglecting my emotional and personal life I could easily become like them. Then he had me notice the men I felt a warm connection to and suggested that I ask them what was happening. One of them was totally in love with me. I had no idea. The other one felt very competitive with the first man and was also attracted to me. So I pursued a relationship with one of them. The doctor said I would be of greater service to the world if I was in a relationship. He said that God didn't care if I was a virgin. That was my opening into being physical.

Nancy: So you began having sexual relationships?

Sister Anne: Yes. I continued a relationship with this man, a priest, until my community transferred me: they told me my theology wasn't sound. I had stopped wearing my veil, and was questioning the theology of obedience. My obedience was to God, not to the whim of my current

Mother Superior. To straighten me out they assigned me
to an ultra-conservative convent. I quickly fell in love with
one of the good sisters, and we were together for over a
year. I think it was her first and last sexual experience.

Nancy: Did she end it?

Sister Anne: Yes, she began to feel guilty. Part of me
felt guilty too, but I had to live my life. I would like people's
approval — it's hard to live without approval. But it's also
hard for me to live without living.

Nancy: And then what?

Sister Anne: During the next ten years I went out with
several men — mostly people in ministry — though I did have
an intense affair with another community member. I was
almost forty when I met Laura, a student at the University
where I was chaplain. We were madly in love. I used to crawl
through her dormitory window to sleep with her, often
returning to the convent in the early morning — hoping no
one had missed me. Sometimes she would stay over in my
room; we'd prop the door closed with a chair since there
were no locks. We were wild: making love on the kitchen
floor, holding hands under the table during dinner with the
community. And we were sworn to secrecy — nobody knew
anything. It was intense for two years. Then the isolation
and constant fear of being discovered overwhelmed her.

Nancy: Yes, it's hard to maintain a relationship under
those conditions. So then?

Sister Anne: Then I met Marie. She came to a group
Laura and I were forming to explore alternative religious
communities. Little did we know. . . .

Nancy: Ah! So you created your own alternative community?

Sister Anne: Yes! And believe it or not, Laura now lives
with us! She and Marie are the best of friends. But it's been
a long process. When I was with Laura, I didn't consider
myself a Lesbian. In fact, when I met Marie I told her I

would love her even if she was a man. She didn't like that at all. Unlike Laura, she was strongly woman-identified and quite comfortable being a Lesbian. I remember when Marie met Laura she said, "So this was your lover." I denied it. Then I realized that she had in fact been my lover. I had had lovers, but was not into naming. In that way I didn't have to deal with what my actions meant politically or socially. All my relationships were highly secretive. They were like dreams rather than reality. It was irrational, but I didn't think I had made love. With Marie I have claimed my basic affinity with women — my Lesbian sexuality.

Nancy: How would you describe your life with Marie?

Sister Anne: Well, my other loves have been secondary to my work. My focus has shifted now, and my personal life with her is primary. We are committed to one another and envision spending our lives together. I'm still a little embarrassed about being sexual. It's hard to let go. I turn it into a play session, which at one time was great; but now it's a pattern, a way to avoid intimacy.

Nancy: We have years of being trained that celibacy is the higher way and that sex is gross.

Sister Anne: Yes. It takes too much time, gets me off the track, takes too much concentration, and it's kind of ridiculous. I don't have much of a sexual appetite. But I am a very sensual person. Tenderness and affection are an important part of our daily life together, and we do share a deep passion.

Nancy: How does Marie feel about you staying in the community?

Sister Anne: She wants me to leave. When I first started living with her I really thought I could stay in the community and carry this relationship on. But now it's apparent that I've got to go one way or another. We need to make some choices. It's not the fear of being exposed — we have a lot of friends who know that we're lovers; we're both out

at work, we have our own life. But there are emotional
and economic issues which keep us from taking the next
steps together. I'm not in any position, for instance, to
move or to buy a house. Technically, I can't own anything;
I can't even have a savings account. So it puts pressure on
the relationship: Marie has more freedom than I do, but
I have a sense of financial security as well as a deeper sense
of emotional security.

I've been a nun for twenty-six years. It's all I know.
I don't know how else to be in the world. I have emotional
ties: my sisters are very important to me. The thought of
leaving is so scary. But I think I'm pushing the limits in
terms of the community knowing about our relationship.
The structures just aren't there — maybe in fifteen years.
Maybe sooner. Marie had a visionary dream recently: The
sisters in leadership discover we are lovers. We are brought
into a room where they are all crying. They love us both,
and though they are upset, they sense that this is the direction the community has to go.

Nancy: Do you think there is a higher percentage of
Lesbians in religious communities than in the society at
large?

Sister Anne: Lesbians in spirit, yes. I believe most nuns
are asexual though. They can't conceive of having anything
but heterosexual relationships; yet they are more suited
for same-sex relationships. But they can't move to that
so they are asexual. Others are real mystics. One sister I
know is definitely a mystic. She gets so much out of the
mystical experience: she's approaching forty and is still
wholesome and happy.

Nancy: What do you see as the relationship between
your sexuality and your spirituality?

Sister Anne: My spirituality has changed over the years.
Institutionalized Christianity tends to separate the spirit

from the body. My experience with feminist spirituality and the Goddess has affirmed my intuition that spirit and body are inseparable. I can see that when I was sexual in the past I felt inhibited and degraded — not fully spiritual. Now my intimacy with Marie involves my whole spiritual/sexual self.

Sister Eileen Brady, 1983

LESBIAN NUN: ON THE BOUNDARY

Eileen Brady
(1969–present)

Many of the groups of women in which I find myself refer to the condition of being on the edge, the fringe, the boundary, as necessary, as life-giving, as rich in ideas. Naming oneself is important; taking on the identity of a name is devastating. How am I able to call myself a nun? Perhaps I am on the edge of being a nun. How am I able to identify myself as a Lesbian? Perhaps I am on the boundary of being a Lesbian.

"Nun" and "Lesbian" are the words that come the closest to describing who I am. However, "nun" is different when perceived by conservative Catholics, or Broadway playgoers, or liberal priests, or women who are my friends. "Lesbian" is different when perceived by psychologists, or moviegoers, or members of the women's community who could outdogmatize the Catholic Church, or women who are my friends.

I identify with Lesbian sensibility and sensuality; I love women. Intimacy and physical tenderness are important to me. But I'm not sure I would fit in the category if "Lesbian" means specific physical behavior, membership in political groups, or other signs of authenticity. I prefer to remain on the fringe of the women's and the Lesbian communities, wary of dress conformity, ritual, and doctrine that can change a community to an institution more concerned with common goal achievement than with personal freedom and development.

In the words of a song by Cathy Winter, "I'm not so sure I want to find just one soul to blend with mine, so I'm looking for some long-time friends." I have experienced the blending of many spirits as a member of the Sisters of Mercy. My friendships in the community are multi-leveled, diverse, and enduring. I love the women who have been with me and with each other through depressions, conflict with authority, firings, jail, prayer, celebrations, and growth in risk and seeking justice.

The Sisters of Mercy of New Hampshire, with whom I have lived for the past thirteen years, are contradictory. We say we are committed to struggle against unjust structures and systems that oppress people; yet we are aligned with the Roman Catholic Church. Is this being in the belly of the Beast or merely being closer to one of the many beasts in patriarchy than to another? I think that, instead of following a male model of the prophet who dies to redeem the structure, we are living on another level of being that is not entirely clear to us but that is preciously alive.

Yet, for all my idealism about the group, it is individual women who have been the basis of hope for me. I have fallen in love, in skin-tingling, soul-searching ways, over and over again. This experience is both mind-boggling and mind clearing. "How can this be?" is replaced by "How can this not be?" as the best question to ask.

There are a variety of responses to the fact that some members of the community identify as Lesbians. Some sisters are disgusted. Some are very happy. Most are silent. Some (including myself in the past) proclaim themselves to be very heterosexual. The groovy religious women of the seventies were involved in "meaningful relationships" with men, thinking it was worthwhile to break down the barriers of the cloister, habit, and rule, and to promote "humanness." I remember the relief I felt when there finally was a man who aroused warm feelings in me. What did that relief say about the deep warm feelings women caused in me up to this time?

Amid dwindling numbers and with seemingly infinite challenges, modern nuns find being called Lesbians or being linked with Lesbian issues as dangerous, as it has been for emerging feminists in every age, and energizing. The image of the nun has been of a woman who sacrifices true happiness (sex with a husband and personal completion in children) for an existence with a group of fearful, frigid females. Some of us are trying to change that stereotype. We want to express the great positive experience of being identified as Lesbians and as nuns. We are strong, caring, powerful women who live with — and love — other women. We share a common history and a constant search together.

I was born in 1947 in ultra-conservative, working-class Manchester, New Hampshire. After graduating with a B.A. in biology, I entered the New Hampshire Sisters of Mercy where I took part in an experimental formation program in which I chose my own graduate program of study, my work, and my living arrangements. I never wore a habit nor had restrictions on my movements.

I have taught in public and Catholic schools and have done parish work, adult religious education, political activism — including an arrest at Seabrook Nuclear Power Plant — and community organizing in a public housing project. For the past two years, I have held a variety of clerical jobs, including two years as typesetter for Persephone Press, a Lesbian-feminist press. For the past ten years, my connection with the institutional structures of Church, other than the Sisters of Mercy, has steadily declined. I live with another Sister of Mercy in an apartment in northern New Hampshire and am part of the movement within my community to bond with other women in and out of religious communities in shared justice concerns.

Section IX

CONVENT VALUES AND LESBIAN ETHICS

Although the patriarchal Roman Catholic Church created the structure of religious communities, the daily reality within convents was and is sisterhood. In our Lesbian/feminist communities we are trying to create elastic boundaries to encompass our developing sense of moral commitment to women. Whereas many of us upon leaving convents denied any value in our apparently repressed religious life, we are now learning to reclaim many convent values as codes of ethics for our Lesbian communities.

Ginny Apuzzo, 1984

GRACE TO EMPOWER

Virginia Apuzzo
(1966–1969)

When I told my father that I was entering the convent, he asked, "What for?" Being the oldest daughter and grandchild in my Italian working-class family both pulled me toward and held me back from the convent. My mother had already had a nervous breakdown. I knew I didn't want to get married, go insane, join the military, or go to jail. I needed time to figure out what to do with my life.

In Eastern cultures there's a period at the end of one's life for contemplation. I thought it was a shame to wait until then. Religious life would give me the opportunity to study and work productively. I could give the community the benefit of my expertise as an administrator, and from them take time to think. Where else could a woman in my day go to escape Con Edison and the A and P? In 1966

321

there was no gay movement or women's movement to identify with.

When I entered the convent at 26, I was a fully professional woman, Chair of the Social Studies Department of a school in upstate New York. I had a bachelor's degree in history and education with some graduate credits. I was fully aware of my homosexual identity when I joined the Sisters of Charity, and I stayed three years searching for answers to fundamental questions.

I thought of religious life as temporary. I didn't know whether it would take one year or twenty years to explore the morality of my homosexual identity. I wanted to know if being gay meant I was going to hell or if I could be a good person. The concept of sins of the flesh had imprisoned me my whole life, but I knew it had absolutely nothing to do with relationships. As I look back at my life, I realize that I've committed very few sins of the flesh. It seems to me now that sin is taking away the capacity of people to be who they are, of constraining us with irrelevant concerns like guilt. Yes, the institutional Church is guilty of the sin of holding people back from being.

When I was a postulant grappling with this whole business of sin and sexuality, one of the saddest incidents I remember was a middle-aged nun coming to my room and saying, "Sister, I tie my hands to the top of my bed at night for fear of committing a sin of impurity." I looked into that woman's face, and she looked like a fourteen year old in her innocence. It occurred to me that no sister I lived with was capable of committing a mortal sin of the flesh. They couldn't sin grievously through sexuality because they had never really embraced their sexuality.

One night a nun came to my bed and tried to crawl in with me. I stopped her and said, "Sister, you don't want to do that."

She said, "Oh, but I do."

I persisted, "No, you don't. You will not like yourself in the morning. It will hurt you tomorrow." That was the same nun who said that she tied her hands to the bed. If the pain that woman had around masturbation was as severe as I think it was, I never could have given in to her impulse. And I had no intention of violating my own vow of chastity. One day, the Mistress of Postulants, who is now the Mother General of the congregation, asked me what I thought about wearing pumps as part of the habit. "Don't you think that pumps speak to our getting in touch with our femininity?" she asked me.

I thought about the many times my mother had called me a tomboy and wanted me to wear different clothes to look like the little girl she wanted me to be. And I said to the Mistress of Postulants, "Sister, if I have to identify with shoe leather to get in touch with my femininity, then I'm in big trouble."

Even with all the confusion about sexuality, I was glad to be in the Church during those dynamic years when the Martha/Mary conflict seemed to fall aside for the sake of making a commitment to work for people who are oppressed. I want to use whatever talents and capacities I have for that work.

Being a nun was painful but productive. I couldn't be doing the work I do now for gay liberation without having learned to channel my energy. I call it grace. The speeches I write don't have grace. But every time I stand up in front of a group to speak, something comes over me reaching out over our distance toward what we can do together joyously. That is grace. It isn't God or Mary or even me. It's the power of the group to effect change.

Gay *pride* should not be gay *smug*. We must be committed to eliminating all oppression. I believe in empowering people — in letting them know how much power they have. Powerlessness is what is corrupt. When we demand that the system change — that homophobia and heterosexism be eliminated — we bring in fresh air. We open the windows — and breathe new life together.

This story is based on an interview in the office of Ginny Apuzzo, the Executive Director of the National Gay Task Force, in New York, June 1983, by Rosemary Curb.

Sr. Mary Mendola, 1968

Mary Mendola, 1980

LIFE-LONG LOVERS

Mary Mendola
(1967–1970)

I prefer "homophile" to "homosexual" when speaking about love relationships in religious life that can and do go on for twenty or thirty years — but in no way include a sexual dimension. That is not to say that I don't believe that love relationships including a sexual dimension do not exist in religious life. But what we are talking about here are homophile relationships within the context of a celibate commitment.

When I look back on my three years in Maryknoll, I remember several of these relationships among women ranging in age from forty well into their sixties. At the time, I was so out of touch with my own emotional life that I never could have identified them as homophile relationships. Now, years later, I can appreciate the richness and the love I saw expressed within some of these "particular friendships" of which religious communities are so afraid. The depth of these love relationships is what sustained many of these women as together they shared ten or fifteen years in the jungles of Africa or South America. They lived their religious lives together, some even retiring together and growing old together as life-long lovers. I would never assume anything sexual in these relationships. The whole orientation of these women was a traditional approach to celibacy. Funny, isn't it? But our sexually-oriented society might learn a lot about loving from just such homophile relationships.

I'm not advocating celibacy, nor can I make any value judgment concerning religious women who have sexually active lives. What I am saying is that we can't invalidate women who choose to live their religious lives committed to a "significant other" within the context of celibacy.

I find my sexual needs grow and change as I grow and change. What remain constant are my emotional needs — for sharing, closeness, and love. I am not celibate, but I do know that what I want is a particular friend and significant other standing next to me in the jungles of Manhattan. Maybe we get lost in our rigid definitions, forgetting that somewhere between celibacy and sexuality is a whole world of intimacy.

I live in Manhattan on the upper West Side. I enjoy a career in non-broadcast television as a video tape writer/ producer. I authored The Mendola Report: A Look at Gay Couples *published by Crown in 1980. I work with the gay press and have spoken on gay issues at conferences and on radio and television talk shows. At forty and greying, I'm happy to be where I am.*

This story is based on an interview with Nancy Manahan in November 1982.

Sr. Joanne Marrow, 1966

Joanne Marrow, 1980

NUN DREAMS: ALLEGORY OF
SPIRITUAL TRANSFORMATION

Joanne Marrow
(1964–1966)

I entered the convent to lead the "perfect life," to live among women, to avoid marriage, to go through medical school, to live adventurously as a missionary in Africa or Korea or South America, and to dedicate my life to the service of women and children. I lived in the Maryknoll cloistered novitiate in Valley Park, Missouri, for two and one-half years until my novice mistress told me it was God's will that I leave. I was twenty-one when I returned home to my family in Chicago on July 21, 1966.

While spirituality as defined by Roman Catholicism cripples the soul, the Church supplies a wealth of symbolism and ritual which can feed the intuitive mind. During my time as a Catholic and a cloistered nun, rituals and symbols

seeped deep into my psyche and defined a space in my unconscious which secular society leaves unfilled.

In 1974 I began recording dreams. In 1976 my dreams
began to use convent and nun symbology. Leaving the convent had been such a painful experience that it took ten
years for my unconscious mind to use these images to speak
to me. My convent dreams hold particular depth and power
for me because they represent a change from my naive
sense of spirituality fostered by patriarchal religion to my
present spirituality based on intuition and experience.

Dream One: February 15, 1976 (The Trial)

I am going to re-enter the convent. I am late. On the
way to the convent, I am waiting for an elevator to go
down. I am impatient because there are crowds. Finally,
I am pushed onto the elevator. As I leave the elevator, I
am confused. I am in a big city and can't figure out if I
should take a subway or a bus. I prefer the subway.

I am sitting at a dinner table with six postulants. The
meal, eaten in silence, is finished. The novice mistress and
the mother general approach me. One says, "Because you
were late, you must undergo a special trial."

A being who could be male or female (Mercury, perhaps?) drives me and another postulant to a park. He turns
to me and says, "You are to be a whore." This is the last
thing I expect. But there is no mistake. I see that I am
wearing a whore's costume.

It is night. My companion and I get out of the car, but
she doesn't act like a whore. She merely accompanies me.
We walk along. I am trying to decide how I can go through
with this. We meet a teacher and his sexuality class. I walk
up to him, squeeze his cheek hard and say, "Hey, big boy,
wanna fuck?" He is startled, and the incident creates quite

a scene in front of his class. We walk on. I turn to my companion and ask her if I was whore-like enough. Still, I don't fuck anyone.

We return to the convent to find out if I have passed the trial. We find the mother general. She won't give us an answer. Instead, she opens a door and begins speaking to the many tropical birds in the room. My mother appears at my side and says, "Let's go in." The four of us enter the room. Mother General shows the birds to my mother. I have the feeling that this was my room before remodeling. It is much nicer now than when I occupied it. I say, "Oh, you turned it into a bird room." It is a nice idea, but the birds shit all over. They are flying freely and the floor is a mess. I don't like this. All the time they are chitchatting about birds, I am waiting to see whether I have passed the trial. I never get my answer. I wake.

Dream 2: April 18, 1976 (Convent on the Move)

I return to the convent. The postulant mistress Sister Anne gives me a professed sister's black veil. I think it is a trial because I know that, as a postulant, I am not supposed to wear a black veil. I am looking through her drawer filled with rubber snakes, snake skeletons, and snakes in formaldehyde.

The convent is now located on a busy intersection with building construction going on. Skyscrapers. A man, shouting, directs the moving of a big scaffolding several stories high. Sister Anne gives me wine to drink, and I am getting high. A man says something about decanting wine when it gets turbid. My glass is turbid, and I want to dump it. Sister Anne is already asking me to try a new orange wine. A bald yogi comes up to say goodbye. He touches my hand and blesses me.

Dream 3: August 5, 1977 (The Pink Belt)

I re-enter the convent. I am given the black postulant's outfit, but I have no belt. I am late for chapel. Finally, I put on a pink belt which I brought with me. It is better than nothing. A friendly postulant smiles and joins me walking into chapel. The novice mistress gasps on seeing me, as if to say, "Oh, no, I have to deal with you again." I realize that I am dreaming. I go up to her and whisper, "You won't have to deal with me for long. I only need three days to get the information I need." I am aware that I am here to find out the true meaning of my convent experience. I go to bed in the dorm but can't stand being here in the convent again. I am rolling side to side in my sleep, and this movement wakes me up.

Dream 4: March 22, 1980 (Perfectly Ridiculous)

I am a nun again. But I wish I weren't, since I like sex. I am told that I am only a weekend nun, so I relax. I can handle a weekend. We are wearing black. Because I am wearing purple shoes, a nun tells me, "You are perfectly ridiculous." I start laughing and jumping: "I am PERFECT! I am PERFECTLY RIDICULOUS!" celebrating the cosmic dance of it all.

Dream 5: May 24, 1980 (Leave the Convent to Sell the House)

I am a nun living in Chicago, where I lived for twenty-two years with my family. I realize that my parents won't sell the house because I am living here. I decide to leave the convent so they can sell the house.

Dream 6: October 24, 1980 (I Must Leave the Convent)

I am a novice, washing the floor of my space in the dorm.

I am conscious of the need to be very quiet because the other sisters are sleeping. I think, "I must leave." But I want to stay until the winter is over. I believe my options will be better in the spring. I dread returning to Chicago and looking for a job in the bitter cold. I realize that I can go to Florida. "No," I think, "I have already lived in Florida. I received my Ph.D. from Florida State University. What I need to do is find a psychologist to work with so I can get my license." Then I realize who I am now.

Dream 7: November 17, 1980 (Left with only a Veil)

I am at home in my parents' apartment where I was raised. I am trying to fix my snotty-looking veil. The rest of my habit has worn away so that I am wearing regular clothes. "I've got to stop being a nun," I think. "This is like being in school!" I am quite involved in the details of the pins, cap, elastic, frame, and the veil, trying to assemble it so worn spots don't show. I wake up thinking how odd it is that I remember the details of the veil so vividly.

Dream 8: November 28, 1980 (Trying to Leave)

I am in the convent, trying to save enough money to leave. I am going over to the professed sisters' territory through complex passageways I've never seen before to try to make a secret phone call.

Dream 9: February 16, 1981 (Lost My Clothes)

I am a nun, and I know I am dreaming. I must get this act together because I want to use this dream information when I wake. I am walking around the dorm in my black housecoat looking for my clothes. Everyone else is at a meeting. I can't go without my clothes. I must remain calm. Sister Anne says she will help me put my veil together.

I am surprised that all the pieces of the veil are grey instead of white. But I feel very relieved by Sister's help.

Dream 10:   December   15,   1981   (Think   Your   Own Thoughts!)

I am a professed nun about to go through the ceremony of being assigned to my first mission. This is a grand leave-taking from the motherhouse. I am kneeling in front of a door. The door opens on a hallway. The hallway is full of flowers. There are priests coming and going. They kid a young priest about going out and getting laid. I am disgusted with their hypocrisy. I know I must eventually go out the door. I don't want to meditate on Christ. I decide that virtues are good topics for meditation. I meditate on faith, hope and charity.

Some nuns present me a card with a riddle: 3 2 _ / 2 3 _ _. I solve the riddle easily. The solution is 3 2 1 /2 3 2 1. I decide I must leave and begin thinking my own thoughts.

Interpretations and Conclusions:

Several patterns emerge in this series of dreams. My personal power grows from postulant, to novice, to professed sister, and finally to freely taking my leave. This progression shows not only an increase in power, but also a change from the restrictions of the patriarchal spirituality to my own feminist perception of self as a spiritual being in the material world.

In the first dreams I feel trapped, confused, and anxious. In my first dream as a postulant, for example, I take a step toward spiritual transformation. By going down the elevator and taking the subway I go deeply into my psyche and travel into the underground of awareness. Forces beyond me push my consciousness into the elevator to be "elevated." Both novice mistress and mother general, matriarchs of the novitiate, representing a higher spiritual authority in my psyche, set up my karma. A messenger from the gods drives me to my trial, which occurs at night because I am "in the dark" about its meaning. My present sexuality is "tried" by the male teacher, a colleague in waking life who pursued me sexually and then became a formidable enemy when I rejected his advances. Although perceived by him as a "whore" or sexually available, I am not. The redecorated room at the convent is my spirituality renewed. Whereas the mother general represents convent spirituality, my actual mother signifies my intuitive elements. The birdshit means that freeing awareness is not clean and clear cut, but a messy process.

In my second dream my postulant mistress, toward whom I felt close, represents my self as an evolved spiritual woman. The drawer of snakes signifies that I already possess the secrets of higher consciousness: kundalini energy is symbolized as snakes. With the spiritual wine, elixir of the gods, I experience reaching a higher plane. The busy intersection and the skyscraper construction indicate that I am integrating materials into a psychic web that reaches to the heavens. The scaffolding indicates that I am still using part of my old convent spiritual structure in my evolution. It will be dismantled and discarded when my new structure is complete. The turbid wine of patriarchal religion has gone sour and must be dumped. The farewell of the yogi is the recognition by the masculine force that he has nothing left to teach me. I am now the builder and teacher.

In several dreams, as in waking life during this period, I see that I am perceived as strange, alien, or difficult. I am misunderstood and alone. In the third dream my pink belt of passionate love stands out against my black dress and brands me the nonconformist among other postulants. But my three days' return to convent burial, after which I move into the symbolic resurrection of waking reality, integrates my consciousness. Eastern philosophies emphasize that we are all dreaming when we think we are pursuing our waking life, and that achieving awareness involves "waking up" from our chronic sleepwalking state. From a dream that I am sleeping, I wake into reality. I open my eyes with a great sense of accomplishment and power.

My fourth dream informs me that sexual expression is compatible with my spiritual life but that I am also comfortable with periods of celibacy. My "under-standing" (shoes) is expressed as the color purple, a color of spiritual transformation. Knowing that I am PERFECT brings me elation and joy.

I progress to making a rational and confident choice to leave the convent. This is a major step in resolving the psychic disintegration experienced on being expelled from the novitiate. In the fifth and seventh dreams I recognize which parts of my moral conscience are inherited from my parents and which are remnants (the worn veil) of convent spirituality. I create the circumstances of my evolution rather than requiring others to force me to leave, as actually happened. As I shift from the victim role towards being a conscious actor, my personal sense of power grows within convent confines.

In the sixth dream I choose the optimum time to leave. I decide to stay through winter in order to hibernate and gather myself. The dream integrates my need to leave the convent with my present concern about getting my license to practice psychology and yields a transcendent realization of who I am now.

In my eighth dream I take my fate into my own hands and save money, my spiritual legacy from the convent, to make the transition more comfortable. The phone call is secret because I must guard my inmost self and continue discovering the complex passageways of my unconscious mind. I think of careers and make decisions about where to go next.

Finally, I go through the process of leaving the patriarchal spiritual structure and I create an original feminist spirituality. Leaving the cloister to work in the world is a joyous event: the doorway is open and the path welcomes me with flowers. I reject the hypocrisy of the priests and patriarchal spirituality. In choosing to meditate on virtues which transcend all religions rather than male images, I am leaving behind guilt, rules of lifestyle, sexual restrictions and helplessness. Solving the riddle represents my logical analysis of the past. I am thinking my own thoughts and developing a lifestyle based on my own morality, valor and power.

I am a professor of psychology at California State University, Sacramento, with a private practice as a clinical psychologist. I live quietly with my lover, three dogs, three cats, and two parakeets. With the help of amazons, I am building a house in the remote Sierra Nevadas as a spiritual retreat.

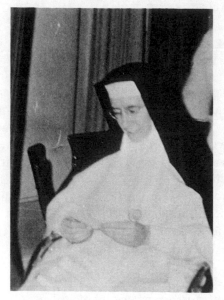

Sr. Mary Teresa, 1957

Hannah Blue Heron, 1981

MYSTICISM: LOVE OR SUFFERING?

Hannah Blue Heron
(1950-1967)

When I was a child, Christian Science Churches were very ascetic. They were built like Greek temples. At the front was a simple lectern large enough for the reader of the Bible and the reader of *Science and Health* by Mary Baker Eddy. The American flag and that of the Church flanked each side, along with tall baskets of cut flowers. Against the wall were chairs; simply painted in gold was the message: GOD IS LOVE. That was all. I knew these words long before I went to school and learned to read.

In Sunday school we were taught at a very young age that God was omniscient, omnipotent and omnipresent. Along with the message of love, the last of these attributes captured my imagination and filled my spirit. I remember lying stomach down across the board of the swing in our yard, swinging and singing, "God is love, God is everywhere. No matter how high I swing, He's already there." I would kick harder and go higher, feeling His loving presence rush through me. Then I would let the "cat die down" slowly, slowly until I was motionless, still euphoric and lost in the presence of His love.

At nineteen when I converted to Catholicism, I rediscovered the pervasive presence of light and love in a delightfully concrete way in Holy Communion. There were to be mystical moments of feeling my essence immersed in love, closely united to each person kneeling by me, and then feeling this love expanding to include everyone in the world, the entire universe.

As a nun, I joyously consecrated my life to this presence each morning as I renewed my vows. Once a week I also had to face the omniscient judge of the confessional, but I did not let this detract from the more joyful, and more real for me, message of the new life of the Resurrection, germinated in me at Baptism, and growing and developing in me each day of my life.

A person seeking the spiritual path in the Church is warned *ad nauseum* about thinking of herself as holy because of the euphoria she sometimes feels during meditation or at Communion. She is put down as being like a child needing a piece of candy to encourage her along the narrow way. She receives this warning even as a postulant, as if they were afraid she might enjoy a bit of ecstasy she doesn't deserve. According to them no one can be a mystic or a saint without much suffering first.

Over the years I developed my own opinion about these euphoric experiences. First of all, in the inmost depths of my soul, I knew they were similar to the euphoria I had experienced in my love-making with my first lover, the woman who had led me into the Catholic Church. Second, I knew these experiences had opened my spirit to a capacity for loving and being loved that I wouldn't have had otherwise. Finally, if euphoria was not holiness, for me it was an effective way to feel close to my Groom, Jesus, and to receive the energy to labor long hours for Him. It did not eliminate suffering from my life, if suffering was, indeed, the secret to sanctity. So, emulating St. Teresa's practical turn of mind, I began again to meditate in such a way as to feel the euphoric joy I had experienced as a child and would treasure as an adult.

I left the Religious of the Good Shepherd in 1967 to begin the tasks of recognizing my Lesbianism and integrating it into my life. I now live in southern Oregon. I am composing a musical fantasy From the Other Side of Madness *and working on an autobiography,* Self Portraits in the Nude. *My story is an excerpt from* That Strange Intimacy, *1983.*

Sr. Mary Theresa, 1970

Joyce, 1983

NO CIRCLE OF WOMAN ARMS
UNDER MOONLIGHT

Joyce
(1967-1972)

A mesh of threads intertwined, weaving and spinning here and there bring me to this point in time. In 1966 I converted to Catholicism and approached religous life a year and a half later attempting to weave my newspun sense of spirituality and life purpose into an orthodox religious frame of reference. Now as a dyke and a witch, I question whether entering the Franciscan novitiate years ago was a misguided detour or a necessary personal passage in my growing spiritual consciousness.

Putting on religious garb marked a transition between patriarchal controlled living and my vision of gynecentric reality. In *The Church and the Second Sex* Mary Daly says, "The nun has always been the image of the old and of the new woman . . . involved in the drama of transition from the era which is ending to the new age." Religious life began my rite of passage from the old to the new woman.

Catholic women are offered no choice but subservience to a male principle: become one man's property in marriage or become a Bride of Christ. Being the sacrificial virgin bride of Christ denied both physical and spiritual be-ing. The ultimate goal was union with the heavenly Other, a sort of holy bondage. My embryonic woman-consciousness recoiled at this option, just as I recoiled from physical union in marriage. How could bondage bring spiritual liberation and growth?

When I entered the convent, religious communities were in the throes of renewal. While nuns were attempting to change their image, lifestyle, and relationships in a radical transformation born of willingness to look squarely at contradictions and confusions, the hierarchy was digging its heels into the security of the old ways.

Toward the end of my four and a half years in the Franciscans, I allied myself with a small group of "radicals." The term seems mildly misplaced now. They were the first to reclaim their woman-names, the ones who called each other friend as well as sister, the ones who hesitantly questioned the tyranny of the Church. Excitedly, expectantly, a barely twenty-one year old naive "little sis," I became one of the group of radicals. Perhaps it was my naivete that allowed me to reach for answers to questions that our superiors did not allow to be asked.

In our struggle I came to a new valuing of myself, my sisters, and the potentially creative force of woman-relatedness. I became an emotional Lesbian without knowing it, slipping into it as easily as one slips into a well-tailored outfit. I was in love with life and my new discovery of sisterhood. I created rituals to celebrate new visions. Of course

I ran headlong into the restraints of the religious system which attempted to separate me from my woman-named sisters and from myself.

Change must be slow and grounded, they said. New discoveries must be sanctioned and fitted back into traditional (male) values. Love between sisters, they warned, will always be called particular friendship and shameful. Self-expression must be disciplined and directed toward the male principle, the Christ and mankind, to avoid sin. There will be no stirrings of the spirit not recognized by the Church, no joyous dance, no circle of arms under the moonlight. That smacks of pagan ritual!

Years later I look back and see their fears. Wandering through fields of change, we radicals had reached a frontier: a strange place with boundaries unclear. The new place was powerful because it sprang from the roots of women's creative energies: mysterious, frightening, buried, and denied release for so long. Those of us who crossed the frontier were labelled unsuited for religious life and eventually divorced from the ranks of the Brides of Christ. But our transformed spirits could now learn to dance and soar in rhythm with the energy which casts off bondage and is forever recreating itself in time and space.

I was born an Aquarian in 1948 in Louisiana. I converted to Catholicism in 1966 and spent four years as a Franciscan nun. I discovered matriarchal spirituality in 1980. I received a Ph.D. in psychology from Florida State University. By occupation I am a psychologist.

CONVENT VALUES AND LESBIAN ETHICS

Conversation with Janice Raymond and Patricia Hynes
(1960–1972 and 1965–1970)

(In October 1983, Rosemary Curb interviewed Pat and Jan in the home they designed and built in Montague, Massachusetts. Jan, whose published work includes *The Transsexual Empire*, is writing a book on female friendship and teaching women's studies at the University of Massachusetts in Amherst. Pat, who founded "Bread and Roses" Restaurant in 1974 in Cambridge, is an environmental engineer who oversees the clean-up of hazardous waste sites for the Environmental Protection Agency.)

Rosemary: Many of our Lesbian friends who didn't enter religious life imagine that being in the convent was a negative experience. If we think in terms of the Church's power over us, then, of course, it was repressive; but somehow that autonomous community of women eluded direct male domination. What about the positive aspects of having been in the convent?

Pat: Whenever Jan and I have talked about our feelings towards nuns when we were growing up, a number of women have said that they had terrible experiences. They found nuns dry, uncaring, and unloving. I'm surprised because I had an incredibly positive experience with nuns as a child. That's why I became one. It was the attraction to grown women who were differnt from the other adult women I saw around me. Single professional women whom I knew lacked the friendship and sense of family with other women that nuns had. And so, not only did I like particular nuns who taught me in grade school, but I loved — and Jan has said this too — being around the convent, seeing the nuns interacting. I felt their excitement with each other and saw everything in their lives fitting together. In the convent everyone had a job — unlike my house where the girls did the housework and the boys were allowed to go free. I saw equal division of work. There were no roles or privileges like my father and brothers had in my house.

Rosemary: You were saying earlier that the experience of living in a community of sisters was so wonderful that you've been trying to recapture it ever since.

Pat: Yes, I think that for a lot of us former nuns, some of the best experiences of our lives were in the novitiate. By the time we were novices, we had adjusted to the regulatory aspects of convent life. We lived with women who shared the same attraction to other women, a common spirit of idealism, and a tremendous amount of good will, high expectations, and erotic energy. Those years remain some of the happiest and brightest that I look back on.

Jan: I came from a family of boys, and it was the experience of sisterhood that initially attracted me to convent living. I went to a girls' high school, but the experience of friendship was very different in the convent.

Pat: I became active in the women's movement soon after I left the convent. Nine years ago when I started "Bread and Roses," a women's restaurant and cultural center, I was trying to re-create the sense of community I had experienced in the novitiate. The spirit of "Bread and Roses" was similar to that of the novitiate. There was a lot of work to do, and it was evenly shared among women. It was a time of high idealism in feminism — of a deeply felt attraction to creating a community. Those were the things I loved best and remembered most deeply about the convent.

Today I carry a sobered and more mature desire for a community of women, never expecting to live again in the sort of physical community that I once had. I try to re-capture that sense of women FOR each other, women as primary, something that goes out beyond one's circle of personal friends, as it did with a religious community. Even with women I didn't know, I sensed our common ideals and common life. I dedicated myself to something larger than all of us. Feminism seemed to promise those things, and I continually hope they will happen. But I have become aware that they will happen only if we create them. Originally my expectation was that feminism would generate sisterhood. I would be part of it, but it would happen because it seemed so inevitable. At this point, I feel much more responsible for making it happen myself.

Rosemary: Working on this book, I've remembered that loving convent community that feminism seems to promise but has never been able to deliver. Does it have anything to do with the dogmatism underpinning religious life?

Jan: I think the realization of convent community had a lot to do with a certain sense of basic boundaries and agreed-upon rules that helped to encourage respect and caring. The failure of convent community, for many women, was a result of these boundaries and rules becoming too restrictive and dogmatic.

Pat: The convent offered the structure of community. You didn't have to create that, nor did you have to sustain it. The community was financially established. Education was guaranteed, at least in my community. You had a job. You had a place to be buried. You had older women who were mentors. You did not have to invent everything as you went along. With feminism, none of the structure is there. Many early feminist institutions, women's centers, and businesses were short-lived because there were no guiding principles of organization. Disagreements often escalated into divisiveness that undid many early attempts to create feminist institutions.

Jan: Disagreement existed in convents, but divisiveness was restricted by the structure we've been talking about.

Rosemary: The agreed-upon ground rules in religious life made it a lot easier for community to exist. What about our deepest common experiences from the convent? Why did we enter? What did we find there that was so wonderful? How does that shared bond still exist in our lives today as Lesbians not living in a physical community and yet who have a sense of extended community — the international Lesbian community and the local community, for example, here in your valley?

Jan: What seemed to be excessive regulation at the same time fostered thoughtful means of communication. We did manual work in silence, but a lot of communication went on. I remember being in a laundry with women and exchanging deep significant looks. I knew what those looks meant. It really uplifted my day. Sometimes it meant the day.

Pat: I remember women inventing ingenious ways of communicating. Jan and I have talked about missing a certain thoughtfulness among feminists. In the convent,

I had a trunkful of thoughtful gifts, the most tender letters and poems. And it was not just the function of being young and in love. It does seem that, under what could be considered very difficult and frustrating conditions, we developed more diverse ways of being aware of one another.

Jan: I was thinking about why the prohibition against particular friendship somehow never seemed to work. The friendship always survived. I remember the standard lectures given by our novice mistress. Although she never uttered the word "Lesbian," she once said "homosexual." She said that women our age would normally be forming relationships with men, and that we should be careful about intimacy with each other because that wasn't normal. At the same time that we were receiving lectures against particular friendships, however, we were encouraged to form spiritual friendships. So we could always rationalize that a particular friendship was actually spiritual because it was invested with more than erotic feelings. Also, there was a third party present — God.

Pat: We did introduce a sense of transcendence into a relationship. There was something holy, something sacred about it. I was always wanting to push a particular friendship over into the spiritual realm so that it wouldn't be wrong and so that I wouldn't be overcome with passion.

Jan: The negative part of particular friendship was the need to justify it. The positive part was that it had a dimension of importance beyond itself.

Pat: I went to a Catholic women's college. Although we slept in rooms together, there were unspoken prohibitions against Lesbianism. While the friendships were very warm and caring, there was no comparison between those and the ones I had in the convent. I had much deeper feelings even for women I was not attracted to. The depth of feeling that women freely gave to one another in the convent created a unique world.

Jan: One of the unfortunate things that happened when I left the convent was that I lost contact with many of the women with whom I'd had intense friendships. Most of them left the convent before I did, and one by one they went straight. Almost as soon as they got out they became immersed in the heterosexual dating scene and eventually got married and are still married. Given the fact that relationships with women were primary in the convent but not the norm in the world, I suppose they were trying to normalize themselves. Maybe they looked back upon their intimate convent relationships as an adolsecent stage they had to go through.

Rosemary: What years were you in the convent?

Jan: I was in for twelve years — from 1960 to 1972.

Rosemary: You entered right out of high school?

Jan: Yes.

Rosemary: And, Pat, you entered after graduating from college?

Pat: Well, I was in twice. I entered after high school and then again after college for five years from 1965 to 1970. I think that Jan's transition from the women's world of the convent to a woman-identified feminist world was fairly smooth in contrast to many women's.

Jan: I was in both worlds for an overlap of three years.

Pat: Some women like myself left sooner than Jan and didn't have the proximity to feminist and Lesbian thinking, which places like graduate school provided. I stepped from a woman-centered existence into "the world," as we called it, as if the convent were not part of the world. I had no support for continuing intense relationships with women. I remember feeling a tremendous loneliness for the community of women I had wanted to get out of. I felt that no one would understand if I kept up those relationships. Looking back, I realize that I was always a Lesbian, at least since high school. I'd had long-term committed involvements with women for years at a time through my high school and college years and then through my convent years. My first experiences with men were after I left. I was intensely curious about sexuality and why it was so prohibited. When I found that I really could not stand one relationship with one man, I had many — I mean dozens. I tried all kinds and types from many races and continents, old, young, agnostics, priests, married men. Looking back I realize I needed twelve or fifteen men to equal one woman. I understand better than Jan what pushed ex-nuns into going into bars and dating and getting married quickly. The only thing normative was heterosexuality. Frantically we tried to erase our convent experience and to ease the strangeness of the world.

Jan: Rosemary, did you say you were married?

Rosemary: Yes, I was one of those who got married within a year of leaving. Although I'd had a sexual relationship with an older sister during my last two years in the convent, it never occurred to me that I could have relationships with women outside of religious life. The passion I'd felt for the woman I left behind, who said she was too old to leave, was nothing like the controlled warmth I felt for the man I married. I told myself that the feelings were different because she had been my first lover and the convent magnified everything.

Pat: Maybe even rarefied everything.

Rosemary: Right, and normal people get married, and . . .

Jan: You gotta grow up.

Rosemary: Exactly.

Pat: Were you conscious of feeling embarrassed in front of the world after you left the convent about the intensity of feeling you had for another woman in the convent?

Many women may even erase the memory of it in themselves; they deny, ignore, and forget it. Did you find yourself doing that?

Rosemary: Oh yes, I erased the convent years. I didn't want anybody to know I was an ex-nun. I felt extremely awkward about my clothes, hair, movements, gestures. I feared that every social blunder I committed betrayed my past. I entered the convent right out of high school. When I left at twenty-five, I considered myself socially retarded because I still had the mannerisms and expectations of a high school girl. The angelic naivete of a nun was also somewhat less than charming for a woman in the politically charged mid-sixties.

Jan: I entered the convent young and stayed twelve years, although during the last five years I wasn't living in community. In graduate school in the late sixties, I was in the midst of campus activism. Feminism was just starting. I was in a Protestant theological school in Boston with women who were beginning to think about the combination of feminism and religion. Many of these women studying for ordination in Protestant denominations were not interested in institutional religion but in this thing we call spirituality. Some were leaving because their feminist consciousness forced them to see how patriarchal religious identification fragmented feminist spirituality. These friendships enabled me to keep my woman-identification and my sense of spirituality (but radically defined). It was exciting to move forward with women who cared about spiritual issues.

Rosemary: How soon did you leave the Church after you left the convent?

Jan: I left the Church before I left the convent. The difficulty was not leaving the Church but the community of women. I felt that I shouldn't leave my friends behind because our bonds were so strong.

Pat: You also wanted to bring them forward with you.
Jan: They wouldn't come. Some of them are still there.
Pat: When I first left in 1970, I was bitter and disappointed. I felt that a dream was broken because that institution was so unbending, so unable to make room for women who wanted to grow. I was heart-broken at leaving women I had wanted to live with for the rest of my life, and angry at the ones who had the power to change the life but wouldn't. Walking back into the world, I was suddenly embarrassed at how parochial I looked and felt. I remembered my community as a group of naive women remote from the world and unsophisticated. I noticed nuns in habits on the street and thought they looked silly, and yet I remembered looking like that and thinking well of myself.

As I moved into feminism and acknowledged my Lesbianism, I began to recapture the convent passion and sense of community with women. Recently I have taken another look at the institution and the women. Last summer I went back to the place where I had been in the novitiate to look up some women I knew. Some of them have moved up in the ladder of authority from mistress of postulants or novices to treasurer and mother general. A woman who had taught me physics in college is now seventy and still teaching fulltime. She runs a planetarium. After spending hours talking with several of them, I departed impressed by these older women who are now running institutions of thousands of women, handling the finances, making decisions about restructuring and reorganizing. They were deeply attracted to the world I move in and asked me direct questions about Lesbianism and feminism. They were curious about the spiritual potential of feminism. I left feeling that they grasped the continuum on which I moved, that they did not see my current life as a radical departure from either the self that they had known or the spirituality that they had seen in me. I felt a sense of integrity with my past. I was happy that they did not see Lesbian feminism as incongruous with religious life in the way my family and many Catholics do. I came away with an understanding of why I had become a nun.

Rosemary: What in your life takes the place of prayer and meditation or the sense of mystical transcendence?

Jan: Feminism itself has taken that place. I don't need a defined period of prayer or meditation anymore. I think the convent really helped to sprinkle that spiritual dimension throughout my activities. That was, after all, defined as the classic habit of prayer. I would not define it that way anymore. I would name it the habit of reflection. I find myself reflecting while I'm teaching or even when looking into somebody's eyes. I've heard women say that they feel a necessity for boundary times with a special liturgy. I don't have that need, but there are dimensions of my life that are very celebratory.

Rosemary: How do you celebrate?

Jan: All sorts of ways. When I've had a terrific class, I linger with my students afterwards and just talk about ideas. Dinner with friends. Feeling alive in very special ways.

Rosemary: Is it a consciousness of yourself existing outside of space and time?

Jan: It's defined by the women around me.

Rosemary: So there's a communal quality to it?

Jan: We have a lot of friends whom we celebrate certain days with, such as solstices or birthdays.

Rosemary: Do you celebrate solstices with any rituals?

Jan: No, we don't. We just get together and have a party.

Pat: Sometimes we use the telescope to look at the stars. At solstice I like to be aware of exactly what is happening in nature, what the solstice is about. What about your sense of the spiritual — for want of a better word?

Rosemary: I think of my spirituality as grounded in the

earth — quite a contrast from the mortification of the flesh I practiced in the convent. I don't go around hugging trees very often, but I do feel that impulse. I've never been initiated into a coven, but I like to call myself a witch because the word carries such patriarchal taboo, and I feel a solidarity with the women who were burned as witches. I've participated in ritual circles celebrating solstices, equinoxes, and full moons at the Pagoda on Vilano Beach north of St. Augustine, my Lesbian separatist spiritual home. Morgana, who started Pagoda in 1977 and who is a close friend, has conducted those rituals and taught me most of what I know of the daily practice of the craft. I've also joined circles led by Starhawk and Z. Budapest, and I've studied their books in designing rituals which I've conducted in my back yard, in my living room, and on the Rollins campus. Leading a ritual circle with women who have never practiced any pagan ceremony gives me a chance to preach my spirituality and practice consciousness raising. I hope every woman who joins my circle emerges joyful and empowered, feeling the life force which connects her to the earth. Even when we raise a cone of power and feel our collective energies spiralling upward, I want us to feel very earthy. Maybe spirituality isn't the right word.

Jan: I still like "religious." In its etymology, there are many meanings, but one of the best is "to tie together." I feel that's what has happened in my own life with feminist spirituality. It has tied a lot of dimensions together.

Rosemary: Aren't you amazed at how many leaders of the Lesbian/feminist movement are former nuns? Do you think convent training gave us daily habits of focus to banish dissipation and distraction with (alas!) a tendency toward obsessive perfectionism? I'm still obsessed with not wasting a minute, and I'm never satisfied that I've done enough. What has stuck with you?

Pat: A few things I've taken with me from the convent

are not bad qualities but were misused or masochistic there. Take chapter of faults. In the convent it was absurd, but I'm now able to name my mistakes, to say when I've done something wrong. I have the ability to apologize or acknowledge that I was wrong and to be clear about it and not feel guilty. I value that in myself.

Jan: I learned much about what Alice Walker has called "the rigors of discretion." For example, people have often said to me, "How did you know she was a shithead right from the beginning?" I really don't know how I knew except that I formed a habit of discretion because there was so much time to cultivate it, and it was so stringently encouraged within the self. We developed an ability to discern who was a friend and who was not. Some feminists call that psychic. I think it is a habit of discernment. I don't mean that I'm always right or that I always recognize the wheat from the chaff; but more often than not, my sense of discernment is accurate.

Pat: A sense of responsibility for carrying your own weight was also inculcated in the convent. If you ate, you were expected to clean up after yourself and to help with preparing dinner. Sharing household tasks is equitable between Jan and me. It wasn't hard to get there. We had no crisis in friendship over responsibilities. Neither of us felt that we were carrying more than the other. I feel grateful for those years of exercising some of my best abilities. I have a capacity for friendship. As with any talent, the more you exercise it, the better you become at it. I look back on those years as five of the best in my life in terms of friendship.

Jan: When I was reading Lillian Faderman's *Surpassing the Love of Men,* I noticed that the reasons romantic friends were attracted to each other also existed in convent friendships. We had a companionship of equals. We were involved in something larger than ourselves.

Pat: Many structures, while rigid, showed some wisdom that I think Lesbian feminists could benefit from. While we lived communally, a sense of privacy was encouraged and enforced. At night when you went to your room, although, granted, you might have liked someone else there, it was good to be able to close your curtains or your door and be in your own space. You were not interrupted.

Rosemary: The rule of silence is what I miss most.

Pat: Without it you wouldn't have had time to think, to study, to pull yourself together. In addition, although there was a sense that everyone in your class was equal and treated the same, as women got older and put in their time, they were relieved of a certain amount of work, which always fell to the younger sisters who had put in less time. Through work, you gradually earned your way to be able to relax. Sometimes in feminism I feel that we can never earn this recognition. Everyone is supposed to be equal forever. Can't we graduate into being mentors to younger women? The levelling that happens in the name of sisterhood or abolishing hierarchy doesn't allow women who deserve respect or recognition to get it.

Jan: I often feel that many of my students are reticent to express individuality. In the name of some kind of amorphous feminist equality, nobody is supposed to stand out.

Pat: In the convent a subtle alternative to that levelling developed. In the same community of sisters, you were able to earn a certain status without being hierarchical.

Jan: One good thing in my community, especially in the novitiate, was the combination of handwork and headwork. I don't just mean doing menial labor of a domestic female sort. We learned tasks such as carpentry, tasks that women of that age ordinarily would not have been doing. Mao's prescription for a good citizen was anticipated in some communities. I can remember having intense daily periods of study and intense periods of manual labor in the same day. The sudden switch was hard, but in the long run it was a nice combination. I learned how to pick up a hammer and perform structural tasks that I probably never would have learned otherwise. There was a lot of wisdom in that.

Pat: It amazes me that I don't remember much jealousy although there were lots of grounds for it because of other women's accomplishments. All of us who were close in my group were proud of each other's accomplishments. There was room for many women to become accomplished, and not at the expense of anyone else. While each of us had our particular friends, we also had erotic or close-to-erotic feelings for many others.

Rosemary: In our quest for Lesbian/feminist ethics, how can we moderate our fervor for political correctness? How can we resist old tendencies toward rigid orthodoxy and celebrate our multicultural diversity? How can we establish values and avoid dogmatism?

Jan: We want to be able to define values and say what shape these values should take without being intolerant or dogmatic.

Pat: And yet we feel a sense of rightness about certain values. We want to set standards that aren't relative and at the same time avoid rigidity. We need elastic boundaries to hold on to, boundaries that can expand.

GLOSSARY

abbey: building or rectangular cluster of buildings joined by covered walks, called cloisters, surrounding an enclosed garden, where a monastic community lives.

apostolate: the office, mission, occupation, or special spiritual project of a religious sister.

asceticism: the practice of rigorous self-discipline and self-denial in order to reach a higher spiritual state.

aspirancy: pre-convent training period for high school girls before entering the postulancy or novitiate.

assembly: meeting held annually by most religious communities to discuss matters pertaining to community life.

band, band members: group of women who enter a community and go through religious formation at the same time.

beatitudes: virtues, such as meekness and peacemaking, celebrated in the gospel Sermon on the Mount by Jesus (Matt. 5:3–12; Luke 6:20–26).

blind obedience: performing without question whatever a superior commands, considered a perfection of the vow or virtue by religious.

canon law (code of): norms or rules used to govern the Catholic Church as an institution, violations of which merit censure or excommunication.

catechism: a book of questions and answers about Roman Catholic theology for children to memorize and recite.

celibate, celibacy: solemn vow taken by priests, variously interpreted as a promise made to God and sanctioned by the Church either never to marry or to avoid all sexual activity.

cell: monastic name for the private room or sleeping place of a nun or monk.

Chapter of Faults: official community meeting for individual sisters to make public confession of violations of the Rule and Constitutions (not sins), to mention faults omitted by others, and to receive a penance to perform as retribution; held weekly or less frequently, usually on Friday.

chastity: one of the three solemn or simple vows made at religious profession, variously interpreted in same ways as priestly celibacy, to channel love toward God alone and one's sisters in general community charity.

cincture: a belt of cord, hemp, or leather used to gather the religious habit at the waist.

cloister: enclosed part of a convent which nuns could not leave, nor outsiders enter without permission.

Communion (Holy): Sacrament of the Eucharist or liturgical celebration in which bread and wine are consecrated and received as the body and blood of Jesus in commemoration of the Last Supper.

community customs: traditional practices in some religious communities such as eating only one meal daily during Lent or kneeling during the chanting of certain psalms.

Compline: the last hour of the Divine Office or communal night prayers concluding with a procession and hymn *Salve Regina* ("Hail, Queen of Heaven") to the Blessed Virgin Mary.

confession: accusing oneself of sin to a priest in the sacrament of Penance (more recently known as the sacrament of reconciliation); or proclaiming faults against the Rule to the community in Chapter of Faults.

congregation: religious community bound by a common rule.

constitution: written regulations for community procedures following the spirit of the major rule. For example, the Dominican Constitutions are based on the Rule of St. Augustine.

custody of the senses: restricting input from the senses in order to be recollected in prayer, such as keeping eyes lowered and hands folded under the scapular.

dark night of the soul: a stage in the ascetical/mystical life characterized by personal desolation and inability to pray, described in writings by Teresa of Avila and John of the Cross.

discipline: whip made of leather straps tipped in metal, small chains, or strands of knotted rope used to flagellate one's bared shoulders, thighs, or buttocks as a penance while reciting penetential psalms; begun in 13th century and continuing, in moderation, until recently.

dispensation: written permission from pope for release from religious vows.

Divine Office: official public prayer of the Catholic Church composed of psalms, hymns, readings, prayers recited in sections called canonical hours such as Matins, Lauds, Vespers, Compline.

doctrine: official teaching of the Catholic Church on any given subject.

dogma: a belief the Catholic Church requries everyone

to accept such as the teaching that the Mother of Christ did not die but was assumed into heaven.

dowry: money given by family when a woman enters a religious community returned to her when she leaves or given to the community when she dies.

doxology: prayer to Trinity which traditionally ends public prayers: "Glory be to the Father, and to the Son, and to the Holy Spirit."

enclosed nuns: women who have taken solemn vows and live their entire lives of prayer and manual labor behind monastic walls.

Eucharist: see Communion (Holy).

examen: a private nightly ritual in most convents: asking ourselves a series of questions examining our consciences for sins and faults committed that day, e.g., "Have I told any lies today?" and "Did I keep custody of the eyes today?"

exclaustration: permission for a religious still under vows to live outside her community temporarily, under jurisdiction of local bishop rather than to her religious superior.

external nuns (externs, extern sisters): uncloistered religious with simple vows who live within a monastery and care for physical needs of the community and serve as liaison with world by answering doors, shopping, etc.

feast days: days of liturgical celebration commemorating events in the lives of Christ, Mary and saints.

flagellation: ascetic practice of expiation and self-discipline from medieval corporal punishment for wayward monks; no longer prevalent in most religious communities.

formation: refers to Sister Formation Movement established in 1957 to improve training of young sisters by integrating spiritual, intellectual, social, and apostolic development.

generalate: convent house where community governor (the Mother General) lives with her General Council.

General Council: official governing body of a religious community, elected or appointed.

General (Mother): head of religious order or congregation (also superior-general) elected for a term of three to six years.

grace: gift or blessing indicating divine favor.

Gifts of the Holy Spirit: distinctive habits that accompany the state of grace such as patience and kindness.

guimpe: a starched cloth covering the neck and the shoulders as part of a nun's habit.

Gregorian Chant: oldest musical art form still in use in the West; single-line melody for Latin texts for biblical prayers, especially psalms.

habit: distinctive garb worn by members of religious communities which identifies their congregation.

hierarchy: organization of ranks and orders in religious communities, such as rank from time and date of entrance into the community.

holy card: small colored religious pictures of God, the Blessed Virgin, or saints, sometimes with prayers or quotations from the Bible, given as gifts to other Sisters on feast days.

Holy Rule: early monastic regulations for community life written by Saints Benedict, Augustine, Dominic, and Francis.

holy water font: ornate container, such as marble stand, filled with water blessed by a priest, which upon entering a church Catholics dip their fingers in and make the Sign of the Cross by touching forehead, chest, and shoulders.

host: round wafer of consecrated unleavened bread, believed to *be* the body and blood of Jesus while appearing to be bread: received as the Eucharist in holy communion and displayed in the monstrance for special adoration.

inclination: formal posture of reverence and submission for nuns during prayers and community exercises;

middle inclination: bowing with upper body perpendicular to the floor; profound incl.: bowing as low as possible.

infallibility: doctrine which proclaims that the pope always speaks divine truth when speaking from his official chair.

J.M.J.: abbreviation for "Jesus, Mary, and Joseph" often written at the top of a page as a dedication.

juniorate: third year of sisters' religious training when they are called "Junior Professed."

leave of absence: period of time away from religious community for some specific purpose.

Lent: season of penance from Ash Wednesday until Holy Saturday in preparation for Easter.

Little Office of the Blessed Virgin: variation of Divine Office.

liturgy: refers to Eucharistic celebration (the Mass) and all public ceremonies, rituals, and prayers.

Matins: first of seven canonical hours, originally called "Vigils" recited at Midnight or in the first half of the night, or at the end of the night just before dawn.

Marian devotions: celebrations, rituals, and prayers, in honor of Mary, the mother of Jesus.

May crowning: custom in Catholic schools during May of walking in procession singing hymns to Mary, and a selected person placing a crown of flowers on a statue of Mary as Queen of Heaven and Earth.

mission: assignment given to a sister or the place to which she is assigned.

mistress (mother, postulant, novice): name given to sister or sisters in charge of religious formation of young sisters.

monstrance: large gold receptacle for displaying the host on special feasts.

mortifications: private penances to control or punish physical desires, such as lust or gluttony, assigned by a superior or confessor or chosen by the individual Sister;

such as fasting, sleeping without a pillow or in a rigid position, or wearing a cord or metal object to cause physical pain.

Mother: a term used for religious superiors.

motherhouse: main convent of religious community, where the novitiate is located and where the older sisters live after their retirement.

mysticism: the experience of intense union with God or ultimate reality.

novena: nine successive days of prayer for a special intention.

novice: candidate for temporary religious profession clothed in the religious habit and spending at least one full year of strictly religious formation.

novitiate: full year or more of religious formation required before religious profession in a special religious house, or part of house where novices live.

obedience: one of three religious vows made by members of religious communities to follow the Rule and constitutions and any orders of superiors.

oratory: convent room set aside for prayer, study, or instruction on religious matters.

particular friendship (P.F.): refers to friendships between two sisters which exclude others; considered harmful to community living and prelude to Lesbian relationship.

parish: local church and geographic area it serves.

pastoral ministry: work done in parish by priests and nuns.

postulant: earliest phase (six months to a year) in religious life before receiving religious name and habit; becoming obsolete.

poverty: one of three vows of religious profession to give up ownership of private property.

presence of God: the practice of stopping work for a moment of prayer or recollection; announcing "Remember,

Sisters, we are in the presence of God," when Sisters are
acting frivolous.

prioress: ruler of a priory or any autonomous religious
house.

prostration: a custom in some religious communities of
lying face down on the floor in front of the assembled body
of sisters, or in front of the superior as an act of penance, or
in front of the Blessed Sacrament as an act of reverence.

province (provincial): a geographic division of a religious
community formed by grouping a number of houses under
one major superior.

reception day: ceremonial day when postulants receive
religious names and habits and become formally admitted
to the community; considered the wedding day when the
religious wearing a wedding gown becomes a "Bride of
Christ" while choir sings "Veni Sponsa Cristi" (Come Spouse
of Christ).

refectory: dining room in religious houses.

rule book (The Rule, The Holy Rule): see Constitutions.

sacristy: room adjoining the altar in a church, where
priests change into vestments and where altar bread and
wine are stored; sacristan: person assigned to care for altar
vestments and objects.

scapular: a length of cloth about shoulder width worn
over the shoulder front and back as part of some religious
habits.

Sign of the Cross: religious gesture of placing the tips
of the fingers of the right hand on forehead, chest, left and
right shoulder tips to trace the pattern of the cross on one's
body; used at opening and closing of prayers and classes.

silence: former common monastic practice of avoiding
conversation except at appointed times and places in order
to pray; always kept in chapel, refectory, dormitory, and
cemetery; ordinary, small, or simple silence during the work
day did not prohibit necessary speech; solemn, sacred, or

profound silence from after night prayers until after breakfast every morning prohibited all speech.

sponsor: a sister in a religious community who makes the initial contacts with the community for a young girl desiring to enter.

stigmata: simulation of the wounds of Jesus crucified in hands, feet, and side in the body of a religious person striving for mystical perfection, considered a great gift of divine favor.

Suscipe: prayer in the Mass, meaning "Receive," which introduces the most solemn section during which bread and wine are changed into the body and blood of Jesus.

veil (taking the . . .): headpiece which symbolizes consecrated virginity; also an expression which refers to a postulant being clothed in the religious habit on Reception Day.

vows (temporary, final, perpetual . . .): promises made to God in public and sanctioned by church hierarchy; at religious profession promises to practice poverty, chastity, and obedience in religious life.

ADDITIONAL READING: NOVELS, NON-FICTION ARTICLES, PLAYS

Compiled by Nancy Manahan

Armstrong, Karen. *Through the Narrow Gate.* New York: St. Martin's Press, 1982. English ex-nun's moving story of her seven years in religious life, pre-Vatican II.

Baldwin, Monica. *I Leap Over the Wall.* New York: Signet, 1950. Classic story of author's twenty-eight years (1913–1941) in a cloister, with wry descriptions of return to secular life. Pp. 82–84, 87, 187–188, and ch. 14 mention particular friends and love between women.

Bernstein, Marcelle, ed. *The Nuns.* New York: Bantam, 1976. Sympathetic non-fiction account of contemporary religious life based on conversations from 1971 to 1975 with over five hundred nuns. Bernstein, cataloguing strict proscriptions against particular friendships, concludes that "cases of Lesbian affection among religious women, consummated or not . . . are the exceptions" (p. 108).

Boswell, John. *Christianity, Social Tolerance and Homosexuality: Gay People in Western Europe from the Beginning of the Christian Era to the Fourteenth Century.* Chicago: University of Chicago Press, 1980. A scholarly cross-cultural history of changing church attitudes toward homosexuality with rare information on same-sex love in medieval religious life. Includes "the outstanding example of medieval lesbian literature," written by one nun to another (pp. 220–221).

Brown, Hester. "Get Thee to the Motherhouse or The Meaning & Significance of Real Bread in the Mass." *Heresies,* 7(2:3), pp. 76–79. Description of a community of nuns and what the lesbian feminist community could learn from them.

Brown, Judith C. "Lesbian Sexuality in Renaissance Italy: The Case of Sister Benedetta Carlini." *Signs: Journal of Women in Culture and Society,* 9:4 (Summer 1984), 751–758. Documented case of a sexual relationship between two seventeenth century nuns, discovered and prosecuted. Forthcoming book (Oxford University Press).

Brownsworth, Victoria A. "Lesbian Nuns: Closeted in the Cloister?" *Philadelphia Gay News,* May 2-15, 1980, pp. 16–17 and May 30-June 12, 1980, pp. 12, 15. Two-part article based on in-depth interviews with lesbian nuns and ex-nuns. First article on the subject to appear in print.

Clarke, Peg. *Potted Love.* Sidney: Crescent Press, 1980. Short novel, set in an Australian boarding school, about an entanglement between a nun and a senior girl.

Cruikshank, Margaret. "Cloister Convents: Breaking Silence." *Gay Community News,* April 30, 1983, pp. 8–9. Interview with Rosemary Curb about lesbians in religious life.

Cruikshank, Margaret, ed. *The Lesbian Path.* San Francisco: Double Axe Books, 1981. Collection includes essays by four lesbian ex-nuns: Jeanne Cordova, Rosemary Curb, Caroline Ferguson, and Nancy Manahan.

Cruikshank, Margaret. "Nuns No Longer: Lesbian Convent Life." *Philadelphia Gay News,* Nov. 12–25, 1982, p. 17. Interview with Nancy Manahan and Rosemary Curb concerning *Lesbian Nuns: Breaking Silence.*

Curb, Rosemary. "Lesbian Former and Present Nuns." *Lesbian Connection,* Vol. V(6) (Sept. 1982), p. 9. Personal background of *Lesbian Nuns: Breaking Silence.*

Curb, Rosemary. "Leaving the Convent." *WomanSpirit,* Fall, 1983, pp. 48–49. Story of author's traumatic exit from religious life after seven years in the Sinsinawa Dominicans.

Curb, Rosemary. "Lesbian Nuns: Patriarchal Suppression or Matriarchal Community? *Women's Studies Quarterly,* Summer, 1985. Comprehensive summary of class and ethnic background, education, attitudes, self-perception, reasons for entering and leaving, years and age in religious life, sexual experiences, and evolution of spirituality. Based on questionnaires and stories submitted for *Lesbian Nuns: Breaking Silence.*

Curb, Rosemary and Hannah Blue Heron. "Sister Mystics." *WomanSpirit,* Fall, 1983, p. 41. Two ex-nuns discuss how their former ascetical practices and Catholic mysticism have been transformed into lesbian spirituality rooted in the beauty and goodness of the earth.

Diderot, Denis. *The Nun.* Trans. Leonard Tancock. London: The Folio Society, 1972. Originally published as *La Religieuse* in 1796. Infamous anti-Catholic novel depicting corruption, sadism, and pathological lesbianism in convents. See Lillian Faderman's *Surpassing the Love of Men* (Wm. Morrow, 1981), pp. 43–46 for a feminist analysis of *The Nun.*

Fraser, Antonia. *Quiet as a Nun: A Tale of Murder.* New York: Viking, 1977. Thriller set in a convent. Much speculation about particular friendships, present and past, within the order.

Glubka, Shirley. "Bless Me, Sister . . ." *Conditions:* Nine, 1983, pp. 46–55. Sensitive short story by a lesbian ex-nun about her sexual relationship with another nun. Explores the significance of naming — and not naming — our actions and feelings.

Goergen, Donald. *The Sexual Celibate.* New York: Seabury Press, 1974. Groundbreaking book, including ch. 7, "The Sexual Life of a Celibate Person." See pp. 77–87 and 188–196 for cautiously positive statements on the value of non-genital homosexual relationships for celibates.

Godden, Rumer. *In This House of Brede.* New York: Viking, 1969. Sensitive novel about a successful middle-aged woman who enters a British convent. Includes an account of a particular friendship between a professed sister and a young novice which is nipped in the bud.

Gramick, Jeannine, SSND. "Lesbian Nuns." *Insight,* Spring, 1978. Reprinted in *Probe,* Vol. VII, No. 6, March, 1978, pp. 5–6. Interviews with two lesbian nuns, ages 45 and 50.*

Gramick, Jeannine, SSND. "Gay and Celibate." *Probe* (National Assembly of Women Religious Newsletter). Vol. IX:4, January, 1980. Summary of lesbian nuns' responses to questionnaire about celibacy and relationships.*

Gramick, Jeannine, SSND. "Cracks in the Convent Closets." *News/Views,* National Sisters Vocation Conference, Nov./Dec., 1982, 1–7. Sensitive article about special needs of lesbian candidates for religious life.*

Gramick, Jeannine, ed. *Homosexuality and the Catholic Church.* Chicago: Thomas More Press, 1983. A collec-

*Available from New Ways Ministry, 4012 29th Street, Mt. Ranier, MD. 20712.

tion of thoughtful articles including "Homosexuality, Celibacy, Religious Life and Ordination" by Robert Nugent, S.D.S. and "Gay Men and Women and the Vowed Life" by Cornelius Hubbuck.*

Griffin, Mary. *The Courage to Choose: An American Nun's Story.* Boston: Little, Brown, 1975. Acknowledges that fear of homosexuality lay beneath convent proscriptions of particular friendships and mourns the resulting "painful isolation" and "warping of personalities." Actual lesbian relationships "were rare indeed, and should have been dealt with honestly and humanely" (p. 155).

Henderson, Nancy. *Out of the Curtained World: The Story of an American Nun Who Left the Convent.* Garden City: Doubleday, 1972. Engaging account of author's six convent years in the 1960s. P. 131 warns against particular friendships; author does not mention having any.

Heron, Hannah Blue. "I Meet the Queen of Hearts." *Common Lives/Lesbian Lives.* Fall, 1983, No. 9, pp. 78–83. Excerpt from forthcoming autobiography (*That Strange Intimacy*) of a lesbian ex-nun.

Homosexuality and Social Justice: Report of the Task Force on Gay/Lesbian Issues. Commission on Social Justice, Archdiocese of San Francisco, 1982. An enlightened 150-page report covering a wide range of issues including the spiritual life of homosexuals, violence against homosexuals, the Latino community, the disabled, youth, and the aged. See ch. 6, "Lesbian Women and Gay Men in Religious Congregations/Orders and Priesthood."

Hulme, Kathryn. *The Nun's Story.* Boston: Little, Brown, 1956. Classic novel of religious life. Depicts a nun's intense relationships with two of her superiors and with a young woman about to enter the order. Book populated by strong single women, none explicitly lesbian.

Ide, Arthur Frederick. *Sex, Women & Religion.* Dallas: Monument Press, 1984. Study of religious teaching on women and sex. See chapter on Byzantine women for mention of lesbians in convents (p. 121).

Ide, Arthur Frederick. *Lesbianism in the Early Religious Orders of the Christian Church to 900 A.D.* Dallas: Monument Press, forthcoming.

Ide, Arthur Frederick. *Lesbianism in the Medieval Nunnery.* Dallas: Monument Press, forthcoming.

Leopold, Kathleen, and Thomas Orians, eds. *Theological Pastoral Resources: A Collection of Articles on Homosexuality from a Pastoral Perspective.* Washington, D.C.: Dignity, 1981. Contains a one-page article entitled "From Abomination to Blessing: The Gift of Being Gay — Reflections of a Gay Woman Religious."

Lersch, Susan. *Sisters.* A play of convent life, including lesbian friendship and one explicit sexual experience between two nuns. Stonewall Repertory Theater, N.Y.C., 1983.

Lewis, Lucy, *The Sister Joseph Memorial Gymnasium.* Full-length drama set in a Catholic girls' boarding school circa 1975. The school principal accuses two students of being lesbians, while she herself is involved with a younger nun. Originally titled *Christ's White Brides* in a 1983 U. of Iowa production. Magic Theater, San Francisco, 1984.

Manahan, Nancy. "A Lesbian Ex-Nun Meets Her Sisters." *Common Lives/Lesbian Lives,* No. 8 (Summer, 1983), 88–91. Account of first national gathering of lesbian ex-nuns (at 1981 Michigan Womyn's Music Festival).

Manahan, Nancy. "Lesbian Nuns and Ex-Nuns: Breaking Silence." *Conference for Catholic Lesbians Newsletter* (later *Images*), Sept., 1983, 1(2), 5–6. Background and content of *Lesbian Nuns: Breaking Silence.*

Manahan, Nancy. "Moving the Mountains." *Communication* newsletter, January, 1984, p. 6. Description of *Lesbian Nuns: Breaking Silence.*

Mancuso, Theresa. "Sisters: A Review." *Images*, 1:3 (December, 1983), p. 14. Glowing review of Susan Lersch play, *Sisters*.

Marlowe, Jane R. "Hail Mary," in *Focus: A Journal for Lesbians*. Nov.-Dec., 1979, pp. 3-9. Tender story of a nun meeting her convent lover, now an ex-nun, with flashbacks to their convent times.

Montley, Patricia. *Sister-Rites*. Full-length drama about a twenty-year reunion of seven members of a convent class with their novice mistress. Church pressure on the remaining nun to give up her work in gay ministry creates a crisis of self-revelation among her ex-nun friends. First place winner: American Theatre Association's Women's Program playwriting competition, 1983, and Colonial Players Playwriting Contest, 1984.

Nugent, Robert, SDS, Jeannine Gramick, SSND, and Thomas Oddo, CSC. *Homosexual Catholics: A New Primer for Discussion*. Washington, D.C.: Dignity, Inc., 1980. Booklet on church teaching, scripture, civil rights, and ministry regarding homosexuals. See pp. 16 ff., "Can a Catholic homosexual person become a Sister, Brother or Priest?"*

Nugent, Robert, ed. *A Challenge to Love: Gay and Lesbian Catholics in the Church*. New York: Crossroad Publishing, 1983. In-depth essays on social, theological, and pastoral perspectives on homosexuality. See Marguerite Kropinak's "Homosexuality in Religious Life" (pp. 245-256) and Mary E. Hunt's "Lovingly Lesbian: Toward a Feminist Theology of Friendship" (esp. pp. 145-147). Good bibliographic references.*

Nuscera, Maria. "Lesbian and Celibate: Journeys in the Dark." *Images*, Vol. 2, No. 1 (March, 1984), pp. 2-3. Account of a lesbian nun's struggles with sexual relationships and celibacy.

*Available from New Ways Ministry, 4012 29th Street, Mt. Ranier, MD 20712.

O'Brien, Edna. "Sister Imelda." *The New Yorker,* Nov. 9, 1981, pp. 48–58. Story of an emotionally intense relationship between a nun and a high school senior girl, as seen through the eyes of the girl.

O'Keefe, Maureen, SSND. *Christian Love in Religious Life.* Chicago: Henry Regency Co., 1965. Although O'Keefe laments proscriptions against deep, loving friendships between nuns, including appropriate expressions of physical affection, she has a long section on dangers of crushes and particular friendships in community life.

Rothbaum, Susan. *Wrestling Dragons.* Forthcoming. Based on extensive interviews with women and men who have left spiritual and other idealistic communities, by co-director of Sorting It Out. Describes entrance, honeymoon period, disillusionment, leaving, re-entering the world, and integrating the experience.

Salm, Luke. "The Vow of Chastity and Moral Theology Today." *Sexuality and Brotherhood.* Ed. Martin Helldorfer. Illinois: National Assembly of Religious Brothers, pp. 19–24. Presents four widely differing answers to the question, "How compatible is sexual activity with the vow of celibacy?"

San Giovanni, Lucinda. *Ex-Nuns: A Study of Emergent Role Passage.* Norwood, N.J.: Ablex Publishing Co., 1978. Sociological study based on in-depth interviews with 20 ex-nuns. Only mention of lesbians is in a footnote: "No respondent indicated she had been intimately involved with a woman" (p. 74).

Sowers, Prudence. "The Habits of Love." *The Advocate,* May 27, 1982, pp. 29–30, 56. Exploration of lesbians in religious life based on interviews with five lesbian nuns and ex-nuns including Virginia Apuzzo, Jean O'Leary and Diana T. DiPrima.

Spark, Muriel. *The Abbess of Crewe.* New York: Viking Press, 1974. Whimsical, irreverent novel about electronic surveillance in a very modern abbey. Lesbian hints, pp. 21, 33, 62.

"Vows of Defiance." *Newsweek,* March 19, 1984, pp. 97–100. Describes strife between increasingly feminist American nuns and the church hierarchy. Mentions the "pain of lesbians in religious orders" (p. 98).

Wong, Mary Gilligan. *Nun.* San Diego: Harcourt, Brace, Jovanovich, 1983. Memoir of author's convent years (1961–1968) and her subsequent marriage, motherhood, and Ph.D. Two accounts of particular friends (pp. 119–125 and 224–226) and an eye-opening 1981 conversation with a gay priest about gay men and lesbian women in religious life (pp. 380–382).

Woods, Richard, OP. "Gay Candidates, the Religious Life and the Priesthood." *Call to Growth/Ministry.* IV:4 (Summer, 1979), 24–43. Discusses whether gay and lesbian candidates should be admitted to religious life, concluding, "there is no intrinsic reason why homosexual candidates should not be admitted . . ." (p. 41).

Resources

Bear and Company, P.O. Box 2860, Santa Fe, NM 87504. Magazine of personal and social transformation. Includes articles incorporating feminist, lesbian and gay Christian perspectives. Back issues only: 3 volumes, 1981–1984.

Communication, a network to promote the integration of personal sexuality and ministry for gay and lesbian religious and clergy. Box 27, Wheeling, WV 26003.

Conference for Catholic Lesbians, P.O. Box 134, Highspire, PA 17034. Goal is "to build a community whose Christian spirituality reflects our lived experiences as feminists, as women, and as lesbians." Publishes a quarterly newsletter, *Images.*

Dignity, Inc., 1500 Massachusetts Ave., N.W., Suite 11,
    Washington, DC 20005 (202/861-0017). In Canada,
    Box 1912, Winnipeg R3C 3R2. Organization for gay
    and lesbian Catholics and other concerned persons.
    Founded in 1969. Publishes a newsletter, *Dignity*.
Integrity, Inc. P.O. Box 2516, Chicago, IL 60690. In Canada,
    P.O. Box 873, Station F, Toronto, Ontario M4Y2N9.
    Organization for gay and lesbian Episcopalians.
Lady Inclination of the Night. c/o Kay F. Turner, SSB
    3.106, Folklore Center, University of Texas, Austin,
    TX 78712. A journal of feminist/matriarchal spirituality.
New Ways Ministry, 4012 29th Street, Mt. Ranier, MD
    20712 (301/277-5674). A Catholic coalition for gay and
    lesbian civil rights. Engaged in education, counseling,
    and workshops on homosexuality. Focus on general
    audiences, including pastoral workers and religious com-
    munities.
SIGMA [Sisters in Gay Ministry, Associated] 1101 Jancey
    St., Pittsburgh, PA 15206. A national support organiza-
    tion for women religious working in pastoral ministry
    to lesbian and gay persons.
Sorting It Out. P.O. Box 9446, Berkeley, CA 94709 (415/
    524-3200). A non-profit organization providing support
    for people who have left spiritual/communal groups or
    gurus/teachers and have unresolved feelings to sort out.
    Welcomes lesbians.
Thesmorphoria. Covenant of the Goddess, P.O. Box 11363,
    Oakland, CA 94611. A periodical of matriarchal religion.
WomanSpirit. 2000 King Mountain Trail, Wolf Creek, OR
    97497-9709. Magazine of feminist spirituality. Back
    issues available.
*Woman of Power: A Magazine of Feminism, Spirituality,
    and Politics*, 121 Inman Street, Cambridge, MA 02139.
    Quarterly journal of essays, interviews, fiction, poetry,

reviews, graphics, and photographs about feminist spirituality and politics.

Cassette Tapes

First Conference for Catholic Lesbians: seven workshop tapes, including "An Overview of SIGMA (Sisters in Gay Ministry, Associated)." CCL, P.O. Box 134, Highspire, PA 17034.

First National Symposium on Homosexuality and the Catholic Church, Nov. 20–22, 1981. Six audio cassettes. Talks were edited for publication in *Homosexuality and the Catholic Church*, ed. Jeannine Gramick. Eastern Audio Associates, Oakland Center, 8980 Route 108, Columbia, MD 21045 (301/596-3900).

Ministry and Homosexual People. Series of eight audio cassettes by Jeannine Gramick and Robert Nugent, including "Homosexuality and Religious Vocation." National Catholic Reporter Cassettes, Box 281, Kansas City, MO 64141.

The Naiad Press, Inc.
P.O. Box 10543
Tallahassee, Florida 32302

Source of Lesbian material. Write
for complete catalog of publications.

A few of the publications of
THE NAIAD PRESS, INC.
P.O. Box 10543 • Tallahassee, Florida 32302
Mail orders welcome. Please include 15% postage.

Lesbian Nuns: Breaking Silence edited by Rosemary Curb and
Nancy Manahan. Autobiographies. 432 pp.
ISBN 0-930044-62-2 $9.95
ISBN 0-930044-63-0 $16.95

The Swashbuckler by Lee Lynch. A novel. 288 pp.
ISBN 0-930044-66-5 $7.95

Misfortune's Friend by Sarah Aldridge. A novel. 320 pp.
ISBN 0-930044-67-3 $7.95

A Studio of One's Own by Ann Stokes. Edited by Dolores
Klaich. Autobiography. 128 pp. ISBN 0-930044-64-9 $7.95

Sex Variant Women in Literature by Jeannette Howard Foster.
Literary history. 448 pp. ISBN 0-930044-65-7 $8.95

A Hot-Eyed Moderate by Jane Rule. Essays. 252 pp.
ISBN 0-930044-57-6 $7.95
ISBN 0-930044-59-2 $13.95

Inland Passage and Other Stories by Jane Rule. 288 pp.
ISBN 0-930044-56-8 $7.95
ISBN 0-930044-58-4 $13.95

We Too Are Drifting by Gale Wilhelm. A novel. 128 pp.
ISBN 0-930044-61-4 $6.95

Amateur City by Katherine V. Forrest. A mystery novel. 224 pp.
ISBN 0-930044-55-X $7.95

The Sophie Horowitz Story by Sarah Schulman. A novel. 176 pp.
ISBN 0-930044-54-1 $7.95

The Young in One Another's Arms by Jane Rule. A novel.
224 pp. ISBN 0-930044-53-3 $7.95

The Burnton Widows by Vicki P. McConnell. A mystery novel.
272 pp. ISBN 0-930044-52-5 $7.95

Old Dyke Tales by Lee Lynch. Short stories. 224 pp.
ISBN 0-930044-51-7 $7.95

Daughters of a Coral Dawn by Katherine V. Forrest. Science
fiction. 240 pp. ISBN 0-930044-50-9 $7.95

The Price of Salt by Claire Morgan. A novel. 288 pp.
ISBN 0-930044-49-5 $7.95

Against the Season by Jane Rule. A novel. 224 pp.
ISBN 0-930044-48-7 $7.95

Lovers in the Present Afternoon by Kathleen Fleming. A novel.
288 pp. ISBN 0-930044-46-0 $8.50

Toothpick House by Lee Lynch. A novel. 264 pp.
ISBN 0-930044-45-2 $7.95

Madame Aurora by Sarah Aldridge. A novel. 256 pp.
ISBN 0-930044-44-4 $7.95

Curious Wine by Katherine V. Forrest. A novel. 176 pp.
ISBN 0-930044-43-6 $7.50

Black Lesbian in White America by Anita Cornwell. Short stories,
essays, autobiography. 144 pp. ISBN 0-930044-41-X $7.50

Contract with the World by Jane Rule. A novel. 340 pp.
ISBN 0-930044-28-2 $7.95

Yantras of Womanlove by Tee A. Corinne. Photographs.
64 pp. ISBN 0-930044-30-4 $6.95

Mrs. Porter's Letter by Vicki P. McConnell. A mystery novel.
224 pp. ISBN 0-930044-29-0 $6.95

To the Cleveland Station by Carol Anne Douglas. A novel.
192 pp. ISBN 0-930044-27-4 $6.95

The Nesting Place by Sarah Aldridge. A novel. 224 pp.
ISBN 0-930044-26-6 $6.95

This Is Not for You by Jane Rule. A novel. 284 pp.
ISBN 0-930044-25-8 $7.95

Faultline by Sheila Ortiz Taylor. A novel. 140 pp.
ISBN 0-930044-24-X $6.95

The Lesbian in Literature by Barbara Grier. 3d ed. Foreword by
Maida Tilchen. A comprehensive bibliography. 240 pp.
ISBN 0-930044-23-1 $7.95

Anna's Country by Elizabeth Lang. A novel. 208 pp.
ISBN 0-930044-19-3 $6.95

Prism by Valerie Taylor. A novel. 158 pp.
ISBN 0-930044-18-5 $6.95

Black Lesbians: An Annotated Bibliography compiled by
J. R. Roberts. Foreword by Barbara Smith. 112 pp.
ISBN 0-930044-21-5 $5.95

The Marquise and the Novice by Victoria Ramstetter. A novel.
108 pp. ISBN 0-930044-16-9 $4.95

Labiaflowers by Tee A. Corinne. 40 pp.
ISBN 0-930044-20-7 $3.95

Outlander by Jane Rule. Short stories, essays. 207 pp.
ISBN 0-930044-17-7 $6.95

Sapphistry: The Book of Lesbian Sexuality by Pat Califia. 2nd
    edition, revised. 195 pp. ISBN 0-930044-47-9 $7.95

All True Lovers by Sarah Aldridge. A novel. 292 pp.
    ISBN 0-930044-10-X $6.95

A Woman Appeared to Me by Renee Vivien. Translated by
    Jeannette H. Foster. A novel. xxxi, 65 pp.
    ISBN 0-930044-06-1 $5.00

Cytherea's Breath by Sarah Aldridge. A novel. 240 pp.
    ISBN 0-930044-02-9 $6.95

Tottie by Sarah Aldridge. A novel. 181 pp.
    ISBN 0-930044-01-0 $6.95

The Latecomer by Sarah Aldridge. A novel. 107 pp.
    ISBN 0-930044-00-2 $5.00

VOLUTE BOOKS

Journey to Fulfillment	by Valerie Taylor	$3.95
A World without Men	by Valerie Taylor	$3.95
Return to Lesbos	by Valerie Taylor	$3.95
Desert of the Heart	by Jane Rule	$3.95
Odd Girl Out	by Ann Bannon	$3.95
I Am a Woman	by Ann Bannon	$3.95
Women in the Shadows	by Ann Bannon	$3.95
Journey to a Woman	by Ann Bannon	$3.95
Beebo Brinker	by Ann Bannon	$3.95

These are just a few of the many Naiad Press titles. Please request a
complete catalog! We encourage and welcome direct mail orders from
individuals who have limited access to bookstores carrying our publications.